D1492151

The Cooking of Japan

The Cooking of Japan

by

Rafael Steinberg

and the Editors of

TIME-LIFE BOOKS

photographed by Eliot Elisofon

TIME-LIFE INTERNATIONAL (Nederland) N.V.

THE AUTHOR: Rafael Steinberg (*far left*), who joined the Editors of TIME-LIFE BOOKS in producing the text, first went to the Orient as a correspondent during the Korean War, shortly after taking a degree at Harvard. Later he was a TIME correspondent in Tokyo and London, and spent several years as *Newsweek*'s Tokyo bureau chief. He is the author of *Postscript from Hiroshima*, a book about survivors of the nuclear bombing, and is at work on novels at his home in Glen Gardner, New Jersey.

THE PHOTOGRAPHER: Eliot Elisofon (*near left*) first went to Japan in 1955 to lecture on photography. He has returned five times, twice to take pictures for major stories on Japan for LIFE. A painter as well as a photographer, Elisofon exhibited his water-colours in Tokyo while he was completing his work for this book.

THE CONSULTING EDITOR: Michael Field (*far left*) supervised the adapting and writing of recipes for this book. One of America's foremost food experts and culinary teachers, he has written articles for leading magazines. His books include *Michael Field's Cooking School* and *Michael Field's Culinary Classics and Improvisations*.

THE CHEF: Toshio Morimoto (*near left*) started as an apprentice in Osaka's famous Kitcho restaurant when he was 15 and was an experienced chef when he left for the United States 12 years later. In 1964 he opened his own restaurant in New York, naming it, by special permission, after its Japanese prototype.

THE CONSULTANTS: Fumie Adachi, director of exhibits programming for the Japan Society in New York, reviewed the text for accuracy. Rand Castile, educational director of the Japan Society, studied the tea ceremony in Kyoto under Sochitsu Sen and served as the expert on this subject. Fumi Inokuma, wife of a distinguished Japanese painter, assisted in planning the still-life food photography. Eiko Yuasa, head of the International Conference Hall in Kyoto, assisted in Japan.

THE SPECIAL CONSULTANT FOR THIS EDITION: Margaret Costa (*left*), born in Southern Rhodesia and educated in England, has been "obsessed" with cooking since the age of six. She abandoned theatre work and a job as staff writer for London's *Sunday Pictorial* to write about food—a career that has kept her busy for 20 years. For some 15 of those years, she has helped to compile Raymond Postgate's *Good Food Guide* to eating out in the British Isles. Today, as the wife of one of London's best chefs, an Englishman trained in the Escoffier tradition, she writes about food, wine and restaurants for half a dozen newspapers and magazines, including *The Sunday Times Magazine* and *The Illustrated London News*.

THE ASSISTANT TO THE SPECIAL CONSULTANT: J. Audrey Ellison, a microbiologist, food analyst and home economist, adapted, revised and tested the recipes for this edition. Mrs. Ellison taught home economics at London University after taking her science degree there. Now, she is consultant to the Norway Food Centre in London and to a number of food manufacturers and importers. She has compiled several cookery books, including *The Great Scandinavian Cook Book*, which she translated from the Swedish and edited for English and American readers.

THE COVER: *Togan-to ebi*, a clear soup with prawn and winter melon (*page 58*).

© 1970 by TIME Inc.
Original English language edition © 1969 by TIME Inc.
All rights reserved.

Contents

Introduction   6

I   The Heritage of a Remarkable Past   8

II   Foods for All Seasons   25

III   The Logic of Japanese Cookery   41

IV   The World's Greatest Seafood   75

V   Simple, Satisfying Home Cooking   107

VI   A Ceremony That Begot a Cuisine   137

VII   Eating Out as a Way of Life   151

VIII   Magnificent Meals in Elegant Settings   183

Appendix   *How to Use Japanese Recipes*   198

A Guide to Ingredients in Japanese Cooking   199

Recipe Index: English   200

Recipe Index: Japanese   201

General Index   202

Where to Find Japanese Foods   207

Picture Credits and Acknowledgements   208

The Recipe Booklet that accompanies this volume has been designed for use in the kitchen. It contains all the 84 recipes printed here plus 31 more. It also has a wipe-clean cover and a spiral binding so that it can either stand up or lie flat when open.

Solving the Mysteries of
Japan's Marvellous Cuisine

As a boy in land-locked, then lakeless, Oklahoma, I had dreamed of the islands of Japan, but both Lafcadio Hearn and Giacomo Puccini were curiously reticent about Japanese *food*. Rumours of "raw fish" fought their way through dust storms and tornadoes, but that whole, salty, underwater world of "sea-food" was for the most part a trickle of misinformation. Squid and octopus. Any difference? Don't they both squirt black ink and who counts tentacles anyway? Sea-urchins and anemones. What the devil are they? Kids? Flowers? Secrets of the sea eluded canning processes, frozen foods hadn't come along yet, and refrigerated transport was fairly unknown. Or did refrigerated wagons simply stop at Kansas City?

The time finally came for me to visit my dream of Japan, and as soon as I set foot on the good ship *Hikawa-maru* in Seattle—oh yes, aircraft were invented but they weren't flying the Pacific—I was confronted with what the passengers called "The Choice". You could have either a full Western meal or a full Japanese one. I asked for Japanese food, got it three times a day and stuck to it for the whole 21 days of the voyage to Yokohama. My motives were mostly brummagem, but partly too, I like to imagine, good sense. I was determined to learn Japanese for, as I now tell the story, I knew war was coming. I have never believed that "you are what you eat" (in Japan they drink snake's blood for longevity), however I am convinced that you can't learn a language without enjoying the food of the nation. Just think of the loss of idiom an English-speaking Japanese might feel if he didn't understand things like a lover being the "cream in his coffee", or something being "as English as roast beef".

Now, in retrospect, I must admit I explored Japan's gustatory and culinary arts the hard way. I tortured myself with *umeboshi*, ultra-sour plums, on deck while watching the sun rise. I snacked on odorous, fermented soya beans, called *natto*, at night before retiring. I even tried again and again those little cakes printed in the shape of flat flowers, which taste dry as chalk and crumble into sandy powder with every bite. But along the way I encountered myriads of delights and miracles of surprising pleasures. *Sukiyaki* and *tempura*, it goes without saying, and noodles too, and *tonkatsu*, which loses totally in translation if you say "pork cutlet". The warmth of bean soup, the dew-like freshness of thin soup, the brilliant clarity of good, first-quality soya sauce, and the thousands of other sauces, each bound, as in a marriage, to its own particular mate. Where else in the cooking world can you have so light, so greaseless, so sparkling a set of flavours and textures that turn into aromas or almost melt as soon as they reach your mouth?

The day soon came when raw fish was on the ship's table d'hôte, and I

6

discovered that it didn't taste raw, or even like fish. And with this conclusion I joined the ranks of astonished foreigners whose numbers increase, like school children and textbooks, year by year. By now the last threshold was crossed, and I was enslaved to Japanese cooking.

My life in Japan proper during those pre-war years was one long restaurant tour. After all, I persuaded myself, I was learning Japanese and it was important to say *kaki*, which means both "oyster" and "persimmon", and wait to see whether the waitress asked, "Raw or fried?" or, "Fresh or sugar-dried?" I shared afternoon teas of *mitsumame* with pretty young girls lapping up rainbow cubes of transparent gelatine swimming in fragrant, sugary water dotted for artistic emphasis with a brown bean or two. In the evenings, I learned to mix *sake* with beer—never touching, of course, the cup with my left hand: *hidarikiki*, the sign of a drunkard so eager to get at the booze he forgets formality and uses either hand in careless haste—drinking and eating with the best of the men until the drink was gone and the concluding rice and soup came on. Back in my homeland, when Japan had turned from a dream into a memory, I found myself missing the very foods that I had not particularly liked. *Mitsumame*, for example.

Several years later I returned to Japan. I was a soldier and, as it happened, was living at the American embassy where I had a large apartment, a small kitchen, and two cooks—one for Western food and one for Japanese. This wasn't entirely my own idea, because it was General MacArthur's policy to rehire all the old, pre-war embassy staff, one of whom had cooked in the western style, but it suited my plans very well. I did a lot of entertaining and invariably offered guests "The Choice". One evening George Sansom, the doyen of Japanophiles and a great scholar, came to dinner. I had known how good Japanese food was, but I hadn't before then known that it was good *for* you, too. Sir George had just arrived after a long absence and hadn't yet adjusted to the climate. Still he insisted on coming, provided I could give him raw fish. "Whenever I have a tummy upset", he explained, "I eat nothing but raw fish for a day and then I'm fine." And so he was.

Today I often find myself "hungry" for Japan, and once it got so bad I cooked up an excuse for a quick trip back just because I was hungry. So, there are dangers in becoming habituated to this great cuisine. However, a book such as this one at last makes possible the impossible: You can now do it yourself in your own home. Here, too, be careful. My own son said to me recently, "Please, Dad. Not *tofu* again!" But just wait until he grows up.

—*Faubion Bowers, author, world traveller and aide-de-camp to General Douglas MacArthur during the early years of the post-war occupation of Japan.*

I

The Heritage of a Remarkable Past

A young mother picnics with her hungry baby in a Kyoto setting that combines two familiar symbols of Japan. Behind her is a cherry tree in blossom; on the left is a box of *sushi*. Sometimes called the sandwich of Japan, *sushi* consists of rice delicately flavoured with sweet rice vinegar, then shaped and wrapped in fish or nourishing seaweed.

For years I have been involved in a love affair with the cooking of Japan, one that grows more intense with each sojourn in that enchanting land. This may sound strange to those Westerners who still labour under long-standing misconceptions that make this distinguished cooking seem utterly and impossibly alien. Before I encountered it personally, and through my Japanese wife became a member of the family, I too shared the false impression that traditional Japanese cooking consisted simply of a great many little dishes and too much fish—that it is mainly an aesthetic production in which taste is sacrificed in favour of beautiful effects and finicky etiquette.

Japanese food is indeed served in small, meticulously prepared portions —but if the portions served at any one meal are less than most of us are accustomed to, there are enough of them to almost equal in value an average Western meal. I also grant that fish plays an important role in Japanese cooking. But while fish, shell-fish and seaweed appear frequently on the menu, they never become monotonous because the Japanese have devised an astonishing number of mouth-watering ways of preparing them.

As for the emphasis on appearance, it is certainly true that the Japanese are adept at giving food an additional excitement through the use of exqui-site dishes and bowls selected for their harmony with particular foods. This dedication to visual appeal actually enhances a meal. For, as your palate is captivated by tastes calculated to set each other off, your eye is intrigued by contrasts of colour, shape and texture.

As a journalist, I have friends in the profession whose work has taken them to other countries famous for their fine cuisine. When at last they

sampled Japanese cooking and compared it with the food they had enjoyed elsewhere, these world travellers invariably characterized Japanese cuisine as uniquely refined, fastidious and subtle; the Japanese themselves refer to it as *sappari*—clean, neat, light, sparkling with honesty. Some gourmets rank the cooking of Japan with that of France and China as one of the world's truly great cuisines. In Japan *grande cuisine* is every bit as *grande* as it is in France; and if Japanese cooking has a relatively limited range of food-stuffs with which to work, it compensates for this lack through the great versatility of its methods.

A reflection of the Japanese sensitivity towards food is the great attention paid to each material being processed—even more consideration than is shown by the French, which is a great deal. Whereas the French and the Chinese tend to blend many ingredients together in one dish, the Japanese generally strive to preserve the intrinsic properties of each so that they may all be equally important in taste as well as in appearance. In a clear Japanese soup, for example, the bit of carrot used as a garnish is quite distinct in taste, colour and shape from the pale-gold sliver of pungent lemon that floats up against your lips as you drink the soup. Each ingredient in the soup is to be relished separately, for its own special character. Moreover, if a dish calls for a strong-tasting garnish such as chopped spring onions or grated ginger, this is added at the last moment—usually by the diner himself —so that its taste will not permeate the rest of the ingredients.

Equally important in Japanese opinion as the method of cooking and the skill in presentation is the message or mood that certain foods are intended to convey. One example is a dish, made for the spring fish festival, whose many ingredients include finely textured slices and cubes of raw tunny fish and sea bream, crisp cucumber strips and shredded radish, sections of boiled lotus root, a spray of cherry blossoms and a willow twig—all arranged to suggest the trees, mountains, rivers and flowers of Japan in spring-time. The decoration of the room in which food is served is changed regularly to suggest a mood or to remind the diners of the rhythm of the seasons. In the coldest days of January, for instance, a painting of plum blossoms may be hung in the *tokonoma*—the alcove found in virtually every principal Japanese room—to remind you that the first flowering tree will be in bloom next month.

Often a Japanese chef will go still further to make his dishes visually

A Land in a Few Brush-Strokes

This stylized map, done in brush-and-ink calligraphic style, suggests the general shape and comparative size of the four islands that make up the major part of Japan. The island chain, about 1,000 miles long, lies between about the same latitudes as Tripoli and Lyon, but the variations in climate are far less extreme. The waters that surround Japan are among the world's richest fishing grounds. Honshu is the most temperate of the islands and has the largest proportion of arable land; it produces three-quarters of the Japanese rice and three-quarters of the population live there. Hokkaido, comparatively cold and thinly populated, is important for dairy products. The islands of Shikoku and Kyushu are sub-tropical, producing mandarin oranges and other citrus fruits.

A Note about This "Different" Volume

In reading and using this book you will find certain differences between it and the other FOODS OF THE WORLD *volumes. For one thing there is a preponderance of seafood in the Japanese repertoire, and the recipes and illustrations reflect this. For another, the recipes are organized into four major sections (see pages 54, 90, 122 and 168) instead of as appendages to each chapter. These recipe sections contain explanatory notes at the beginning of each category of dishes. By reading these and the discussion of menu planning on page 198 in the Appendix —as well as the author's enlightening text—you will find that many aspects of Japanese cuisine that may have seemed mysterious become perfectly clear.*

There is a culinary glossary in the appendix, but for your convenience, near the beginning of each chapter there are also brief glossaries that translate Japanese terms not fully defined in the text. There is no chapter glossary with this opening chapter because Japanese terms are defined in it when first used.

—The Editors

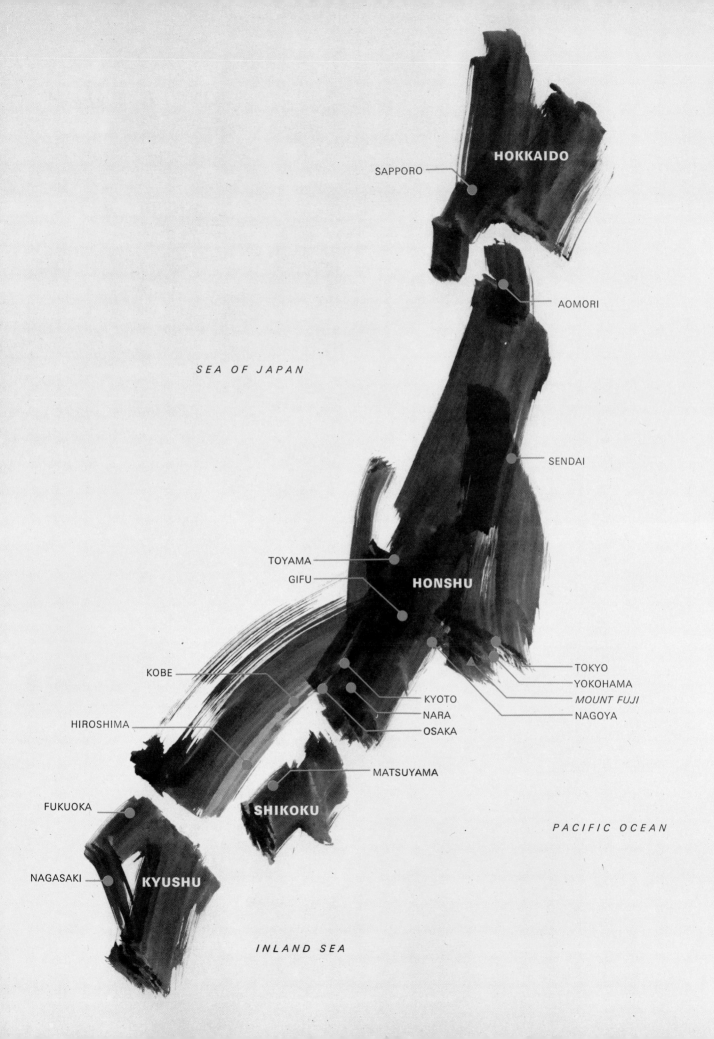

HOKKAIDO

SAPPORO

AOMORI

SEA OF JAPAN

SENDAI

TOYAMA

GIFU

HONSHU

TOKYO
YOKOHAMA
MOUNT FUJI
NAGOYA

KOBE

KYOTO
NARA
OSAKA

HIROSHIMA

MATSUYAMA

PACIFIC OCEAN

FUKUOKA

SHIKOKU

NAGASAKI   KYUSHU

INLAND SEA

appetizing, perhaps by lining a plate with several freshly washed maple or chrysanthemum leaves or by adorning it with a pine sprig or a crisp green leaf scissored into a series of arrow-like points. Then he decides how to set the food within the pattern of the plate and its ornamentation, sometimes at an angle in order to lead the eye to an accompanying dish, or squarely in the centre to emphasize the food's self-containment. Moreover, he aims at making every arrangement unique, and in this way keeps himself constantly creative. As Kaichi Tsuji, chef and owner of one of Tokyo's outstanding Japanese restaurants and the author of many books on Japanese cuisine, once declared: "A great presentation is fine the first time, but less so the second time. To repeat it a third time . . . is to go back to the kindergarten."

To understand how this unique approach to eating developed and reached its present peak of sophistication, we must know something about the forces that shaped its growth. For like the culinary habits of other nations, those of Japan are a reflection of the country's climate and geography, its ethnic inheritances, the ebb and flow of its history, its religious beliefs.

While their origin is uncertain, it seems likely that most of Japan's early settlers were immigrants from the arid, wind-blown steppes of northern Asia. When they crossed the water from Siberia or from Korea, they found verdant islands with a generally temperate climate and abundant rainfall, surrounded by coastal waters teeming with fish. The gratitude that the early

On a sunny day in May, women workers harvest the first (and best) crop of green tea leaves on a plantation in the Ujidawara district, near Kyoto. The shears they are using, with a bag attached to the right-hand blade to catch the snipped leaves, are an innovation in tea harvesting. They are used mainly to cut the outer leaves; the rest are still gathered by hand. A second crop will be picked in July and a third one in September. The women's costumes are similar to those worn by rural women throughout Japan.

Overleaf: Reflected in the shallow water that covers the fields of newly transplanted rice shoots, a farmer (*foreground*) carries a pail of insecticide to scatter over them. He and his neighbours co-operated in creating the irrigation system, but the rice fields are still individually owned. Thatched roofs like those in the background are still found in parts of rural Japan.

settlers must have felt for the beneficence of their new land probably helped to create a desire to live in harmony with nature; these feelings became a fixed characteristic of the emerging Japanese people, a trait that has left an indelible imprint on every aspect of Japanese culture.

In time, this simple reverence for nature developed into a cult dedicated to the worship of a pantheon of natural spirits. Wherever there was a tree or rock with an unusual shape or a stream murmuring over stones, there a divine presence was said to dwell and a primitive temple was erected; there the people made offerings of rice—Japan's staple crop in antiquity as it is today—and *sake*, a beverage made by fermenting rice and then distilling it.

The nature worship of the early Japanese—which eventually evolved into the Shinto religion still widely practised in Japan—was essentially a hymn to the god-given fertility of the land. At the spring and autumn festivals, prayers asking for good planting weather and bountiful harvests were directed to the appropriate deities. One of the most important of these deities was the food goddess, Ukemochi-no-kami. Also held in high esteem was Inari, the rice god. Even today hundreds of thousands of miniature shrines dedicated to him can be seen throughout rural Japan.

The food goddess yielded first place to the goddess of the sun, legendary grandmother of Jimmu, the first emperor of Japan and founder of the dynasty that has reigned for more than 2,600 years. Nonetheless the food goddess remained an important figure of worship, a symbol of the respect with

Continued on page 16

13

which a hard-working, frugal people regarded their most vital resource. For the ancient Japanese, like their descendants today, could not afford to be casual about food. Japan has never produced any surplus, for only about 16 per cent of this mountainous land is suitable for cultivation. Consequently the earliest Japanese diet was sparse and simple, consisting mainly of rice, fish, vegetables, seaweed, salt and fruit, augmented occasionally by venison, wild boar or game birds.

Even in modern Japan the ancient respect for the sacredness of food still prevails. The poetic Shinto Prayer for the Harvest is regularly recited, beseeching the gods for "crops in ears long and in ears abundant, things growing in the great moor-plain, sweet herbs and bitter herbs, things that dwell in the blue sea-plain, the broad of fin and the narrow of fin, seaweed from the offing, seaweed from the shore. . . ." Every year the emperor and empress of Japan observe the chief national festivals, celebrations centuries old that give thanks for plentiful crops. These are called *Niiname Sai*, or "The Tasting of the First Fruits", and *Kanname Sai*, or "The Divine Tasting". In modern industrialized Japan with its ability to import any necessary foodstuffs from all over the world, the emperor and empress observe the festivals largely as a matter of form because it gives a sense of continuity to their line. But in the past, royal participation was a much more serious matter, for a poor rice crop could mean severe hardship to millions of Japanese.

Other nations with natural resources as limited as those of Japan have compensated by importing the things they lacked. But the Japanese, an insular people whose sea-bordered archipelago lies three times as far from the Asian continent as the British Isles lie from the continent of Europe, pursued a policy of either enthusiastically accepting ideas from the outside world, or shutting the world out entirely for centuries at a time.

This oddly vacillating policy profoundly affected not only Japanese eating habits but Japanese life in general. During those periods when the country's doors stood open, the free flow of ideas, products and techniques from abroad enabled the Japanese to be selective, sifting out and retaining only those features of other cultures that they found especially attractive or useful. And during their centuries of withdrawal, they concentrated on reshaping what they had borrowed, blending it with the best of their own native civilization to create the exquisitely refined Japanese way of life that became manifest in its art and literature, architecture and gardening, and in the preparation and serving of food.

Japan's first and most significant period of contact with the outer world began around the sixth century A.D. when Japan, still semi-barbaric despite centuries of sporadic contacts with China, suddenly awoke to the merits of the highly sophisticated civilization of its neighbours. In the seventh and eighth centuries, when T'ang Dynasty China was becoming the world's most advanced nation, Chinese cultural influence on Japan—especially with regard to the beliefs and practices of Chinese Buddhism—reached astounding proportions. The impact of China is still evident in Japanese art and architecture, ideographic written language, literature, techniques of government, taxation and city planning, and—not least—in its cuisine.

Perhaps the most important food innovation contributed by China was the soya bean, which in various guises is still the foundation stone of Japanese cooking. Another Chinese acquisition was tea, which became Japan's national beverage. Tea reached Japan around the year 800 and was first used there in powdered form as a medicine or as a drink reserved for aristocrats and priests. Tea was to have an important impact on Japanese cooking, but one that would not be felt until the 15th century.

This flow of influences from China came to an early end towards the middle of the ninth century, when the T'ang Dynasty was in decline. But as the Japanese moved into a long era of insular seclusion they began to refine their borrowings and turn them into the elegant Japanese civilization.

The focus of that civilization was the imperial court at Japan's ancient capital of Heian-kyo, later known as Kyoto, and the 400 years following the foundation of the city in 794 are known as the golden age of Japanese culture. The Heian age was a time of aristocratic ideals, and never perhaps in the history of any people have the poetic and the practical been so intimately married. Many of the interests that preoccupy the Japanese to this day took shape during that era, among them poetry, subtle colour combinations, graceful manners, beautiful ceramics. The Heian nobles wrote and exchanged poems on paper whose shades were chosen to convey their moods, practised scent-blending as a fine art, held banquets in lovely gardens beside flowing streams and often followed them with excursions to admire wild flowers, to view the moon or to listen to the almost imperceptible sounds of falling snow. Every aspect of their lives, from their love affairs to their dining habits, was governed by an almost incredibly elaborate code of etiquette.

But while the Heian age was ultra-refined, it was not gastronomically opulent. The diet of the aristocrats and the common people alike mostly consisted of the rice, fish, fruit and vegetables eaten by their ancestors. To make this simple fare as poetic as possible, the Heian nobles added romantic ingredients such as fern-frond tips and devised various ways of presenting food that were calculated to enhance its visual appeal, thus infusing Japanese cuisine with one of the qualities that would for ever after make it unique.

After the golden age of Japan came centuries of violent civil strife that saw the rise to power of a class very different from the poetic Heian courtiers —the warriors called samurai. Although these fighting men were realistic and hard-bitten in the field, they were not averse during their periods of leisure to adopting the elegant table etiquette of the imperial court and the artistic presentation of food. Since their ranks included men of lesser birth as well as nobles, this refinement began to reach the lower levels of Japanese society, a process that was speeded up during the 15th century with the perfection by the Japanese imperial court of a Buddhist-inspired ritual known as the tea ceremony. In the tea ceremony, a small gathering of friends enjoy tea and food served in a mannerly, graceful fashion by their host amid simple but beautiful objects and in a tranquil atmosphere. Over the centuries this ceremony became not only the basis of a whole branch of cooking called *kaiseki ryori*, or tea-ceremony cooking, the *grande cuisine* of Japan (*Chapter 6*), but it also influenced Japanese architecture, decorative style and dining etiquette.

The standards of dining were also refined in that they reflected the taste-

17

fully frugal quality of Japanese life. Even noblemen were expected to leave their bowls and plates absolutely clean, to the extent of tucking fruit pips and fish bones into the sleeves of their kimonos. The Japanese still consider a dish with unfinished food unsightly, although inedible remains are not now hidden in one's sleeve but are replaced in the dish as tidily as possible.

Towards the mid 16th century, Japan was brought face to face with a totally new influence—this time from Europe. The first Europeans known to have reached Japan were three Portuguese travelling in a Chinese junk that was blown ashore by a typhoon in the early 1540s. The Japanese received them cordially, and their war-lords quickly copied Portuguese fire-arms, thus adding a new element to samurai warfare. After the castaways had returned home with the news of their welcome by an agreeable, highly cultivated people, other Portuguese travellers soon set sail for Japan to begin a lucrative trade between the Chinese and Japanese ports.

While the early Portuguese traders were enchanted by the Japanese and their civilized ways, the Japanese saw the newcomers as little better than barbarians. They invited the Europeans to their homes but were appalled by the manners of these pale, long-nosed, meat-gobbling foreigners. A provincial lord, writing of his impressions of the Portuguese traders, described them as understanding "to a certain degree the distinction between Superior and Inferior, but I do not know whether they have a proper system of ceremonial etiquette. They eat with their fingers instead of with chopsticks such as we use. They show their feelings without any self-control. . . . They are people who spend their lives roving hither and yon. They have no fixed abode and barter things which they have for those they do not, but withal they are a harmless sort of people."

This condescending view of Europeans changed for the better after 1549 when well-educated Jesuit missionaries, backed by the Portuguese crown and determined to convert the Japanese to Christianity, began to arrive in Japan. The Jesuits noted that the Japanese, following Buddhist beliefs, still ate practically no meat but a good deal of fish, and that they cultivated a variety of grains—notably rice—and many kinds of vegetables. They also noted that the Japanese made plentiful use of herbs and fruit, including dried fruit, in their meals. What the Japanese ate was obviously good for them, for a leading Jesuit reported: "These people live wonderfully healthy lives and there are many aged."

But the European missionaries and traders unfortunately made the error of meddling in Japanese politics. This threat to the feudal system, added to Japanese fears of an invasion by Spaniards based in the Philippines, resulted in the expulsion in 1638 of all Europeans except for a few Dutch traders, who were permitted to remain but were kept under close watch. An occasional Dutch merchant ship was allowed to land its cargo, but all other foreigners were forbidden to enter Japan, and no Japanese could leave on pain of death. The islands' doors were now locked more securely than ever against the rest of the world, and they remained so until the arrival of Commodore Perry more than two centuries later.

Although the Portuguese were gone, they left behind their recipes for deep-fried foods that came to be known as *tempura*. The word *tempura* itself provides a clue to its origin. In his book *Talking Your Way around the World*,

Shintoism, the ancient religion of a nature- and ancestor-worshipping people, is still closely identified with the bounty of land and sea in Japan. On the opposite page, Shinto priests stand before bottles and casks of *sake* that they have blessed. This rite takes place annually in April at the Matsunoh shrine in Kyoto.

Overleaf:
A newly built oyster boat has been purified in a Shinto ceremony that includes placing a lacy bamboo stalk trimmed with straw and paper in the stern. Presumably, the boat will now be protected as it lowers into Hiroshima Bay the racks of scallop shells in which oysters are cultivated.

Continued on page 22

the philologist Mario Pei says: "The Portuguese, as good Catholics, rejected meat on Ember Days, which they called by the Latin name of Quattuor Tempora, the 'four times' of the year. They asked instead for seafood, usually shrimp. Eventually the name *tempura* became attached to the fried shrimp the Portuguese favoured on these days. Thus did the ancient Latin word for 'times' turn into the Japanese word for shrimp fried in batter."

In characteristic fashion, the Japanese refined the Portuguese method, using a lighter batter and a lighter oil. Today Japanese deep-fried foods have a delicacy unmatched anywhere in the world.

After the 1850s, when Japan ended an almost unbroken millennium as a tightly enclosed nation, the Japanese suddenly found much to admire in the dynamic civilization of the West. They rushed headlong into learning all they could about the ways of Westerners, especially their advanced science and technology, and by the early years of the 20th century Japan was well on its way to becoming the industrial giant we know today.

Along with Western technology and science, the eclectic Japanese also borrowed Western food styles, including the eating of meat. As new dietary ideas became popular and the majority of the people gradually abandoned Buddhist regulations forbidding the consumption of meat, chicken, pork and beef began to appear more and more frequently on the Japanese menu. Before very long the Japanese were raising some of the world's finest beef cattle, and steak—or chicken—had become the principal ingredient in the most internationally famous Japanese dish—*sukiyaki* (*page 134*). In Japan's principal cities restaurants serving dishes imitating those of the West are now enormously prosperous, and the chefs of some of the better ones have learnt the art of Western cooking in France. By the early 1960s Tokyo had more than 2,000 restaurants that served exclusively Western-style food. And the fact that such restaurants are rivalled in popularity by those specializing in a Japanese version of Chinese cooking reflects the growing cosmopolitanism of Japanese tastes in food.

Since their close contact with American eating habits during the United States occupation of Japan following the Second World War, the Japanese have been particularly enthusiastic about American foods. A United States food fair held recently in Tokyo drew half a million people, and today you can have *aisukurimu*—Japanese for ice-cream—or ham and cheese sandwiches almost anywhere in Japan. Bread, toast and fried eggs have made similar inroads on the traditional diet. But these changes in food preferences have had at least one serious side effect: an increasing number of Japanese are fat; until a few years ago it was unusual to see an over-weight person in Japan. The notable exception were the *sumo*, Japan's professional wrestlers, who deliberately attain their enormous girth through a special diet.

While Japanese appetites have become cosmopolitan, the traditional fine cooking of Japan is still widely practised by present-day Japanese, who treasure it as an integral part of their national character. A Japanese separated from his national diet for any length of time feels lost, listless and uprooted. Only with his traditional dishes featuring freshly caught fish, nourishing seaweeds, steamed rice, succulent mushrooms gathered in the uplands and the shimmering white curd made from soya beans can a Japanese feel the sea, mountains and plains of his homeland.

It seems surprising, in this rapidly shrinking world of the 20th century, that only recently have Westerners—Americans more than any others—reversed the usual order and begun to borrow gastronomically from the Japanese. Japan's manufactured products have been known nearly everywhere for years. Films, television and the ease of travel by plane have familiarized millions of foreigners with many aspects of Japanese culture. But it was not until relatively recently that Japanese cooking began to be widely appreciated abroad for what it really is—a unique and highly refined art to be relished by both the eye and the palate. There were only one or two Japanese restaurants in New York City until the Korean War, when thousands of American troops discovered Japanese dishes on their native ground. As a result of their experience of Japanese food during the 1950s the number of Japanese restaurants in New York multiplied dramatically. In London, so far, there is only one Japanese restaurant open to the public; in Paris there are four—and both cities have private restaurants or clubs whose clientele are all Japanese.

There are various reasons for this belated appreciation. One of them is that Americans for a long time confused Japanese with Chinese food, which had been known in America ever since the navvies from southern China helped to build the trans-continental railways during the latter part of the 19th century. Japanese immigration, on the other hand, was slight until 1900, and so Japanese cooking had little opportunity to reveal its distinctive character.

Probably the most significant reason for both America's and Europe's tardy recognition of Japanese cooking, however, has been the Japanese themselves. While they eagerly assimilated Western technology, in matters pertaining to their traditional culture they tended to regard things Japanese and things foreign as lovers without a common language. This attitude still prevails, often keeping the casual tourist from discovering the finest elements in Japanese cooking.

The emphasis on subtlety of taste, aesthetic appearance and traditional ways of serving may make Japanese cuisine seem too formidable to be attempted at home. The surprising truth is that it should be every housewife's delight, for most of its dishes, far from being difficult, actually allow great freedom and rich opportunities for creativity in cooking.

All cookery books devoted to Japanese cooking stress this freedom. The recipe for a specific dish will give methods and seasonings and then add "this method can be used with prawns, crab, lobster, any white fish, etc."— often listing as many as eight or ten possible foods for which the method might be suitable. Where different foods require a slight variation in method, this is also noted and may consist of signals telling you to "cook only until it changes colour" or "cook until transparent white but not opaque white". It is such telling signals that will enable you to recognize those small but crucial differences that add up to perfection.

An old Japanese saying holds that if you have the pleasant experience of eating something that you have not tasted before, your life will be lengthened by 75 days. I like to believe that there is truth in this, and that the pleasures of discovering the cooking of Japan will prolong by many years the lives of those who explore its many byways.

II

Foods for all Seasons

Young maple leaves and a
red felt picnic cloth provide
a springtime setting for this
300-year-old *bento* box and
its nested contents. The
food has been meticulously
prepared for a festive picnic
by a professional chef. It
includes chestnuts, duck,
fish cakes, prawn balls,
kelp and such seasonal
favourites as clams (*on the left of
the main box*) and quail eggs
(*in the tray, centre front*).

Suddenly, on a raw day in early February, the strawberries arrive in a
torrent. Fruit sellers all over Japan shove other products into a corner and
cover their shelves with a rich, red carpet—boxes and boxes of the biggest,
juiciest, sweetest strawberries in the world—while editorial writers and
television commentators remind readers and listeners of the seasonal thing
to do. For a few weeks it seems as if no other fruit exists in Japan.

In elegant restaurants, when most of the dishes have been cleared away
and the geisha are tuning up their samisen, the sated diners are revived by
the sight of five or six huge, glistening strawberries, set before them on a
black or dark-green dish. If the occasion is informal enough and sufficient
sake has been consumed, the attending geisha and the waitresses will oblig-
ingly spear the strawberries with toothpicks and pop them seductively into
the mouths of the weary customers. In tiny noodle shops, in *fugu* restaurants, which generally limit their menus to varied preparations of the
globe-fish called *fugu*, even in the *sushi* snack shops, which normally serve
no dessert at all, strawberries are presented at the end of the meal as a matter
of course. No housewife in Japan would feel that she was doing right by her
family unless she offered strawberries as often as she could afford them.

Almost as abruptly as they come, the strawberries disappear, not to be
seen again until a little later in the year. The Japanese do not often preserve
them or make jam out of them, and only recently have frozen strawberries
reached a few luxury shops. Strawberries are eaten fresh or not at all; to the
Japanese they are as much a part of the late winter season as pancakes to us
are part of Shrove Tuesday. The Japanese would be as startled to be served

Japanese-English Glossary

DAIKON: *giant radish*
MOCHI: *rice cake*
OBI: *a broad sash worn with kimono*
SASHIMI: *slices of raw fish*
SHOYU: *soya sauce*
SUSHI: *vinegared rice topped with raw fish or wrapped in laver*
SUKIYAKI: *a simmered beef dish*
TOKONOMA: *an alcove for displaying objects*
YUZU: *a citrus fruit rather like a lime*

strawberries in late summer as we should be to find Christmas pudding in a picnic hamper at Ascot.

It's not just because strawberries are at their best in February that the Japanese go on a strawberry binge every year; hot-house cultivation could make the berries available for most of the year with little sacrifice of taste. To the Japanese, in their unending quest for harmony with nature, a food simply cannot be separated from its season: to do so would risk throwing the universe ever so slightly out of its pre-ordained rhythm. There are scores of Japanese foods—fruit, fish, vegetables, even sweets—that belong unalterably to certain seasons, and the enjoyment of which, at the right time, the Japanese approach with almost reverent fervour. In Japan every season has its food and, to some extent, every food has its season. Some years ago a Japanese friend of mine was dumbfounded when I happened to mention the variety of frozen foods available in American supermarkets. "But is it safe to eat foods out of season?" she asked.

We of the West go to such lengths to defeat and "tame" nature that it is hard for us to appreciate a culture and a cuisine that still change with the elements. The Japanese ride the seasons instead of battling them. To a Westerner shivering in an unheated Japanese house in winter this "oneness with nature" may seem absurd, but if he can survive until dinner time, a bowl of *tamago dofu* (seasoned egg custard) served in a hot soup, and a few cups of hot *sake*, may give him a different perspective.

Eating egg soup and eating strawberries in season may not be a mystical experience for us, but by responding to the rhythm of the seasons the Japanese unite themselves with the divine forces of the universe. Even non-religious Japanese feel the need for this. Nowadays, many Japanese have abandoned such traditional seasonal pastimes as moon viewing, fire-fly catching, and listening for the pop of the first lotus blossoming; there's just too much noise and smog and concrete in the way. Cut off from these manifestations of nature by central heating, air-conditioning and urban sprawl, urban Japanese have come to rely even more heavily on their seasonal foods to keep the channels open to the cosmos. And as might be expected, their emphasis on each food in its season produces some gastronomic miracles.

But merely serving foods at certain times of the year is not enough. To squeeze every possible drop of seasonal mood and meaning out of a meal, the best Japanese restaurants maintain separate sets of dishes and serving utensils for each season. They insist that the patterns of their waitresses' kimono and *obi* always reflect the season—red leaves in autumn, for example, and blossoms in the spring—and they carefully change the flower arrangement and the hanging scroll in the *tokonoma* of each guest room every few days or more often, not only to harmonize with the food to be served and to suit the particular guest but to match the season outside.

Many Japanese dishes, moreover, are prepared and arranged to look like some seasonal symbol. It is in tea-ceremony food (*Chapter 6*) that this combination of taste, ingredients and appearance reaches its artistic peak, but the idea shapes and colours a wide range of ordinary Japanese foods, adding another aesthetic dimension to the Japanese enjoyment of the seasonal changes in light and weather.

One of the first signs of spring, for instance, is the *uguisu mochi*, or nightingale cake. You see it, usually clutched in the fist of a small, happy child, only when the nightingale breaks his winter silence. Like other sweet rice cakes this soft and chewy confection is made of pounded rice meal and sugar and is filled with sweetened bean paste. This one, however, is cut roughly in the shape of the bird and lightly dusted with green bean powder.

A few weeks later, when the cherry trees are about to blossom, a sweet *mochi* wrapped in cherry leaves appears. The leaves are removed before eating, but their delicate fragrance permeates the cake and lingers on the tongue.

By cherry-blossom time the season is well under way and the Japanese have already eaten many spring foods such as bamboo shoots, for instance. Although these crisp, refreshing slivers of young bamboo are now available canned all the year round, the fresh ones are at their tenderest in the spring, and their appearance in *sukiyaki*, in one of the compartments of the *bento* picnic boxes, and in various kinds of rice dishes always signifies this season.

Early in the spring some elegant restaurants take a trout called *kawamasu*, which happens to be at its best when the plum trees are in bloom, and doubly commemorate that brief moment of the year by producing a dish in which chunks of the salt-grilled trout (*page 177*), garnished with seasonal leaves, are arranged on a blossom-shaped plate so that they look like part of the plum blossom itself.

To Toyama Bay, on the coast of the Sea of Japan, April brings the tender "fire-fly" squid, a tiny phosphorescent creature that appears nowhere else in Japan. Every evening for three or four weeks the bay sparkles with millions of the squid coming in to shallow water to spawn. Toyama residents and sightseers from the cities swarm out in boats to marvel at the display and watch the fishermen pull in their full, glittering nets, which look like huge clusters of diamonds. Most of these squid are consumed raw, as *sashimi*, right at Toyama, since they cannot be kept fresh long enough for shipment.

In May the Japanese gourmet turns his attention to tea, for it is then that the *shincha*, the highly prized first new leaves of the tea bush, are plucked and sent to market. This is not the leaf for the tea ceremony—which is taken from special ancient plants—but the everyday green tea that the Japanese drink morning, noon and night, at home and at work, before meals, with meals and after meals—and which when offered to a visitor, must be sipped before any business can be done. Green tea—Japan tea, or *Nihon-cha*, as the Japanese themselves call it to distinguish it from *kocha*, or the black tea, drunk by most of the rest of the world—is considered so essential a beginning that most Tokyo coffee shops will serve you, unasked, a free cup of tea before they bring your coffee, even if you have ordered nothing else.

Shincha, new tea, makes a brighter-coloured brew than tea picked later in the year, and the Japanese claim that it has a mellower flavour. If the new leaves lie around too long, they lose their unique freshness, so *shincha* can be enjoyed only in May. During the season, tea lovers from all over Japan descend on the tea plantations in Shizuoka, about 110 miles south-west of Tokyo, to taste *shincha* brewed fresh from the plucking. Tens of thousands of tea connoisseurs who can't make the trip order growers to ship them, every year, a choice selection of new leaves as soon as they are picked.

A Japanese can be just as fussy about his tea as any elderly English lady.

Onlookers, including a local policeman, watch Japanese school children salvage frost-bitten persimmons for their owner after an early snowstorm in October. This particular species of persimmon—a small, astringent type—is usually picked in the autumn and peeled and dried, but these ripened on the tree and fell victim to the cold.

Shincha, the Japanese say, must be brewed for one to two minutes in water between 140° and 160°F., and the cups must be warmed to the same temperature beforehand. Ordinary tea requires about 180°, and only the cheapest grades, *bancha*, are exposed to water near the boiling point. If, when the tea is poured, the leaves and stems float on the surface, then the tea has not steeped enough; if they sink and lie flat on the bottom, it has been steeped too long. Ideally, the particles should remain suspended near the bottom of the cup—preferably, say the purists, in a vertical position!

From the tea sipping at Shizuoka, the travelling epicures might journey on to Gifu, between Nagoya and Kyoto, to be on hand for the first taste of the finest seasonal food on the Japanese calendar: *ayu*. The *ayu* is a small freshwater fish that looks for all the world like a river trout and tastes like a fish for the gods. From mid-May, when the *ayu* season opens, until the season peters out in various parts of the country at different times in the autumn, the *ayu* and its praises are literally on everyone's lips. It has such a

28

distinct, sweetish, satisfying taste that the first time I had it I found it hard to believe that I was not eating some carefully concocted culinary masterpiece; it didn't seem possible that the unprepossessing little fish lying before me with skin and bones intact had produced all that flavour. But the only thing the chef had done, after gutting the fish, was *shioyaki* (*page 177*), salt-grilling the fish, the simple Japanese cooking method (*Chapter 3*) that brings out the best in any fish; it was merely my untrained palate that had looked for artifice where nature had already achieved perfection.

The *ayu* is an egalitarian fish. In the cities the greatest restaurants serve it proudly on proper dishes, surrounded by just the right seasonal herbs and grasses. But it tastes just as good in the dozens of flimsy, temporary stalls that pop up every summer along the banks of Japanese rivers to serve freshly caught *ayu* to the common folk—and to unlucky fishermen.

It is not the *ayu* alone that attracts visitors to Gifu in the *ayu* season, for the fish is found almost everywhere in the country, but the remarkable technique of catching *ayu* with trained cormorants, large, long-billed aquatic birds remarkably skilled at catching fish under water. The technique has survived at Gifu centuries after falling into oblivion in other parts of the world.

Cormorants work on moonless nights, tethered to their handlers by long strings. Rings around their necks prevent them from swallowing any but the smallest fish they catch. In the eerie light from torches on the handlers' boats, the obedient birds swoop low over the river, diving in a twinkling to snatch fish from the water, darting to and fro in apparent confusion. A handler may run as many as 12 cormorants at once, somehow managing to prevent his birds from snarling each other's lines or the lines from other boats. One at a time he pulls them back to disgorge their gulletfuls of *ayu*—which are transferred immediately to accompanying restaurant boats and served afloat, salt-grilled or raw, to foreign tourists who have come to look and marvel and to Japanese tourists who have come to eat and look.

Connoisseurs believe that the *ayu* is at its best in late August and early September, when cooling weather puts a layer of fat on the fish. But the Japanese are so eager to get at the *ayu* early in the season and they consume so many of the fish before midsummer, that by August they are slightly fed up with it—although they will never admit to being tired of *ayu*.

Before that happens, the Japanese have briefly abandoned *ayu* for a midsummer fling with eels. Unlike ordinary fish, eels don't lose their fat in the summer, and since fatty fish is considered superior, eels are preferred to other leaner seafoods during the hot weather. What is more, they are fantastically rich in vitamin A. Split, boned, skewered on bamboo and grilled over charcoal in a special sweetened soya sauce called *tare*, the eels become a toast-brown dish called *kabayaki*, which in any season, with or without rice, is pungent, heady fare. It is easy to understand why it is so popular.

What is harder to understand, however, is why so many modern Japanese slavishly obey an old superstition that orders them to eat eels on a particular day of the year. On the Chinese lunar calendar, eel day is *Ushinohi*, the Day of the Ox in the *Doyo* season—the dog days—and it falls in late July or early August. For reasons lost in antiquity, the Japanese believe that eels eaten on *Ushinohi* cure illnesses and enable one to survive the heat of summer. Some authorities suggest that the custom derived from the idea that eels would

Overleaf: The patchwork quilt of land on Innoshima island in the Inland Sea shows the manner in which Japanese farmers rotate their crops to the best advantage. The white sections are fields of chrysanthemums, which are processed into an agricultural insecticide that is sold throughout Japan. These plants do not thrive if they are planted in the same soil year after year. Therefore next season's chrysanthemums will be planted where the brownish-yellow wheat and green leaf vegetables now grow.

drive out evil spirits on a day that is astrologically propitious. A more likely explanation is that the whole thing was dreamed up a couple of centuries ago by an eel-shop proprietor in Edo—old Tokyo. If this is true, it was the most successful promotional scheme in Japanese history.

On *Ushinohi* eel restaurants are jammed from morning to midnight, and some customers have to eat standing up. Politicians and other celebrities get themselves photographed smiling over skewered *kabayaki*, and television comedians work eels into their routines. "Have you had your eels yet?" is the standard greeting when meeting friends on *Ushinohi*. Office workers, having eaten eels at lunch, stop at eel restaurants on their way home to collect a parcel of pre-cooked *kabayaki* for the family, for eels are too slippery and difficult for the ordinary housewife to handle.

Oddly, eel eating on *Ushinohi* is one old custom that flourishes more strongly in the sophisticated cities than in rural districts. Country folk don't seem to need a special day to remind them of the seasons. But the vast majority of Japanese in the cities really seem to believe that they must eat a helping of eels on the appointed day or else risk illness, and so every year they happily devour nearly 800 tons of eels in 24 hours. And lo, most of the eel eaters do indeed survive the summer heat.

While eels are keeping the Japanese healthy, a variety of other summer dishes are keeping them cool. *Tofu*, or soya-bean curd, cooked with other foods during most of the year, finally becomes a dish in its own right in the hot weather. Served on ice, and flavoured with soya sauce and flakes of *katsuobushi* (dried bonito), chopped spring onions and ginger, the cold, custard-like *tofu* makes an excellent—and non-fattening—light summer lunch. Another favourite food for fighting the heat is *zarusoba*, iced buck-wheat noodles (*page 131*). The slithery greenish-brown noodles are piled on a little bamboo tray and dipped before eating into a special sauce made of soya sauce, *mirin* (sweet *sake*), *niban dashi* (a soup stock; *page 54*), and garnished with chopped spring onions, and bits of *nori* seaweed.

The Japanese have too high a regard for their green tea ever to imbibe it cold. Instead, on hot summer days, they drink a kind of cold "tea" made by brewing roasted barley grains in a teapot. Just what makes their *mugicha* so refreshing I cannot say, but it does have a tonic effect. Nowadays, carbonated drinks and ice-cream are as popular in Japan as anywhere else, but a plate of *zarusoba* and a cup of *mugicha* still win my vote on one of those awful, sultry August afternoons in Tokyo.

Autumn arrives suddenly, in early September, and not even in the concrete jungle of Tokyo do you need a menu to tell you that the season has changed. The summer vanishes overnight and you wake up to what most Japanese consider the finest season of the year—cool, dry air, the sky scrubbed blue, and a hint of changing colours on the trees, on the kimonos of the women, and on the cup that holds your morning tea.

The first—and perhaps the most important—gastronomic event of autumn is the September appearance of *matsutake*, which may very well be the world's most delicious mushroom. Certainly no other mushroom I have eaten ever tasted like steak. A smaller fungus, the *shiitake*, is by far the most common mushroom in Japanese cookery, but to the Japanese the huge *matsutake*, often measuring eight inches across, is the mushroom king, and

    Continued on page 36

This "frost-spotted" model house suggests winter, the season when strips of abalone are grilled at table on a hot stone.

The Right Food Honoured at the Right Season in the Right Setting

The Japanese reverence for nature, which manifests itself at every turn, is perhaps most frequently perceived in the serving of food. For to the Japanese food is the most essential product of nature and therefore an especially favoured object of respect. Kaichi Tsuji, a noted chef and master teacher of Japanese *grande cuisine*, puts it this way: "Food should be prepared to do honour to the essence of the materials chosen". By this he means that food is appropriately honoured when it is served in season and when its full flavour is brought out without the addition of anything alien to its inherent taste. Great chefs like Kaichi Tsuji further enhance the delights of fine food by devising exquisite presentations that please the eye as well as the palate; seen above is one example of their skill in this regard and others are pictured overleaf. While certain Western dishes depend on seasonal foods for their excellence, seasonal Japanese dishes go a step further by creating a subtle interplay of substance and symbolism. To be sure, the season dictates the food to be used, but it is the chefs who invent compatible settings that make the finished dishes a charming salute to a particular time of the year.

33

MAY: FESTIVAL FOOD

In Japan the fifth day of May is
Children's Day. But the day was
formerly dedicated to boys, and some
of the festive food still reflects this
emphasis. Special stress is laid on
manliness and courage. Here the food
is served on a mottled porcelain
plate set into a teak frame. It consists
of prawns shaped like samurai
warriors' helmets (*top centre*),
accompanied by green circlets of
cucumber cut to simulate an
ancient coat of arms suitable for an
adventurer; of rice and sea bream
wrapped in bamboo leaves and
seaweed, with crisp ginger spears
(*left*); and roast duck, mushrooms
and green soya beans (*right*). The box
holds a special feast-day sweet.

AUGUST: HORS D'ŒUVRE

To combat the debilitating effect of
summer on the appetite, this meal
uses psychological as well as culinary
weapons. The cool appearance of the
glass dish sets the mood for a light
hot-weather meal. Green maple leaves
placed beneath a transparent tray are a
summery base for (*counter-clockwise
from the top*) smoked salmon, sea
urchin and white meat of sea bream,
bean curd, green soya beans and fried
chicken. Next to this array is a pitcher
of *sake*. The lace-like crystal dish
offers visual refreshment with its
green *nori* seaweed, cucumber stuffed
with plum paste, and raw prawns. On
the right on the yellow dish are salted,
dried bonito. On the long green leaf
are cucumber and river trout.

SEPTEMBER: MOON FOOD

The autumnal colours of this traditional meal, together with the warm *sake*, bring joy to Japanese viewing the moon during the semi-annual Tsukimi festival. The red lacquer bowl contains *akadashi* soup, whose base of *dashi* and red soya-bean paste is the starting point for many variations. Above it are steamed abalone and cucumber with a special soya sauce. In the quartered tray, the dish holds grilled rock trout. The chicken, shaped from rice, has an eye made of a green pea. In the blue-rimmed dish are fern fronds, boiled bamboo shoots and two bean-curd balls. On the upper right are prawns, eel and burdock cylinders and half an egg that represents the moon surrounded by clouds.

DECEMBER: EXOTIC CASSEROLE

Winter brings a solid dinner whose sombre colours befit the season. In the pot on the upper tray are thick slices of white *daikon* radish, reddish octopus and *konnyaku*, a jelly-like food made from devil's tongue. The fluted bowl contains a hot prepared mustard —stinging by Japanese standards; numbing to unwary Westerners —with which the morsels are gingerly anointed. The uncovered bowl holds *akadashi* soup, also encountered above, here varied by the addition of bits of mushroom and *daikon*. In the covered bowl is rice. The oblong plate offers raw sea bream surrounded by three different garnishes. Diners dip the raw fish into the grated *daikon* in the tiny bowl to add a tangy flavour.

they properly make as much fuss over it as they do about strawberries in the spring and *ayu* and eels in the summer.

Matsutake grows in red pine forests. In districts thus favoured, such as that around Osaka and Kyoto, *matsutake* gathering is one of the happiest festivals of the year. Thousands of local people, their ranks swelled by Tokyoites who zip down on the new super-express, their mouths watering, swarm through specially reserved forest areas carrying *sake*, rice and cooking pots. There are family groups, factory and office excursions paid for by the boss, and clusters of businessmen, accompanied by geisha or bar hostesses hired for the day, on the expense account, to provide even more zest to the outing. They pick their *matsutake*, preferably those with the crown only half opened, cook them on the spot and savour the taste, with *sake* and laughter, under the trees.

Most Japanese, who can't afford the time and money to go to the *matsutake*, need only wait and the *matsutake* will come to them. At the peak of the season the *matsutake* turns up everywhere. Even restaurants that never serve another mushroom all the year round offer *matsutake* to keep their regular customers from straying. Housewives cook it at home, *sukiyaki* houses add it to their ingredients, restaurants offering a Japanese version of Western cookery serve it like a meat dish, on a plate with vegetables, while chefs at the great restaurants spin subtle webs of taste to complement the hearty flavour of the mushroom. Often *matsutake* will be cooked only with *tofu*, which is so bland that no extraneous taste will mar the mushroom's purity. To many Japanese, however, *matsutake* marinated in soya sauce and sweet *sake*, and then grilled, is a filling, satisfying meal in itself. Others prefer it in *dobin mushi*, steamed with chicken, fish and ginkgo nuts in small earthenware pots, one for each person. *Matsutake meshi*, rice cooked with mushroom, is the simple dish of the pine-forest picnics.

In Japan as elsewhere, autumn is also the season for fruits and nuts. In modern times, Western fruits such as apples, pears, grapes and, for late-summer eating, peaches have been introduced to the country, and Japanese orchards produce delicious crops. But for the tradition-conscious Japanese, the fruit that truly spells autumn is the bright orange *kaki*, or persimmon, ripening in farmyards and on hill-sides all over Japan.

Fresh, the *kaki* is segmented and served as a dessert all the autumn long; its taste lies somewhere between an apple and an apricot. Dried, the *kaki* becomes a winter staple, excellent for between-meal nibbling, and an indispensable part of the New Year holiday. *Kaki* is rich in vitamin C, and since ancient times the Japanese have recognized its medicinal properties as well as its seasonal beauty and taste. Persimmons are said to be an effective, quick antidote for over-indulgence in *sake*. Old-timers in some parts of the country still prescribe *kaki* leaves for coughs, high blood-pressure and various digestive upsets.

October brings chestnuts and ginkgo nuts, the latter peculiar to the Orient. In the Kansai, the Osaka-Kyoto area, chestnuts go into an autumn dish called *fukiyose*, a colourful mixture of nuts, prawns, *matsutake* and vegetables, arranged to suggest a pile of autumn leaves. Some rural areas celebrate a chestnut festival, cooking the nuts in rice and making a special sweet rice cake flavoured with chestnuts. In some of the poorer mountain districts of

Japan, boiled and mashed chestnuts are made into everyday dumplings.

The little ginkgo nut is used in soups and cooked dishes all the year round but the Japanese eat it for its own sake in the autumn. Before they can get to the meat of the nut they must wash off a soft, outer covering. Then a hard white shell is cracked. Finally, after roasting, a filmy inner skin comes off, revealing the green gem within. Traditionally a family gathers around the hibachi on autumn evenings to roast ginkgo nuts over charcoal and eat them hot. Nowadays the nuts are also used to bring a whiff of autumn and a mood of nostalgia to some of Tokyo's Western-style bars.

For those Japanese who care deeply about every aspect of their food, November is the memorable moment when rice, freshly harvested, tastes best. Country people who have moved to the city send home in November for a sack of the early rice of their district, and even housewives who have lived all their lives in town know that the moist new rice, distinguished by a special name, *shinmai*, needs less water for cooking.

Rice is something more than a staple food for the Japanese. For centuries it was their standard of wealth; feudal fiefs were ranked according to their rice yield and samurai were paid in rice. Even today shrines to Inari, the rice god, are the most ubiquitous in Japan and an integral part of the folk culture. The very word for "meal" in Japan is *gohan*—rice—and a Japanese doesn't feel he has eaten until he's had his bowl of rice.

Imposing a decorative design, the criss-crossed bamboo strips form the protective wrapping of carefully boxed fresh *shiitake* mushrooms. Harvested both in the spring and autumn, *shiitake* are in demand, fresh or dried, for their subtle flavouring and visual interest.

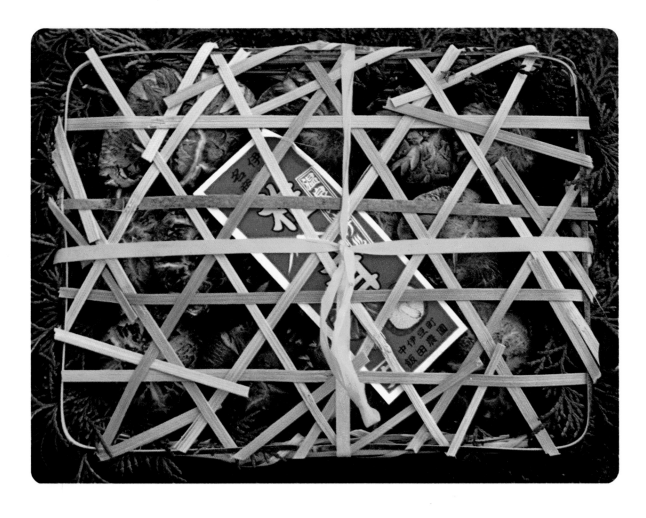

Sometimes, for variety, the Japanese will pour different sauces over their rice or cook it with other ingredients. But the freshly harvested *shinmai* is almost never "spoiled" this way, for the Japanese insist that they find in it a taste and goodness that speak of the season, the land and their heritage.

All through the autumn, as the ocean waters cool and spawning ends, fattened fish check in on schedule and take their places on the Japanese menu. One of the first to arrive is the *kamasu*, a species of barracuda, followed quickly by *samma*, a mackerel-pike. By December, most of the scores of varieties of sea creatures that nourish Japan are in plentiful supply (*Chapter 4*).

Winter is the time for white-meat fishes, raw, grilled and deep-fried (*tempura*). It is the season for warming fish stews, like the *sampei jiru* of far-northern Honshu and Hokkaido: a thick salmon soup with vegetables. In winter, *fugu*, the dangerous globe-fish (*Chapter 4*), is at its best and hot *sake* at its most effective. And it is on winter evenings that you are most likely to hear plaintive, reedy wail of the noodle seller's horn; for although the Japanese eat noodles—both buckwheat *soba* and the heavier wheat variety called *udon*—all the year round, hot noodles, served in dozens of combinations of fish, meat and vegetables, are best in cold weather.

Foods cooked at the table, like *sukiyaki* and *mizutaki* (*page 134*), flourish in the winter months. *Mizutaki* is made with chicken; a similar dish, made with beef, is called *shabu shabu* (*page 135*), because that is the sound the sliver of raw meat makes as you hold it in your chopsticks and swish it around in a pot of boiling chicken stock and *dashi*. When the meat is lightly cooked you remove it, dip it into a special sauce of *shoyu*, grated *daikon*, ground sesame seeds, *yuzu* juice and other ingredients, and enjoy it. Then the winter vegetable *hakusai*, which we call Chinese cabbage, and *tofu* are boiled in the same liquid and, after they are eaten, *udon* noodles are sometimes added to the rich broth remaining and eaten as a final course. The secret of *mizutaki* lies in the dipping sauce, and many restaurants specializing in this item guard their recipes jealously.

The seasonal star of the winter scene is something much more simple: the tangerine, or mandarin orange, called *mikan* in Japanese. The *mikan* is one of several citrus fruits grown in Japan, but except for expensive imported delicacies it is almost the only fresh fruit of any kind available all through the winter—until that magic moment when the strawberries arrive. Legend has it that there were tangerines in Japan 2,000 years ago; history records the presence of the fruit for at least 600 years, and centuries before science discovered vitamin C the Japanese were using *mikan* juice as a cold tonic.

From late December until early spring, tangerines are on every table, on sale in little net bags at stalls in the underground, and often served with the cup of tea that precedes all business discussions. On New Year's Day they join rice cakes as a standard holiday offering—and if the Shinto deities are at all like their descendants, they are hugely appreciated, for the Japanese devour the fruit in tremendous quantities. I have seen a family group of about ten children and adults, gathered on the New Year, casually polish off an entire crate of *mikan* in one happy, chatty, informal—and eminently healthy—afternoon. In a way, the Japanese regard the *mikan* through the winter as a flame-coloured symbol for the rising sun that will come back again in the spring to warm the earth and its people.

Opposite:
The best, biggest and most expensive strawberries of the season reach the markets in February and signal the end of winter. These berries grow on steep terraces in the mild Pacific climate of Shizuoka prefecture on the main island of Honshu. The box containing the 12 giant specimens in the foreground will fetch about a guinea. The 20 smaller berries in the other box will cost considerably less.

III

The Logic of Japanese Cookery

A variety of cutting and cooking techniques produced the displays in this delightful autumn *bento* box. The foods range from the simple *kimeyaki* (*top left*) and *temarizushi* (*top right*) to the elaborate *igaguri* (*below left*). The carrot "maple leaf", the lime "flower" cradling red caviar, and the ginkgo-nut leaf made of *fu* all serve to carry out the autumnal theme.

After thinking about the reluctance of some of my friends to venture into Japanese cooking, I have decided that their hesitancy is largely a matter of nomenclature. I have complete sympathy with them, for the unfamiliar language can create difficulties with the names both of the ingredients and of the techniques. It takes an effort of will to bear in mind that—despite the similarity in sound—*shioyaki* means food sprinkled with salt before grilling, while *sukiyaki* is a dish prepared by simmering, and has nothing to do with grilling. In time the pieces do fall into place as it becomes clear that there is a logic in the organization of Japanese cooking, and in its language.

The most important lesson to be learnt is that of the ubiquitous role of the soya bean. Generally considered by foreigners to be the most humble of vegetables, the soya bean is in fact the king of the Japanese kitchen. One might almost say that the Japanese cuisine is built upon a tripod of soya-bean products: *miso*, a fermented soya-bean paste; *tofu*, a custard-like soya-bean cake; and soya sauce, used both to season foods as they are being cooked and to make dipping mixtures that enhance the flavours of foods when they are being eaten.

Miso has a distinctive taste that sets its mark on other ingredients. And it forms a vital part of hundreds of Japanese dishes. *Miso* appears in many guises on Japanese menus starting with a favourite breakfast dish, *misoshiru*, the rich soup for which *miso* is essential. *Miso* may be an ingredient in a marinade for vegetables and fish and is also used in some recipes as part of a dressing in which foods are grilled. Because every maker of *miso* varies the proportions of the ingredients according to his taste and because *miso* im-

41

proves with age—it can be kept in wooden vats for as long as a decade without spoiling—to a sensitive palate no two *miso* will taste exactly alike.

The second great soya-bean product in Japanese cooking is *tofu*, which looks like, and has the consistency of, firm but fragile cakes of whitish custard. To outsiders, *tofu* comes close to being tasteless; the Japanese look upon it as a softener for other flavours as well as a separate taste. It is sautéed, boiled, grilled; used to garnish soups; rolled in cornflour and deep-fried; scrambled with eggs; mixed with sesame seed. So versatile is it as an accompaniment to almost the entire range of Japanese foods that some restaurants take great pride in preparing only dishes that make use of this protean ingredient.

Until recently the foreigner wishing to cook with *tofu* had to find an oriental food store whose owner gets his own supply. For *tofu*, even when refrigerated, spoils after three or four days. Happily, the Japanese have learned how to make instant, powdered *tofu*, which is reconstituted by mixing with boiling water and a coagulating agent included in the package. The powder can be stored, without refrigeration, almost indefinitely, and reconstituted *tofu* will stay fresh in the refrigerator for as long as 10 days. The flavour of reconstituted *tofu* is at least as satisfactory as that of the fresh variety. *Tofu* is also now available in tins, and although it has slightly less flavour than the instant product, its texture makes it desirable for certain dishes.

The third member of the soya-bean triumvirate is *shoyu*, or soya sauce, whose ingredients include not only soya beans but also wheat or barley, salt, water and malt. Its preparation is rather complicated and hardly worth the effort, for it can be bought at almost any supermarket. The Japanese, like the Chinese who invented it, use soya sauce as a dip, as a seasoning for cooking liquids, and as an ingredient in marinades. But for the Japanese, soya sauce is their all-purpose seasoning, as important to their country's cuisine as salt is to Western foods. One word of caution: Insist on soya sauce imported from Japan; neither the artificially flavoured domestic nor the heavier Chinese versions are at all satisfactory in Japanese cooking.

The soya bean's only important rival is rice. In Japan, rice occupies an even more important place than wheat and wheat products do today in the Western world. In fact, a meal without rice in some form would be just about unthinkable; it is hardly surprising, therefore, that a great deal of space is devoted to rice recipes in Japanese cookery books. But since rice is so intimately connected with family eating, we will discuss its preparation in Chapter 5.

Other ingredients frequently used in the preparation of vegetables, seafood, meat and fowl include: mild rice vinegar; sesame oil; the sweet rice wine called *mirin*; the stronger rice wine called *sake*; a green horse-radish powder called *wasabi*; *daikon*, the giant white radish that resembles the white turnip in taste; the strips of dried gourd called *kanpyo*; *gobo*, or burdock root; and *shirataki*, a preparation made from a yam-like tuber.

Japanese cooks also use such familiar seasonings as salt, pepper, mustard, sugar, spring onions, chives, onions and other foods found in most European kitchens. But there was a time, not so very long ago, when anyone interested in preparing Japanese meals had to write to importers in order to obtain the unfamiliar ingredients. Today, however, the situation has improved. Almost all the ingredients mentioned in this book are available at the retail shops run by the importers Mikadoya and Cydilda in London (*page 207*).

Once the foreigner who has decided to explore Japanese cooking has been introduced to the ingredients that are used only in this cuisine, the time has come to learn the methods by which the people of Japan prepare their meals. As they usually cook meat and vegetables in small pieces, the Japanese have never developed the arts of baking and roasting; they do, however, boil, steam, fry and grill, using techniques quite similar to Western ones but with just enough variation to produce their own distinctive and sophisticated cuisine.

Take grilled fish, for example. In most of the world, it is usual to baste fish with butter while it is being grilled to keep it moist. This is never the case in Japan. There, fish is often salt-grilled by the method called *shioyaki*, and I have never eaten elsewhere a moister or tastier grilled fish. Like so many Japanese cooking methods, this is very simple. The fish is salted and then set aside for 20 to 30 minutes before cooking. It is then placed in the grill, skin side up, where it remains until the skin becomes golden brown. The fish is then turned over so that its flesh is exposed to the flame. The dish is ready to eat when there is a flow of milky-white juices from between the flakes of the flesh. At precisely this point, the fish must be removed from the grill; another minute or two of the heat will dry it out.

This method of grilling works with just about any kind of fish one can name. The only requirement is that there be some skin on the fish, for under the skin lies a thin layer of fat that is worked on by the salt. The fat melts and protects the flesh from the heat and moistens and flavours the fish. From their experience with the *shioyaki* method, Japanese cooks have learned to avoid fish that has been skinned and boned. A great deal of flavour lies in the bones and under the skin, flavour that is imparted to the flesh during grilling. The Japanese know this and therefore do very little filleting. But the Japanese do cut away the skin and bones when a fish is to be deep-fried for *tempura*, or on most occasions when it is served raw as *sashimi*, or in some dishes that require boiling with strong soya sauce.

Shioyaki grilling is not limited to fish. A number of other foods, particularly chicken, are enhanced by this quick and simple method. But there are other types of grilling done in Japan. One sure-fire method, relatively well known abroad, is *teriyaki*, which means "shining grill". This is almost as simple as salt-grilling, but it does require a marinade made up of soya sauce and *mirin*, usually in equal proportions, although proportions and ingredients may vary and sometimes chicken broth is added for delicacy and to prevent scorching. With some *teriyaki* dishes the marinade does triple or even quadruple duty, serving as a flavouring agent before cooking, a basting sauce during cooking, a glaze to complete the dish, and sometimes as a dipping sauce after cooking. The final results of *teriyaki* grilling (*pages 175, 176*) are dishes with a mild, delicate and sweet flavour.

As in all Japanese cookery, timing is of the utmost importance in *teriyaki* grilling. It matters not whether foods are grilled, boiled, steamed or fried; the relationship between the thing being cooked and the degree of heat it is receiving remains uppermost in the minds of Japanese cooks. A good

Basic Japanese Ingredients

The Japanese ingredients listed below and illustrated overleaf are described further on page 199. Nearly all are available (*page 207*).

1 *Kome* (Japanese rice)
2 *Sake* (rice wine)
3 *Su* (rice vinegar)
4 *Mirin* (sweet *sake*)
5 Canned vegetables: *top left, konnyaku*; *centre, shirataki* (both made from the same plant root); *right, takenoko* (bamboo shoot); *bottom*, sliced *renkon* (lotus root)
6 *Junsai* (slippery vegetables)
7 *Gobo* (burdock)
8 *Azuki* (red) and *kuromame* (black) beans
9 *From left: Goma* (black and white sesame seeds), *ginnan* (ginkgo nuts)
10 *Goma-abura* (sesame oil)
11 *Tsukemono* (pickles): *clock-wise from top left*, large pickled plums, pickled yellow radish, red pickled ginger, small pickled plums
12 Mushrooms: *from left, nameko, matsutake*, dried *shiitake*
13 *Fu* (wheat-gluten croûtons)
14 *Udon* (thick wheat noodles)
15 *Hiyamugi* (thin noodles served cold)
16 *Somen* (thin wheat noodles)
17 *Harusame* (transparent noodles)
18 *Daikon* (white radish)
19 *Uni* (prepared sea-urchin)
20 *Aonoriko* (powdered green seaweed)
21 *Shoga* (ginger root)
22 *Kona sansho* (Japanese pepper)
23 *Hichimi togarashi* (seven-pepper spice)
24 *Clock-wise from top right: sansho* (Japanese pepper leaf), Aji-no-moto (MSG), *takano tjume* (small whole red peppers), *karashi* (mustard)
25 *Shoyu* (Japanese soya sauce)
26 *From top: aka miso* (red soya-bean paste), *shiro miso* (white soya-bean paste), *tofu* (soya-bean curd)
27 *Kombu* (dried kelp)
28 Pre-flaked *katsuobushi* (dried bonito)
29 *Katsuobushi* (dried bonito)
30 *Nori* (dried laver)
31 *Wakame* (dried seaweed)

17

18

31

29

30

28

27

15

19

20

13

16

21

26

22 23 24 25

example of this principle is the care with which some Japanese prepare a dish as simple as eggs fried sunny side up. First they brush the pan with sesame oil and heat it until it is sizzling. This done, they break the egg into the pan and move the pan around so that the heat is evenly distributed. When the egg white has set, the Japanese pour one teaspoon of cold water around the egg. The reason for this is simple: the egg whites, being thinner than the yolk, cook much faster. The cold water retards the cooking of the whites, preventing them from getting too hard while the thick yolk slowly heats through. Thus the entire egg cooks at a single speed.

Until comparatively recently, eggs as they are eaten in the West played only a small part in Japanese cuisine. But the popularity of egg dishes has been growing. In fact, a wide variety of egg dishes is now available in the better restaurants and in sophisticated households. One of my favourites is the Japanese version of the omelette. Called *tamago dashimaki* (*page 178*), the dish consists of layer upon paper-thin layer of egg, each layer cooked in an oblong pan for a few seconds and then rolled around the previous layer. Although it requires painstaking attention to cooking time and a dexterity that comes only with practice, the result is worth the effort. Served either hot or at room temperature and garnished with grated *daikon*, it makes a perfect lunch dish, light, delicate and delicious.

Beef, like eggs, is not an important element in the diet of most Japanese because it is just too expensive—good cuts are about 12s a pound, while the best cost more than £4—but there is no better or more tender beef in the world. The best cuts are cooked very plainly. One way is to fry the steaks in an iron frying pan or on a griddle and then serve them with a dipping sauce called *pon-su*, which is half soya sauce and half lemon or lime juice. Another popular method is to grill the steaks on a wire net over charcoal, the meat having been dipped in a sauce made of equal parts of thickened soya sauce and *mirin*. Whether fried or grilled, the steaks themselves are always cut thin, no more than a quarter inch thick.

It is ironic that beef *sukiyaki* (*page 134*), the most widely known Japanese dish, should be part of a culinary tradition that makes relatively little use of meat. The word *sukiyaki* (pronounced *skee-yah-kee*) means "grilled on the blade of a plough". This name reveals the origins of the dish, for in times past farmers in the field, or hunters in the wild, often killed animals and cooked their meat over an open fire on whatever utensils were available, such as a ploughshare. However, modern *sukiyaki* is wrongly named, for *yaki* refers to grilled foods and today's dish is not grilled. In fact it straddles two categories of Japanese cooking: *nabemono*, which applies to dishes cooked at the dining table, and *nimono*, which means boiling in seasoned liquid. *Sukiyaki* is both cooked at the table and simmered in seasoned liquid.

As an element of *nabemono* cooking, *sukiyaki* is a rather important dish; within the gargantuan *nimono* category it is merely one of hundreds. There are at least 15 major subdivisions of this grilling method—each characterized by a different kind of seasoned liquid, and each embracing a host of dishes. One familiar *nimono* technique is merely to cook meat or vegetables in lightly salted water. However *nimono* liquids run the gamut from stocks strongly flavoured with seasonings that include ginger, sugar and *sake* to broths so mild that only a hint of their taste is present in the cooked food.

46

Nimono methods can be used with nearly every kind of foodstuff. One of the simplest, yet most tasty, of *nimono* dishes is called *kimini* (*page 122*). In this dish, shelled prawns are quickly blanched and then rapidly cooked in a boiling liquid containing *niban dashi* (a soup stock; *page 54*), *sake*, sugar and salt. After the few moments it takes for the prawns to become pinkish white, indicating that they are firm and almost done, beaten egg yolks are poured over them, the pot is covered, and the prawns steamed for two minutes. In that short time the egg yolks form a rich glaze.

One *nimono* subdivision combines two categories of the art: *umani*, which means boiling in a liquid that is quite sweet, and "interrupted cooking", in which one of several means is used to halt the cooking process, permitting the food to cool before cooking is completed. To make one of my favourite *umani* dishes (*page 123*), vegetables such as carrots, bamboo shoots, *shiitake* and green peas are combined with strips of boned chicken breast and all are lightly sautéed together in oil. Then the ingredients are taken off the heat and boiled in a mixture of *dashi*, sugar and soya sauce until the liquid has evaporated and the vegetables and fowl are coated with, and penetrated by, the cooking liquid. This dish is great for picnics, for it can be made in advance, eaten at room temperature and requires no dipping sauces.

Interrupted cooking—which may seem unnecessarily complicated—has two purposes: to cook out the bitterness of some foods in one liquid and then to complete the preparation in a second; and to maintain an exact control over the preparation process so that the ingredients cook evenly both on the outside and within. This awareness that the inside and outside of foods cannot cook at the same speed explains why the Japanese and other oriental peoples avoid working with large pieces of meat and vegetables.

Another cooking technique that is very popular in Japan is steaming. This method is simple and the foods prepared in this manner are both nourishing and rich in flavour. Properly steamed vegetables are crisp and their natural flavour and nutrients remain virtually intact. For the Japanese, steaming takes the place of the casserole cooking when all the ingredients are to be prepared together. But instead of our casserole's blending of tastes, each element in the steamed Japanese "casserole" retains its own unique flavour though it may be subtly modified by the other ingredients.

There are two basic Japanese methods of steaming. The first, called *mushi*, involves food suspended on a plate over boiling water. In many *mushi* dishes, the ingredients are simply seasoned with salt before being steamed, and the end product is a dish that tastes rather bland. However, the Japanese dip each morsel into one of several sauces before eating it. The dipping sauce imparts a distinct flavour while the steamed ingredient provides texture and body, together with just enough taste of its own; each *mushi* food is clearly different from all the others, even when the same dipping sauce is used in every case. Most *mushi* dipping sauces are easy and quick to prepare; if you make several for a *mushi* meal, your guests can experience a wide variety of flavour and texture combinations. (*See Recipe Index.*)

Mushi foods acquire slightly more taste during steaming when they rest in a bath of *sake*. As the food steams so does the wine, and the vapours of the *sake* permeate the meat, vegetables or fish, imparting to them a flavour so subtle that the dipping sauce remains an essential element.

A second kind of steamed foods, *chawan mushi*, or foods steamed in egg

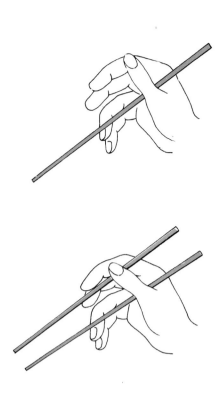

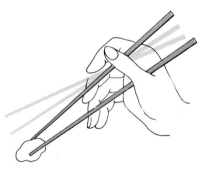

AT EASE WITH CHOPSTICKS
As the top drawing shows, place a chopstick in the crook of the thumb, about one-third of the way down from the thicker end of the stick. It should rest on the inside tip of the ring finger. Then (*centre*), place the second chopstick so that it lies between the index and middle fingers like a pencil; press it against these fingers with the cushion of the thumb. Keep the point of the top stick extended a little past the point of the lower stick. Keeping the lower stick motionless, move the upper stick down to meet the lower, and grasp the food by bending the index and middle fingers as in the bottom drawing. This is only one of several workable ways of using chopsticks.

MSG and the Oriental Food Syndrome

In many of the recipes throughout this book, MSG—a crystalline powder—is called for in the ingredients list as a flavour enhancer. You may have read recently of the "Chinese restaurant syndrome", in which MSG, monosodium glutamate, was identified as the culprit. After eating in Chinese restaurants—which use MSG more extensively than do Japanese —some diners have on occasion complained of burning sensations, a feeling of pressure in the chest, and facial tightness or numbness. Usually these symptoms occur after eating soup or another first course on an empty stomach. They rarely last more than an hour. The cause appears to be the use of ¼ teaspoon or more of MSG per serving, a greater amount than is ordinarily specified for portions in this book. When used as indicated, MSG should produce no discomfort for most people.

custard (*Recipe Booklet*), requires no dipping sauces. Since the ingredients to be bathed in custard are properly seasoned before cooking, dipping sauces are unnecessary, for they would interfere with the flavour.

Whichever method of steaming is used, the key to success is to prevent the steam that condenses on the lid from falling on the ingredients, for this would dilute the delicate flavours. The Japanese employ several specially designed kinds of steaming pots to forestall the possibility of disaster, but an ordinary pot with a lid is a satisfactory substitute; simply place a folded tea towel over the pot before covering it, and the towel will catch the condensation as it falls from the lid. As the towel becomes saturated, it should be replaced. For *chawan mushi* dishes, the Japanese use a special lidded earthenware cup; tea or custard cups covered with foil will serve just as well.

One Japanese cooking technique that is rarely attempted by foreigners, though it is simple enough, is called *mushiyaki*. As the name implies, this is a hybrid form, combining elements of steaming and grilling. Unlike other steaming techniques *mushiyaki* uses no water; instead the steam is supplied by the food's own moisture. I particularly enjoy one form of this category called *horakuyaki*. In Japan this is made in a *horoku*, a thick, unglazed pottery bowl hard to find in Europe; a conventional unglazed casserole with a tight-fitting lid makes a perfectly adequate alternative.

In *horoku* cooking a layer of salt is sprinkled over the bottom of the pot, which is then heated to a high temperature. Bits of beef, fish, shell-fish or vegetables are placed on the salt, and the pot is covered and returned to the heat. The hot salt causes the moisture inside the food to turn to steam, and this steam, in turn, cooks the ingredients.

When the Japanese serve the steamed or grilled or fried dishes that we might consider a main course, they usually accompany them with a kind of salad. Of salads there are two basic types: *aemono*, mixed things, and *sunomono*, vinegared things. In *aemono* dishes, several raw or cooked ingredients are tossed together with one of many dressings or sauces that are sticky and thick, rather like mayonnaise in texture, though the ingredients are quite different. These dressings generally use *tofu* or *miso* or ground sesame seeds as their principal ingredients. A very simple but tasty *aemono* dish is spinach dressed with sesame seeds and *niban dashi* (*Recipe Booklet*).

Although some *aemono* recipes do contain vinegar, it is in the *sunomono* category that vinegar stars. Most *sunomono* dishes have as their main ingredients raw, crisp vegetables—such as sliced cucumber or grated white radish—and a cold cooked fish or shell-fish. *Sunomono* dishes are given a thin dressing made of rice vinegar, plus *dashi*, sugar and soya sauce.

I have left to the last a discussion of *agemono*, or fried things, according to many the pride and glory of Japanese cuisine. The Japanese deep-fry in batter, they deep-fry without batter and they pan-fry in oil. While these methods are familiar to us, there is little similarity between the results achieved by Japanese and Western cooks. Our fried foods can be heavy and greasy. Japanese fried foods, on the other hand, are as light as air and as delicate as a soft spring breeze. The difference lies in the centuries-old techniques that bring out the most subtle of flavours inherent in each food.

Take *tempura* for example. This Japanese dish is known throughout the world, though mostly in the form of deep-fried batter-coated prawns. In fact, almost any food can be used to make *tempura*—chicken, fish and all vegetables except those that are particularly watery, such as white radish, cabbage and cucumbers. *Tempura* (*page 103*) is almost the perfect dish to start on, for its preparation combines many of the principles of Japanese frying and its taste puts it at the highest peak of Japanese culinary accomplishments. For the Japanese the preparation of oil for frying is almost an art in itself; they blend various kinds of oils with all the painstaking care of a scent manufacturer in order to impart to the ingredients the exact taste favoured by the chef. Every *tempura* cook has his own favourite blend of oils. One blend I know of is a mixture of 85 per cent cotton-seed oil, 10 per cent olive oil and 5 per cent sesame-seed oil. Another combines groundnut oil with sesame-seed oil and olive oil in proportions of 75 per cent, 20 per cent and 5 per cent respectively. My own favourite blend is simple indeed: 70 per cent peanut oil to 30 per cent sesame oil.

While the oil is heating up, the Japanese cook coats the *tempura* ingredients with batter, which may contain a variety of ingredients but almost always includes egg, ice-cold water and flour. The trick here is to get the batter as cold as possible; generally it is placed in a glass bowl surrounded by ice. Each morsel of food is lightly coated with this thin batter— so thin that the colours of the food show through, thus adding a visual element to the gastronomical delight—and the morsels are quickly popped into the hot oil, which should be 375°F. As it hits the hot oil, the icy batter literally explodes, puffing up and swelling so that the food inside is partly cooked in its own self-generated steam and partly cooked by the oil.

Tempura is one of the very few Japanese dishes that should always be served straight from the pan. Anyone preparing it should chop up the ingredients beforehand, divide them into individual portions, and cook one portion at a time. The deep-frying process is so rapid that the first guest to be served will hardly have got well under way before the last guest has received his plate. After each portion has been prepared, do as the Japanese do and skim off whatever residue of batter and food may remain in the oil. In this way the oil is kept fresh for longer use, there is no malodorous smoke from left-over bits of batter and food, and most important of all, there is no possibility of including bits of burnt scraps in later servings.

One other point must be taken into consideration. Never attempt to cook too much food at any one time; the *tempura* ingredients should never cover more than half the pan, for overloading will lower the temperature of the oil and slow down the cooking with soggy morsels as the sad result.

If the rules are followed, *tempura* is indeed easy to prepare. So easy, in fact, that there is no need to shy away from making a true *tempura* feast. Pork and chicken, eel and red snapper, prawns, scallops and mussels, mangetout, green pepper, okra and mushroom, aubergine and sweet potatoes— all these and more can be included. An authentic *tempura* meal includes at least six ingredients and can have as many as 14, picked not only for their variety of tastes but also for their differences in colour, shape and texture. All are eaten with dipping sauces (see *page 104* for *tempura* dips).

Despite the ease and speed with which *tempura* can be made, it ranks among the great dishes of the world. If Japanese cookery had produced nothing of note other than *tempura*, this alone would have been sufficient to secure Japan a place of honour in the affections of the gourmet.

Basic Japanese Kitchen Tools

The Japanese treat their tools used for cooking with the same respect that they pay to the ingredients themselves. There are special knives for raw fish, for boning fish, for slicing vegetables and for slicing *tofu*. Although a few of the kitchen tools shown here are available in London shops, Western knives, mixing bowls, graters and skimmers make perfectly acceptable substitutes. On the right, chef Toshio Morimoto, consultant for *The Cooking of Japan*, uses the cutting knife for vegetables as he demonstrates how to peel a *daikon* in a single thin, continuous sheet; the end result, illustrated by the rolled-up carrot, is then finely shredded.

Shown above is an array of some of the specialized knives and cooking utensils used by Japanese cooks.

1 Sashimi knife and scabbard
2 Rectangular omelette pan
3 Boning knife for fish
4 Slicing knife for fish
5 Cutting knife for vegetables
6 Cooking chopsticks
7 *Tofu*-slicing knife
8 Skimmer
9 *Suribachi* (serrated mixing bowl) and wooden pestle
10 *Sodare* (bamboo) mat
11 Grater

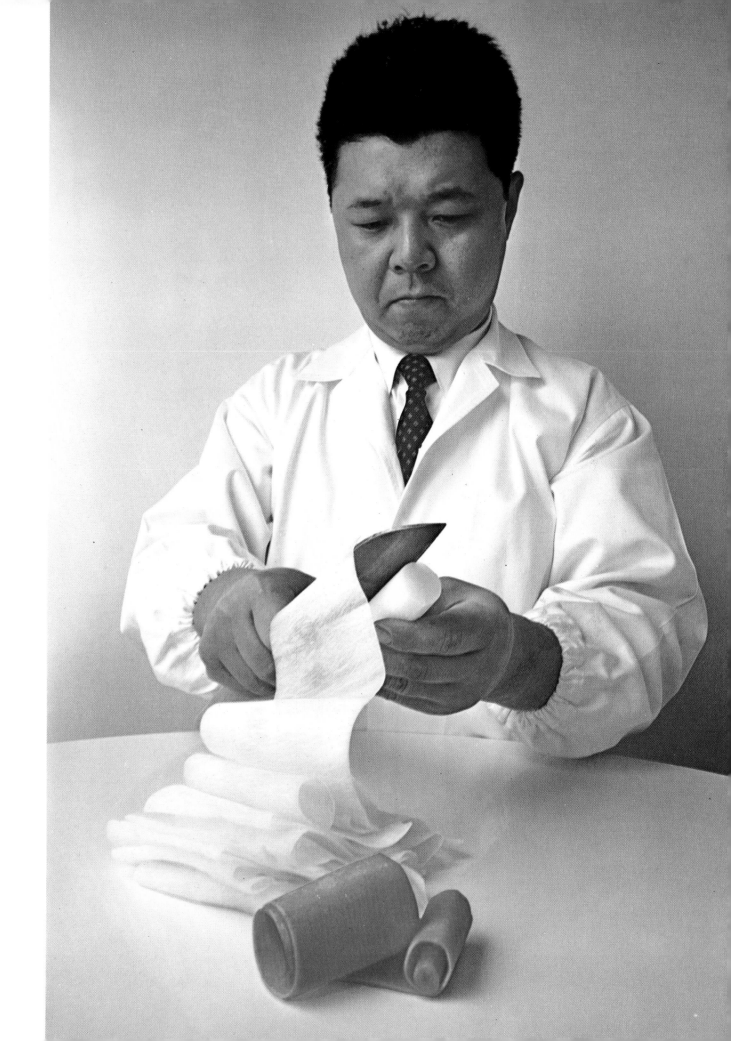

The Fine Art of Cutting and Slicing

Three of the vegetables in the vertical rows on the right should be instantly recognizable to the Western cook, even if some of the end products of their cutting are not. Others are unashamedly exotic in appearance as well as in flavour—but all are basic ingredients in Japanese cooking.

1 In the first row is a *daikon*, one of the commonest Japanese vegetables. A small section of this giant white radish is shown at the top; just below it is a round slice. This can then be halved, quartered, trimmed or shaped into a square or into dice. Or it can be held in the hand and cut into one thin continuous sheet (*page 51*), which is then finely shredded (*bottom*).

2 The carrot in the second row can also be cut in many ways, the simplest being in thin rounds. To cut obliquely, as in the bottom half of the long carrot, make a diagonal cut straight down, shift the carrot to the right, and cut again. Besides being decorative, the oblique cut also provides a greater surface area for seasonings to permeate. The sheet of carrot has been cut as on page 51; this can then be shredded or cut into various-sized strips.

3 The first step in preparing cucumber is almost always to cut it in half lengthways and to scoop out the seeds and pulp. The smaller section has been partially peeled, leaving strips of green skin that will add colour to a dish. Cucumber most frequently appears in thin slices.

4 A canned bamboo shoot can be seen at the top of the fourth row; just below it is a whole bamboo shoot cut obliquely. More frequently, however, the base of the bamboo shoot is cut off and the tapering top cut in half lengthways. The base of the bamboo shoot can then be halved or quartered.

5 In row five is a lotus root—at the top, a fresh root, and below it a slice, which is available in cans. This can be trimmed or cut in any of the ways shown.

6 The last two rows show the long, tapering *gobo* root, of which even the parings, (illustrated at the centre edge of the page) are used by the economical Japanese. To the right of the whole root are *gobo* sections and various ways of slicing them.

7 In the far right-hand corner is an ordinary turnip—cut in an extraordinary way. The whole turnip is peeled and placed between two chopsticks. It is sliced thin to within ⅛ inch of the bottom side—the chopsticks help to prevent cutting through—and then turned a quarter turn and cut similarly. Then it is quartered.

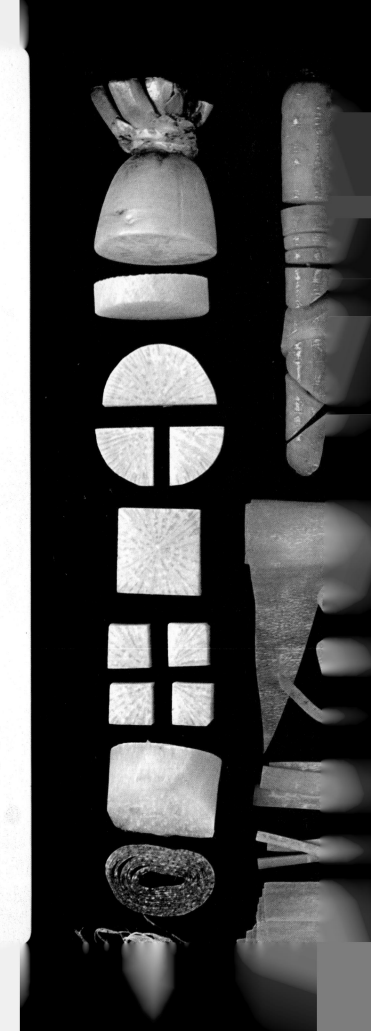

3   4   5   6

7

Dashi and Owanrui: STOCKS AND SOUPS

Aemono and Sunomono: MIXED FOODS AND VINEGARED SALADS

Bento and Zensai: PICNIC FOOD AND HORS D'ŒUVRE

There are three basic types of soup in the Japanese cuisine: the clear soup usually served at the beginning of a meal; the slightly thicker and sweeter "miso" soups, flavoured with red or white soya-bean paste, often served towards the end of a Japanese meal; and the more elaborate soups—almost ragouts—which are substantial main courses at lunch or dinner.

Ichiban Dashi   一番出汁
BASIC SOUP STOCK

"Ichiban dashi" is a cornerstone of Japanese cooking—the Japanese equivalent of our chicken and beef stocks. Like them, it is used as the cooking stock for many meat, poultry and fish dishes and becomes a soup in itself with the addition of various garnishes. "Ichiban dashi" is made easily and quickly from packaged, easy-to-store items.

To make 4 pints

4 pints cold water
A 3-inch square *kombu* (dried kelp), cut with a heavy knife from a sheet of packaged *kombu* and washed under cold running water
½ oz. pre-flaked *katsuobushi* (dried bonito)

Pour 4 pints of cold water into a large saucepan and bring it to the boil over a high heat. Drop in the *kombu*, let the water come just to the boil again, then immediately remove the *kombu* from the pan with a perforated spoon and set it aside. Stir the *katsuobushi* into the boiling water and turn off the heat. Let the stock rest undisturbed for about 2 minutes, until the *katsuobushi* sinks to the bottom of the pan, then skim off any surface scum with a large spoon. Place a double thickness of cheesecloth or a clean cloth napkin in a sieve set over a large bowl, pour in the stock and let it drain through undisturbed. Remove the *katsuobushi* and set it aside.

The stock may now be used as the base for a soup or stew, or as a cooking base. Although best if freshly prepared for each occasion, *ichiban dashi* can remain at room temperature for up to 8 hours without appreciable loss of flavour. Or it can be cooled to room temperature, covered with a sheet of plastic and refrigerated for as long as 2 days.

NOTE: The cooked *kombu* and *katsuobushi* may be discarded, or they can be used in the preparation of *niban dashi* (*below*).

Niban Dashi   二番出汁
COOKING STOCK FOR VEGETABLES

"Niban dashi" is an economical way to use the left-over ingredients of "ichiban dashi" for an equally good but weaker stock. "Niban dashi" is used instead of water for cooking vegetables.

To make 2 pints

A 3-inch square cooked *kombu* (from *ichiban dashi*, above)
⅛ pint cooked *katsuobushi* (from *ichiban dashi*, above)
2 pints cold water
3 tablespoons pre-flaked *katsuobushi* (dried bonito)

Put the cooked *kombu* and *katsuobushi* with 2 pints of cold water into a medium-sized saucepan, and bring almost to the boil over a high heat. Add the additional 3 tablespoons of uncooked *katsuobushi*, reduce the heat to its lowest point and simmer uncovered for about 5 minutes. Place a double thickness of cheesecloth or a clean cloth napkin in a sieve set over a large bowl, pour in the entire contents of the pan and let the stock drain through undisturbed. Discard the *kombu* and *katsuobushi*.

Although *niban dashi* can be used at once as a cooking stock for vegetables, it can also be kept for 8 hours at room temperature. Or it can be cooled to room temperature, covered with a sheet of plastic and refrigerated for as long as 2 days. Because *ichiban* and *niban dashi* look nearly the same, it is best to label their containers if they are not to be used at once.

Sumashi Wan すまし椀
CLEAR SOUP WITH TOFU AND PRAWNS

To serve 6

PREPARE IN ADVANCE: 1. Bring ¾ pint of water to simmering point over a high heat in a small saucepan. Add the cubes of *tofu* and the square of *kombu* and let the water return to simmering point. Then immediately remove the pan from the heat and set it aside until ready to serve.

2. Bring ¾ pint of lightly salted water to the boil in another saucepan. Drop in the spinach, sprinkle lightly with MSG, and let the water return to the boil. Then remove the spinach with a perforated spoon and run cold water over it. Squeeze the spinach to remove its excess water and dry on kitchen paper. Reserve the pan of cooking water.

3. To butterfly the prawns, first cut them three-quarters of the way through along the length of their inside curves. Then spread them out and gently flatten them with the side of a cleaver or the flat of a large, heavy knife. Dip the prawns one at a time into the cornflour to coat them lightly and evenly, then shake off any excess.

Bring the pan of reserved spinach water to the boil over a high heat. Add the prawns and boil them briskly for about 30 seconds. Drain them through a sieve and set them aside.

TO COOK AND SERVE: Bring the *sumashi* to the boil in a medium-sized saucepan. Add the prawns, return to boil for about 15 seconds, and drain.

Arrange a prawn, a spinach leaf, a cube of *tofu* and a thin strip of lemon rind in the bottom of each soup bowl. Fill each bowl three-quarters full of the hot soup, pouring it carefully down the side of the bowl to avoid disturbing the decorative arrangement.

THE ALTERNATIVE GARNISH for the *sumashi wan* is a chicken ball instead of the butterflied prawn. Prepare the chicken balls as follows:

Put the ½ pound of minced chicken, 1½ teaspoons of the soya sauce, ½ teaspoon sugar, a dash of *kona sansho* (or finely ground black pepper) and 1 egg yolk into a *suribachi* (mixing bowl) or mortar and mix vigorously with a pestle until the mixture is smooth. Roll the mixture into 6 small balls with lightly moistened hands.

Put ⅜ pint of cold water, 2½ teaspoons *sake*, 1 scant teaspoon soya sauce and a 2-inch square of *kombu* into a small pan and bring to simmering point over a moderate heat. Drop in the minced chicken balls, lower the heat, and poach gently for about 6 to 7 minutes until firm. Place 1 chicken ball in each soup bowl in place of the prawns, add the spinach and lemon, and fill the bowls as described opposite.

A 6 oz. cake fresh, canned or instant *tofu* (soya-bean curd), cut into 6 equal parts
A 2-inch square *kombu* (dried kelp), cut with a heavy knife from a sheet of packaged *kombu* and washed under cold running water
Salt
MSG
6 spinach leaves
6 medium-sized prawns (16 to 20 per lb.), shelled and de-veined (*see page 168*)
1 oz. cornflour
2½ pints *sumashi* (*page 58*)
A 2-inch piece lemon rind, cut into long, very narrow strips

ALTERNATIVE GARNISH
½ lb. minced white meat of chicken
2½ teaspoons Japanese soya sauce
½ teaspoon sugar
A dash of *kona sansho* (Japanese pepper), or substitute freshly ground black pepper
1 egg yolk
2½ teaspoons *sake* (rice wine)
A 2-inch square *kombu* (dried kelp), cut with a heavy knife from a sheet of packaged *kombu* and washed under cold running water

Soups—from Breakfast to Dinner

The red and white *miso* soups shown directly below—clear soups flavoured with soya-bean paste—are favourite breakfast foods with the Japanese, although they may also play a savoury role at lunch or at dinner. Opposite are examples of more formal soups, elaborately garnished with seafood, eggs and vegetables. The garnishes in the *miso* soups below are only suggestions—other possibilities, together with the recipes for the soups and garnishes, are found on page 59.

AKADASHI
Red *miso*-flavoured soup, garnished here with thinly sliced white *daikon* radish and tiny rings of spring onion.

SHIRO DASHI
White *miso*-flavoured soup, with a neat tie of *kanpyo* —gourd shavings—topped by a dab of hot mustard.

HAMAGURI USHIOJITATE
Clear clam soup (*page 58*)
with a garnish of a tiny
mushroom and a paper-thin
round of lime.

UMEWAN
Clear soup (*page 60*) with a
slice of rolled egg, sea bream,
prawn, mushroom, carrot
and aromatic *sansho* leaf.

To serve 6

1 scant teaspoon salt
12 sprigs fresh watercress or young
  spinach leaves stripped from their
  stalks
A 3-inch square of *kombu*, cut with a
  heavy knife from a sheet of
  packaged *kombu* and washed under
  cold running water
12 small, fresh cherrystone clams,
  scrubbed under cold running water,
  or substitute 12 cockles
6 small white mushrooms
2½ teaspoons Japanese soya sauce
MSG
6 very thin slices lime or lemon

To serve 6

SUMASHI (clear soup)
2½ pints *ichiban dashi* (*page 54*)
1¼ teaspoons salt
½ teaspoon Japanese soya
  sauce
1 scant teaspoon *sake* (rice wine)
MSG

GARNISH
A 1¾-lb. winter or honeydew melon
6 medium-sized raw prawns (16 to
  20 per lb.), peeled and
  de-veined (*see page 168*)
1 scant teaspoon salt
A 2-inch piece lime rind, cut into 6
  very thin strips

To serve 4

A 2-lb. sea bass, filleted but with
  the skin left on
½ teaspoon salt
5 teaspoons cornflour
2½ teaspoons *sake* (rice wine)
A 7-oz. bottle *junsai* (wild
  vegetables)
1½ pints *sumashi* (*above*)
4 very thin slices of lime

Hamaguri Ushiojitate   蛤うしを仕立

CLEAR CLAM SOUP WITH MUSHROOMS

PREPARE IN ADVANCE: Put ⅜ pint of cold water, ½ teaspoon of salt and the watercress or spinach leaves into a small saucepan. Bring to the boil over a high heat and boil for 1 minute. Drain through a sieve and set the leaves aside.

TO COOK: Put 2½ pints of cold water, the *kombu* and the clams into a medium-sized saucepan. Bring to the boil over a high heat, then remove the *kombu* with a perforated spoon and discard it. Let the soup boil for about 2 minutes until the clams open, meanwhile skimming off any scum that rises to the surface. Stir in the mushrooms, soya sauce, ½ teaspoon salt and a few sprinklings of MSG. Boil for 30 seconds, then remove from the heat.

TO SERVE: Place 2 clams in their shells into each of 6 soup bowls. Garnish with 2 sprigs of the watercress or spinach, a mushroom and a slice of lemon or lime. Fill each bowl with the hot broth, pouring it down the side of the bowl to avoid disturbing the decorative arrangement. Serve at once.

Togan-to Ebi   冬瓜と海老

CLEAR SOUP WITH WINTER MELON AND PRAWNS

PREPARE IN ADVANCE: 1. Cut the rind off the melon. Score the peeled side of the melon by making shallow cuts ⅛ inch deep lengthways and then crosswise at ⅛-inch intervals. Then cut the melon into six 1½-inch squares.

2. Drop the prawns into ⅝ pint of boiling water, add 1 scant teaspoon of salt, and boil uncovered for about 5 minutes, until they are pink and firm. Drain and plunge the prawns into cold running water to cool them quickly. Drain again and set the prawns aside.

TO COOK THE SUMASHI: Bring 2½ pints of *ichiban dashi* just to simmering point over a moderate heat in a medium-sized saucepan. Immediately reduce the heat to low, stir in the salt, soya sauce, *sake*, and sprinkle with MSG.

TO ASSEMBLE AND SERVE: Drop in the melon squares, and simmer them uncovered for about 15 minutes, until they are tender and show no resistance when pierced with the tip of a small, sharp knife.

Place a square of melon in each of 6 soup bowls and top with a prawn and a strip of lime rind. Fill each bowl with soup, pouring it down the side of the bowl to avoid disturbing the decorative arrangement.

Botan Wan   牡丹椀

CLEAR SOUP WITH SEA BASS

PREPARE IN ADVANCE: 1. Cut the fillets in half crosswise and place them skin side down on a chopping board. Cut them crosswise at ⅛-inch intervals almost down to the skin, using a sharp, heavy knife, but do not cut through it. The sliced fish will open up when poached and resemble a peony, or *botan* in Japanese.

2. Sprinkle the fish lightly with ½ teaspoon of salt; then sift 5 teaspoons of cornflour over it evenly through a sieve or sifter.

TO COOK: Bring ¾ pint of water to the boil in a small saucepan. Poach the fish, one piece at a time, by placing it on a wide fish slice, lowering the slice into the boiling water for 15 seconds, then sliding the fish on to a heat-proof dish. When all the fish has been poached and arranged side by side, sprinkle the pieces evenly with 2½ teaspoons of *sake*. Now steam the fish for 5 minutes, either in an oriental steamer or in the improvised steamer on page 180.

Meanwhile, bring ¾ pint of water to the boil in a small saucepan. Add the *junsai* and return to the boil. Strain at once and discard the water.

TO SERVE: Cook the *sumashi* over a moderate heat until it reaches simmering point. Divide the *junsai* evenly among 4 soup bowls, add a piece of the steamed fish to each and garnish with a thin slice of lime. Fill each bowl with the hot soup, pouring it down the side of the bowl to avoid disturbing the decorative arrangement. Serve at once.

Misoshiru　味噌汁
CLEAR SOUP WITH SOYA-BEAN PASTE

"Miso" soups—clear soup flavoured with white and/or red soya-bean paste—are sweeter than other Japanese soups and are usually served towards the end of a formal Japanese meal. All are made in precisely the same way, and may be garnished with a selection of the garnishes listed below.

PREPARE IN ADVANCE: Place the 2½ pints of *dashi* in a medium-sized saucepan and set a sieve over the pan. Rub the *miso* (*aka, shiro* or a combination of the two) through the sieve with the back of a wooden spoon, moistening it from time to time with some of the *dashi* to help to force it through more easily.

TO COOK AND SERVE: Bring the soup to simmering point over a moderate heat. Then remove from the heat and stir in a small pinch of MSG.

Pour the soup into bowls, add a garnish (*below*) and serve at once. If the soup seems to be separating, stir to blend it again.

Misoshiru No-mi　味噌汁の実
MISO SOUP GARNISHES

Prepare the garnishes for *miso* soups before the soup is heated.

Soak the firm *wakame* in a bowl of warm water for 15 minutes. When soft, strip the leaves from the tough central vein and discard the vein. Chop the leaves coarsely and set them aside. Bring the *miso* soup to simmering point, drop in the *wakame*, simmer for 1 minute, then pour into individual soup bowls. Garnish with the sliced spring onions and serve.

When the soup simmers, drop in the *tofu* and simmer for 1 minute. Pour into soup bowls, garnish with spring onions, and serve.

Cut the 1-inch piece of *daikon* (or the icicle radish or turnip) into strips ⅛ inch wide by about 2 inches long. Cover the strips with cold water in a small pan and bring to the boil over a high heat. Reduce the heat to low and simmer for about 5 minutes until the vegetables are tender but still slightly firm. When the *miso* soup begins to simmer, drain the *daikon* and add it to the soup. Pour into individual soup bowls, and garnish with the spring onions.

Soak the dried croûtons in cold water for about 10 minutes, until they are soft. Squeeze them gently to rid them of their moisture. Bring the *miso* soup to simmering point, drop in the croûtons and simmer for 1 minute. Pour the soup into individual soup bowls, add a drop of the mustard paste to each bowl, and serve at once.

To make 2½ pints of each

AKA MISO (summer *miso* soup)
2½ pints *ichiban dashi* (*page 54*)
4 oz. *aka miso* (red soya-bean paste)
MSG

SHIRO MISO (winter *miso* soup)
2½ pints *ichiban dashi* (*page 54*)
½ lb. *shiro miso* (white soya-bean paste)
MSG

AWASE MISO (combination *miso* soup)
2½ pints *ichiban dashi* (*page 54*)
4 oz. *shiro miso* (white soya-bean paste)
4 oz. *aka miso* (red soya-bean paste)
MSG

To serve 6

WAKAME AND SPRING ONIONS
½ oz. *wakame* (dried seaweed)
1 spring onion, including the green stalk, sliced into very thin rounds

TOFU AND SPRING ONIONS
A 6-oz. cake of fresh, canned or instant *tofu* (soya-bean curd), cut into ¼-inch dice
1 spring onion, including the green stalk sliced into very thin rounds

DAIKON AND SPRING ONIONS
A 1-inch piece of *daikon* (Japanese white radish), peeled, or substitute 1 large icicle radish or white turnip, peeled
1 spring onion, including the green stalk sliced into very thin rounds

FU AND MUSTARD
18 *kohana-fu* or *yachiyo-fu* (pressed wheat-cake croûtons)
1 scant teaspoon powdered mustard, mixed with just enough hot water to make a thick paste and set aside to rest for 15 minutes

Umewan

梅椀

CLEAR SOUP WITH ROLLED EGG, VEGETABLES AND FISH

"Umewan", known as a "large 'sumashi'", is a delicate but satisfying main-course soup. Although there are many steps involved in its preparation, many of them may be done in advance.

To serve 6

4 eggs, well beaten
Salt
MSG
1 scant tablespoon vegetable oil
3 large *shiitake* (dried Japanese
    mushrooms)
½ teaspoon sugar
2½ teaspoons Japanese
    soya sauce
1 small carrot, scraped and shredded
¼ pint plus 1½ tablespoons *niban
    dashi* (*page 54*)
6 medium-sized raw prawns (16 to
    20 per lb.), in their shells
4 oz. fillet of sea bream, with skin
    left on (divided into 6 slices)
5 teaspoons cornflour
2½ pints *sumashi* (*page 58*)
12 young spinach leaves or 6 sprigs
    watercress
A 2- to 3-inch strip of lemon rind,
    cut into 6 small circles

PREPARE IN ADVANCE: 1. Beat 4 eggs with ⅛ teaspoon of salt and a sprinkling of MSG in a mixing bowl until they are well blended. Lightly coat the bottom and sides of a large, heavy frying pan with about 1 tablespoon of oil using a pastry brush or kitchen paper. Heat over a moderate heat until a drop of water flicked on to the surface evaporates instantly.

Pour about 3 tablespoons of the eggs into the pan, and tip it backwards and forwards gently for a few seconds until the bottom is evenly covered and the eggs have coagulated into a thin film. Tilt the pan up over the heat, roll the omelette in to a tight, thin cylinder using chopsticks or the side of a table fork. Then slide it on to kitchen paper to drain and make similar rolled omelettes with the remaining eggs.

One at a time, place the omelettes on the edge of a bamboo mat or heavy cloth napkin and roll the omelette in the mat 2 or 3 turns. Squeeze the mat tightly around the omelette roll to firm it, then remove the mat and set the omelette roll aside to cool.

2. Soak the *shiitake* in 1½ pints of water for at least 1 hour in a medium-sized saucepan. Then bring to the boil over a moderate heat. Add ½ teaspoon of sugar and 2½ teaspoons of soya sauce, and boil for about 20 minutes uncovered until the liquid is a deep brown and has reduced to about 4 tablespoons. Cool to room temperature.

3. Drop the carrot shreds into ⅜ pint of boiling water and boil 2 to 3 minutes. Pour off the liquid and replace it with 3 tablespoons of the *niban dashi*. Add a pinch of salt and a sprinkling of MSG and cook another 2 to 3 minutes, stirring from time to time. Set aside.

4. Drop the 6 prawns into ⅝ pint of boiling water, add 1 scant teaspoon of salt, and boil uncovered for 5 minutes. Drain and plunge into a bowl of cold water to cool them quickly.

Shell the prawns and, using a small, sharp knife, de-vein them by making a shallow incision down their backs and lifting out the black or white intestinal vein. Set the prawns aside.

5. Sprinkle the fleshy side of the fillets with ½ teaspoon of salt and dip them into the cornflour to coat them lightly and evenly. Shake them to remove the excess cornflour, then drop them into ¾ pint of boiling water. Boil for 1 minute, then add 6 tablespoons of *niban dashi* and ⅛ teaspoon of salt. Cook for another 3 to 4 minutes, remove the fish from the water with a perforated spoon, and set aside on a plate.

TO SERVE: Slice the rolled egg cylinders crosswise into rounds 2 inches long and place 3 pieces in the bottom of each soup bowl. Add 1 prawn per bowl, 1 sliver of fish, a sprig of watercress or 2 spinach leaves, ½ *shiitake* and a few strips of the carrot.

Heat the 2½ pints of *sumashi* to a simmering point. Fill each bowl three-quarters full of the hot soup, pouring it carefully down the side of each bowl to avoid disturbing the decorative arrangement; garnish with a circle of lemon rind and serve at once.

Satsuma Jiru 薩摩汁
MISO-FLAVOURED PORK AND VEGETABLE STEW

To serve 6

PREPARE IN ADVANCE: 1. Bring ⅜ pint of water to the boil in a small pan and drop in the diced pork. Cook uncovered 10 seconds, then drain and set aside.

2. Cover the pork bones with 2½ pints of cold water in a fairly large, heavy saucepan. Bring to the boil uncovered, then reduce the heat to its lowest point and simmer for 30 minutes, skimming off the foam as it rises to the surface. Strain the broth through a sieve lined with a double thickness of cheesecloth or a clean cloth napkin. Return broth to pan and set aside.

3. Bring ⅜ pint of water to the boil in a small saucepan and drop in the *konnyaku*. Return to the boil, then drain immediately and set aside.

4. Steam the mushrooms for 4 minutes in an oriental steamer or in the steamer substitute described on page 180. While the mushrooms are still hot, cut away and discard the stalks and slice the caps into the thinnest possible strips. Cool to room temperature.

5. If you are using the *gobo*, peel it with a rotary vegetable peeler to make 3 tablespoons of peel. Discard the root.

TO COOK: Drop the *konnyaku* into the pan of reserved pork broth and bring to a slow boil over a moderate heat. Add the carrot and *daikon* strips and raise the heat. Bring to a full boil, and add the diced sweet potato and mushroom strips. Skim off the foam with a large spoon and add the pork. Cook for 5 minutes, then reduce the heat to moderate and, with the back of a spoon, rub the *miso* through a sieve directly into the soup. Stir in a few sprinklings of MSG. Stir in the optional *gobo* peelings just before serving.

TO SERVE: Transfer the soup to a large serving bowl, sprinkle spring onions over the top and add a few sprinklings of seven-pepper spice.

TO MAKE NAGASAKI JIRU: Omit the *aka miso* flavouring. Stir in 5 tablespoons of soya sauce instead. Lower the heat and add a sprinkling of MSG. Stir in the *sake*, and the optional *gobo* peelings. Serve as described opposite, substituting a few sprinklings of white pepper for the seven-pepper spice.

The ingredients for Satsuma Jiru (to serve 6):

- ½ lb. boned loin of pork, cut into ¼-inch dice
- 1 lb. pork neck bones
- 1 section canned *konnyaku* (gelatinous vegetable root), cut into strips ¼ inch wide and 2 inches long
- 2 *shiitake* (dried Japanese mushrooms)
- 1 *gobo* (burdock), washed (optional)
- 1 medium-sized carrot, scraped and cut into strips 2 inches long and ¼ inch wide
- A 1-inch piece *daikon* (Japanese white radish), scraped and cut into strips ¼ inch wide and 1 inch long, or substitute 1 large icicle radish or white turnip, peeled and cut into ¼-inch-wide strips
- 4 oz. sweet potato, peeled and cut into ½-inch dice
- 4 oz. *aka miso* (red soya-bean paste)
- MSG
- 1 spring onion, including its green stalk, sliced into thin rounds (about 3 tablespoons)
- *Hichimi togarashi* (seven-pepper spice)

NAGASAKI JIRU (alternative seasoning)
- 5 tablespoons Japanese soya sauce
- MSG
- 5 teaspoons *sake* (rice wine)
- Ground white pepper

Ushio Jiru うしを汁
CLEAR SOUP WITH SEA BREAM

"Ushio jiru" is an unusual soup, deriving its delicate flavour from the fish head, which Europeans usually discard. The body of the sea bream may, of course, be used for another purpose (see "umewan", opposite).

PREPARE IN ADVANCE: Discard the bony jaw part of the sea-bream head and cut the rest of the head into 2-inch chunks. Sprinkle lightly with salt, drop into the boiling water, and let it cook for 10 seconds. Drain and rinse the fish thoroughly under cold running water.

TO COOK: Put 1½ pints of cold water, the fish chunks and the *kombu* into a medium-sized saucepan. When the water comes to the boil, remove and discard the *kombu*. Regulate the heat so that the stock barely simmers, and skim the scum from the surface with a perforated spoon. Simmer about 3 minutes, then stir in 1¼ teaspoons of salt and the MSG.

TO SERVE: Place a few pieces of fish in each bowl and garnish with a slice of lime and a few slivers of celery. Fill each bowl with the hot soup, pouring it down the side so as not to disturb the decorative arrangement.

To serve 4

- A sea-bream head (from a 2-lb. sea bream), split open and cut in half
- Salt
- 1¼ pints boiling water
- A 2-inch square of *kombu* (dried kelp), cut with a heavy knife from a sheet of packaged *kombu* and washed under cold running water
- MSG
- A 5-inch piece of celery stick without leaves, cut lengthways into the thinnest possible strips and chilled in a bowl of iced water
- 4 very thin slices of lime

61

The recipes in this section are for "aemono" and "sunomono". "Aemono" means mixed things: vegetables, fish or poultry mixed and tossed with dressings and sauces. "Sunomono" means vinegared things: vegetables alone or with fish in vinegared dressings. The categories overlap somewhat, but both encompass small dishes meant to accompany main dishes and to complement them in taste, texture and colour. Europeans might experiment with them as first courses or salad courses.

Kani Sunomono 蟹酢の物
CRAB MEAT IN VINEGARED DRESSING

PREPARE IN ADVANCE: 1. Peel the cucumber partially, leaving occasional ¼-inch strips of green peel to add colour to the finished dish. Cut the cucumber in half lengthways, scoop out the seeds with a small spoon, and slice the halves crosswise into paper-thin slices.

Put 6 tablespoons of cold water and 1 scant teaspoon of salt into a small bowl, and add the cucumber slices. Let them soak for at least 30 minutes at room temperature. Then drain the cucumbers and gently squeeze them with your hands to rid them of any excess moisture.

2. If you are using crab meat, pick over it and discard any cartilage and bits of bone. Shred it finely with a large, sharp knife. If you are using abalone, slice it very thinly.

TO ASSEMBLE AND SERVE: Divide the cucumber and crab meat or abalone into small individual bowls. Wrap the grated ginger in a piece of cheesecloth and squeeze the ginger juice over each bowl. Serve with the *sambai-zu* dipping sauce, as a first course or as part of a Japanese meal (*page 198*).

To serve 6

1 large cucumber
1 scant teaspoon salt
12 oz. fresh or canned crab meat
    or abalone
2½ tablespoons coarsely grated fresh
    ginger root

DIPPING SAUCE
6 tablespoons *sambai-zu* (*page 64*)

Goma Joyu-ae 胡麻醤油和え
SOYA AND SESAME-SEED DRESSING WITH FRENCH BEANS

PREPARE IN ADVANCE: 1. Snip off and discard the ends of the French beans (or mange-tout) and cut them into ½-inch lengths. Drop them into ¾ pint of lightly salted boiling water, reduce the heat to moderate and cook briskly, uncovered, for about 8 to 10 minutes, until the beans are tender but still slightly resistant to the bite. Drain and run cold water over them to stop them cooking and set their colour.

2. Put the *dashi*, sugar, ¼ teaspoon of salt, a sprinkling of MSG, 1½ teaspoons of *sake* and ¼ teaspoon of soya sauce into the same pan. Bring to the boil over a moderate heat, add the French beans (or mange-tout) and return to the boil. Then remove the pan from the heat and cool to room temperature.

3. Heat 2½ tablespoons of *sake* to lukewarm over a high heat. Remove the pan from the heat and ignite the *sake* with a match, shaking the pan gently until the flame dies out. Pour the *sake* into a small bowl and cool to room temperature.

4. Add the *sake*, 1½ teaspoons of sugar and 5 teaspoons of soya sauce to the previously prepared sesame paste, and mix together thoroughly.

TO ASSEMBLE AND SERVE: Pour the sesame dressing into a large bowl, add the drained French beans or mange-tout and toss together until the vegetables are thoroughly coated. Taste for seasoning and add more salt if necessary. Serve at room temperature in small bowls, as a first course, a salad or as part of a Japanese meal (*page 198*).

To serve 6

1 lb. French beans, or 1 lb.
    fresh or defrosted frozen
    mange-tout
Salt
⅜ pint *niban dashi* (*page 54*)
2½ teaspoons sugar
MSG
1½ teaspoons *sake* (rice wine)
¼ teaspoon Japanese soya
    sauce

DRESSING
1½ oz. white sesame seeds, warmed
    and ground into a paste (*see
    shira-ae, step 5, opposite*)
2½ tablespoons *sake* (rice wine)
1½ teaspoons sugar
5 teaspoons Japanese
    soya sauce

Shira-ae 白和え

TOFU AND SESAME-SEED DRESSING WITH VEGETABLES

To serve 6

PREPARE IN ADVANCE: 1. Bring ⅜ pint of water to the boil in a small saucepan and drop in the shredded *konnyaku*. Return to the boil, then drain immediately and cool to room temperature.

2. Bring another ⅜ pint of water to the boil and drop in the loaf of *tofu*. Simmer uncovered over a moderate heat for 5 minutes, drain, and cool to room temperature. Then wrap the *tofu* in a tea towel or napkin and squeeze it gently to rid it of its moisture. Rub it through a sieve set over a bowl with the back of a wooden spoon.

3. Soak the shredded carrots in 3 tablespoons of cold water and ½ teaspoon of salt in another bowl for about 30 minutes. Drain, squeeze dry, and set aside.

4. Heat 1 teaspoon of vegetable oil over a high heat in a small saucepan until a light haze forms above it. Stir in the *konnyaku*, *dashi*, ½ teaspoon of the sugar, the rest of the salt, a few sprinklings of MSG and ⅛ teaspoon of soya sauce, and bring to the boil. Boil uncovered until the liquid has reduced to about half. Cool to room temperature.

5. Heat a small frying pan over a high heat until a drop of water flicked across its surface evaporates instantly. Add the sesame seeds and, shaking the pan almost constantly, warm them until they are a pale gold and their aroma is released. Grind to a paste in a *suribachi* (serrated mixing bowl) or, more easily, pound them at high speed in an electric blender with ⅛ teaspoon of soya sauce. Transfer the sesame-seed paste to a mixing bowl and stir in the reserved *tofu*.

TO ASSEMBLE AND SERVE: Drain the *konnyaku* and its sauce through a sieve set over a small bowl. Stir 5 teaspoons of the sauce into the sesame-seed paste. Then stir in 2½ teaspoons sugar, ¼ teaspoon salt, a few sprinklings of MSG, the drained *konnyaku*, and the reserved grated carrot.

Serve as a first course or part of a Japanese meal (*page 198*).

2 pieces canned *konnyaku* (gelatinous root vegetable), drained and shredded
1 loaf fresh, canned or instant *tofu* (soya-bean curd)
1 small (3- to 4-inch) carrot, scraped and shredded
1 scant teaspoon salt
1 teaspoon vegetable oil
6 tablespoons *niban dashi* (*page 54*)
3 teaspoons sugar
MSG
¼ teaspoon Japanese soya sauce
2½ tablespoons white sesame seeds

Sesame seeds, ground against the ribbed surface of a *suribachi* with a wooden pestle, quickly release their oil and turn into a paste.

Sambai-zu

三杯酢

RICE-VINEGAR AND SOYA DIPPING SAUCE

To make about 6 tablespoons

2 tablespoons rice vinegar
2 tablespoons *niban dashi* (*page 54*)
1 tablespoon sugar
1½ teaspoons Japanese soya sauce
⅛ teaspoon salt
MSG

TO PREPARE: Put the rice vinegar, *niban dashi*, sugar, soya sauce and salt into a small enamelled or stainless-steel saucepan and sprinkle lightly with MSG. Bring the sauce to the boil, uncovered, over a high heat, stirring constantly. Then immediately remove the pan from the heat and set the sauce aside to cool to room temperature.

TO SERVE: Serve the *sambai-zu* in tiny individual cups or dishes, as a dipping sauce for *kani kyuri ikomi* (*page 66*), *kani sunomono* (*page 62*) or *shime saba* (*opposite*).

Suzuko Mizore-ae

すずこ みぞれ和え

RED CAVIAR WITH "SLEET" DRESSING

The dressing of grated radish and lemon juice has a faintly iridescent sheen and reminds the Japanese of sleet. Its pungent flavour makes an excellent foil for the highly salted red caviar.

To serve 6

½ lb. *daikon* (Japanese white radish), peeled and finely grated or substitute ½ lb. grated icicle radish or white turnips
2½ teaspoons fresh lemon juice
¼ teaspoon salt
MSG
6 oz. red caviar

GARNISH
6 sprigs parsley
6 thin slices lemon

ALTERNATIVE GARNISH
6 wedges of lemon
Japanese soya sauce

TO ASSEMBLE AND SERVE: Put the *daikon*, lemon juice, salt and a few sprinklings of MSG into a mixing bowl. Gently fold in the red caviar without crushing the eggs. Divide the mixture equally among 6 small bowls or dishes and garnish each serving with a sprig of parsley and a thin slice of lemon.

Serve *suzuko mizore-ae* at room temperature as a first course or part of a Japanese meal (*page 198*).

NOTE: In Japan, the ingredients in *suzuko mizore-ae* are often served separately rather than mixed together. Put about 3 tablespoons of the *daikon* dressing into each bowl and next to it, 1½ tablespoons of red caviar. Garnish with a wedge of lemon and season with soya sauce to taste.

Namasu

なます

DAIKON AND CARROT IN VINEGAR DRESSING

It is said that whenever lords and "daimyos" of an earlier era invited guests to dine with them for the first time, this simple salad was served as a first course—to indicate that the food to come was not poisonous in any way.

To serve 6

½ lb. *daikon* (Japanese white radish), peeled and shredded, or substitute ½ lb. icicle radish or white turnips, peeled and shredded
1 small carrot (about 3 inches), scraped and shredded
2½ teaspoons salt
¼ oz. pre-flaked *katsuobushi* (dried bonito)
2½ teaspoons rice vinegar, or substitute 2½ teaspoons mild white vinegar
1½ teaspoons sugar
MSG

PREPARE IN ADVANCE: 1. Put the *daikon*, carrot, ⅜ pint of cold water and salt into a small mixing bowl. Stir thoroughly, then soak the mixture for at least 30 minutes.

2. Meanwhile, put half of the *katsuobushi* into a small pan. Cook uncovered over a low heat, for 3 to 4 minutes, stirring constantly, to dry the *katsuobushi* further and to release its flavour. Transfer the cooked *katsuobushi* to a *suribachi* (a serrated mixing bowl) or to a mortar, and grind or pound the flakes to a fine powder. Shake the *katsuobushi* through a sieve on to a sheet of greaseproof paper and set aside.

TO ASSEMBLE AND SERVE: Drain the *daikon* and carrot, squeeze them dry, and place in a mixing bowl. Add the vinegar, sugar and a few sprinklings of MSG, mix thoroughly, then stir in the powdered *katsuobushi*.

Serve at room temperature in individual bowls, either as a first or salad course or as an accompaniment to *shime saba* (*opposite*).

64

Shime Saba しめ鯖

MACKEREL IN VINEGAR DRESSING

PREPARE IN ADVANCE: A day beforehand, sprinkle the fish on both sides with salt and place the fillets in a deep glass, enamelled or stainless-steel baking dish large enough to hold them in one layer. Cover with a sheet of plastic and refrigerate 8 hours or overnight. Then remove any remaining bones with tweezers.

Put the vinegar, water and sugar into a small bowl and pour over the fish. Marinate at room temperature for 15 minutes. Then place the fish on a chopping board and slice the fish diagonally into ½-inch-wide pieces.

TO SERVE: Divide the fish into 4 portions and arrange the slices side by side on individual plates or in small soup bowls. Garnish each portion with 1½ tablespoons of *namasu* and a sprig of parsley. Sprinkle each serving of fish evenly with grated ginger and accompany with individual bowls of *sambai-zu*. *Shime saba* will serve four as a first course or as part of a Japanese meal (*page 198*), or it will serve two as a main course for lunch.

To serve 4

1½ lb. mackerel, cleaned, scaled and filleted, but with skin left on
5 teaspoons salt
5 tablespoons rice vinegar, or substitute 3 tablespoons mild white vinegar
¼ pint plus 5 teaspoons cold water
1¼ tablespoons sugar

GARNISH
6 tablespoons *namasu* (*opposite*)
4 sprigs parsley
1 scant teaspoon finely grated, scraped fresh ginger root

DIPPING SAUCE
6 tablespoons *sambai-zu* (*opposite*)

Nameko Mizore-ae なめこ みぞれ和え

SLIPPERY MUSHROOMS WITH "SLEET" DRESSING

PREPARE IN ADVANCE: 1. Bring ¾ pint of water to the boil in a small saucepan. Add the *nameko* and return to the boil. Drain in a sieve and plunge the sieve into cold water to cool the mushrooms quickly.

2. Put the *daikon*, rice vinegar and salt into a small mixing bowl.

TO ASSEMBLE AND SERVE: Fold the mushrooms into the dressing and stir gently to coat them well. Divide the mushrooms among 6 small bowls, and sprinkle each serving with the grated lime rind. Serve at room temperature as a first course or part of a Japanese meal (*page 198*).

To serve 6

14 oz. canned *nameko* (slippery mushrooms)
1 to 2 inches *daikon* (Japanese white radish), peeled and finely grated (about 2½ oz.), or substitute 2½ oz. grated icicle radish or white turnips
1 scant teaspoon rice vinegar or fresh lemon juice
⅛ teaspoon salt
1 scant teaspoon grated lime rind

Silver-edged mackerel, flanked by *namasu* and grated ginger (*right*) is served with *sambai-zu* dipping sauce (*recipes opposite*).

Kani Kyuri Ikomi 蟹胡瓜鑄込み

CUCUMBER STUFFED WITH CRAB MEAT AND PICKLED GINGER

To serve 4 to 6

2 cucumbers, about ½ lb. each
    and about 2 inches in diameter
5 teaspoons salt
16 sprigs watercress or flat-leaf
    Italian parsley
2 oz. canned crab meat,
    picked over to remove any bones
    or cartilage, then flaked
1 piece (¼ oz.) bottled *beni shoga*
    (red pickled ginger), shredded
3 tablespoons *sambai-zu* (*page 64*)

PREPARE IN ADVANCE: 1. Peel the cucumbers lengthways with a rotary peeler or small, sharp knife, but leave occasional ½-inch green strips to add colour to the finished dish.

Rub the cucumbers with 5 teaspoons of salt and set them aside in a bowl to marinate for 15 minutes. Then hold them under cold running water and wash them free of salt.

Pat them dry with kitchen paper. Trim the ends and remove the pulp and seeds from the centre of the cucumbers using a teaspoon or melon scoop. The resulting tunnel in each cucumber should be about 1 inch in diameter.

2. Bring ⅜ pint of water to the boil in a small pan and drop in the watercress or parsley. Cook for about 15 seconds, just long enough to wilt the leaves. Then drain and run cold water over them.

TO ASSEMBLE: To measure correctly how much stuffing each cucumber will hold, place 1 cucumber at a time on a chopping board and lay half the crab meat in a straight line alongside it. Press the flakes of crab meat together with your fingers to make them adhere. Arrange half the watercress or parsley down the length of the crab meat and half the pickled ginger in a long strip beside it.

Slit the cucumber lengthways along one side and, holding it open with your fingers, use chopsticks or your hands to insert the filling into the opening. Press the cucumber firmly but gently to seal it.

TO SERVE: Carefully slice the cucumbers into ½-inch rounds, arrange them on individual serving dishes, and pour a little of the *sambai-zu* dipping sauce into each dish.

Serve the *kani kyuri ikomi* at room temperature as a first course, as part of a Japanese meal (*page 198*) or to go with drinks.

Holding the slit cucumber open with one hand, use chopsticks or tongs to fill the hollowed-out shell with crab meat, watercress and red pickled ginger. Slice the stuffed cucumber (*right*) into ½-inch rounds and serve as an hors d'œuvre or first course.

Neri Shiro Miso
練り白味噌

WHITE MISO DRESSING

To make about 1½ pints

Although 1½ pints of "miso" dressing may seem a large amount to make at one time, it is used extensively in Japanese cooking and if tightly covered will keep as long as six months at room temperature.

30 oz. packaged *shiro miso* (white soya-bean paste)
10 oz. sugar
⅜ pint *sake* (rice wine)
2 egg yolks

TO COOK: Put the *miso*, sugar and *sake* into a medium-sized saucepan and bring to the boil over a moderate heat, stirring constantly. Lower the heat and simmer for 30 minutes, stirring from time to time to prevent the dressing from burning.

Remove the pan from the heat and quickly beat in 2 egg yolks, 1 at a time. Immediately dip the bottom of the pan into a large bowl of iced water to cool the dressing rapidly. It may be used at once in *nuta-ae* (*Recipe Booklet*), *nasu karashi sumiso-ae* (*Recipe Booklet*) or in *kinome-ae* (*below*), or it may be stored in a tightly covered jar at room temperature for future use.

Kinome-ae
木の芽和え

BAMBOO SHOOTS WITH GREEN SOYA DRESSING

To serve 6

PREPARE IN ADVANCE: 1. To prepare a whole bamboo shoot—which is superior to the sliced variety—place it on its side, cut off the base, then cut the base in half horizontally. Cut the tapered top lengthways in quarters, then cut all of the pieces into ½-inch dice. Bring ⅜ pint of water to the boil, drop in the bamboo dice and return to the boil. Boil uncovered for about 10 minutes, until the bamboo shoots show no resistance when pierced with the tip of a sharp knife. Drain and set aside.

10 oz. whole or sliced canned *takenoko* (bamboo shoots), drained and scraped clean
⅜ pint *niban dashi* (*page 54*)
1½ teaspoons sugar
2 teaspoons salt
MSG
5 teaspoons *sake* (rice wine)
A 2-inch square of *kombu* (dried kelp), cut with a sharp knife from a sheet of *kombu* and washed in cold running water
4 oz. fresh spinach leaves stripped from their stalks
3 tablespoons white *miso* dressing (*above*)
¼ teaspoon *kona sansho* (Japanese pepper)

Sliced bamboo shoots need only be cut into ½-inch dice, boiled for 2 to 3 minutes, then drained.

2. Put the *niban dashi*, sugar, ¼ teaspoon of the salt, a few sprinklings of MSG, the *sake* and the *kombu* into a medium-sized saucepan. Bring to the boil over a high heat, stirring constantly, and add the bamboo shoots. Return to the boil and cook briskly, uncovered, until nearly all of the cooking liquid evaporates. Then cool to room temperature.

3. Wash the spinach leaves thoroughly and pat them dry with kitchen paper. Grind or pound the leaves to a paste in a *suribachi* (a serrated mixing bowl) or use a pestle and mortar, adding the rest of the salt gradually as you proceed.

Alternatively, chop the leaves finely with a large, sharp knife and mash them with the salt in a bowl.

4. No matter how you have made the spinach paste, stir ⅜ pint of cold water into it and transfer it to a small saucepan. Bring it to the boil over a high heat, then pour the mixture into a sieve set over a mixing bowl and drain. Discard the liquid.

TO ASSEMBLE AND SERVE: Pour the *miso* dressing into a bowl and rub the spinach paste through a sieve into the dressing with the back of a wooden spoon. Then stir the mixture until it turns a soft, delicate green. Sprinkle with ¼ teaspoon of *kona sansho* powder, add the bamboo shoots, and stir together gently. Serve at room temperature in individual small bowls as a first course or as part of a Japanese meal (*page 198*).

The following recipes are "bento"—or picnic food—and "zensai"—Japanese hors d'œuvre. Because they are all small portions of delicate food, many of the recipes can be used for either purpose. The main point of picnic food, however, is that it can be served at room temperature and stand on its own, without a sauce. When used as "zensai", these recipes can, of course, be served hot and with a sauce.

Kamaboko 蒲鉾
STEAMED FISH LOAF

To make 24 *zensai*

A 3-inch square of *kombu* (dried kelp), washed under cold running water
1½ oz. flour
10 to 11 oz. plaice or other white-meat fish fillet, without any skin or small bones
1 teaspoon salt
2 egg whites
3 tablespoons *mirin* (sweet *sake*), or substitute 2½ tablespoons pale dry sherry

GLAZE
1 egg yolk
1 scant teaspoon *mirin*, or substitute 1 scant teaspoon pale dry sherry

PREPARE IN ADVANCE: 1. Cover the *kombu* with 6 tablespoons of cold water and soak for 30 minutes in a small bowl. Add the flour, mix to a paste with a wooden spoon, and set aside.

2. Cut the fish into small pieces and purée them, a few at a time, in an electric blender. Then transfer the purée to a bowl and beat into it the salt, egg whites, *mirin* and the flour-*kombu* liquid using an electric beater or wooden spoon. Continue to beat until smooth.

3. Lightly oil a 1¼-pint cake tin or ovenproof baking dish with a pastry brush or kitchen paper and line the bottom of the tin or dish with a sheet of aluminium foil. Add the fish mixture and spread it evenly over the foil with a rubber spatula. Rap the tin on a table to remove any air pockets.

TO COOK: Preheat the oven to Mark ¼: 250°F. Place the pan of puréed fish in a shallow roasting tin and pour enough boiling water into the roasting tin to come half-way up its sides. Cook the fish loaf uncovered in the middle of the oven for about 50 minutes, until the fish is firm to the touch. Turn off the heat, keep the oven door closed, and let the fish cake rest for 10 minutes.

Preheat the grill. Put the egg yolk and *mirin* into a small bowl and brush it evenly over the top of the fish with a pastry brush. Slide the pan under the grill and watch it closely as it browns lightly. Brush again with the glaze and grill again for another minute, repeating the process twice more until the fish becomes encrusted with a thick golden glaze. Cool to room temperature.

TO SERVE: Run a knife around the inside of the pan. Cut the fish cake into slices ½ inch wide by 1 inch long, and transfer to a serving dish. *Kamaboko* is served at room temperature as an hors d'œuvre, part of a picnic box, or as a first course.

Kamo Sakamushi 鴨酒蒸
SAKE-STEAMED DUCK

To make about 24 *zensai*

2 whole boned duck or chicken breasts, with the skin left on (*see pages 176-177*)
1 scant teaspoon salt
2½ teaspoons *sake* (rice wine)

PREPARE IN ADVANCE: Place the boned duck or chicken breasts skin side up on a flameproof dish and sprinkle them with 1 scant teaspoon of salt. Cover with a sheet of plastic, refrigerate and marinate for at least 3 hours.

TO COOK: Preheat the grill to its highest point. Meanwhile, pour the *sake* over the duck and steam for 7 minutes in either an oriental steamer or the steamer substitute described on page 180.

Remove the plate of duck from the steamer and slide it under the grill about 3 inches from the heat. Grill for about 2 minutes until the breasts have turned a rich golden brown.

Cool to room temperature, then cut the breasts into ¼-inch slices. Serve as an hors d'œuvre or as a first course.

68

To prevent prawns from curling as they cook spear them along their inner curve with toothpicks or small skewers. After cooking, peel and de-vein them. Then cut three-quarters of the way through along the inner curve and flatten the prawns butterfly fashion.

Ebi Kimizushi

海老黄味ずし

PRAWN SUSHI WITH EGG YOLK

To make 6 *zensai*

6 medium-sized, raw, unshelled
   prawns (16 to 20 per lb.)

MARINADE
3 tablespoons rice vinegar, or
   substitute 3 tablespoons mild
   white vinegar
4 tablespoons water
1 scant teaspoon sugar
¼ teaspoon salt
MSG

FILLING
4 egg yolks
1¼ teaspoons sugar
¼ teaspoon salt
2½ teaspoons fresh lemon juice
MSG

TO COOK: Leaving the shells of the prawns intact, insert toothpicks along their inside curves to prevent them from curling as they cook. Drop the prawns into ¾ pint of boiling water and cook briskly, uncovered, for about 3 minutes until pink and firm. Drain in a sieve and cool quickly under cold running water.

Remove the toothpicks and peel the prawns, leaving the last section of shell and the tail attached to each one.

De-vein the prawns by making a shallow incision across their tops with a small, sharp knife and lifting out the black or white intestinal vein with the point of the knife.

Butterfly the prawns by cutting along their inner curves three-quarters of the way through, spreading them open and flattening them lightly with the flat blade of a large knife or cleaver.

Put the vinegar, water, sugar, salt and a few sprinklings of MSG into a mixing bowl and stir together thoroughly. Add the prawns, turn them about in the marinade to moisten them well, and marinate at room temperature for about 1 hour.

Drop the 4 egg yolks into a small saucepan, and beat them lightly with a fork. Remove 2½ teaspoons of the egg yolks, and set them aside in a small bowl.

Add ¾ pint of water to the remaining yolks, stir thoroughly, and cook over a moderate heat for about 10 to 15 minutes until the yolks are firm and hard-boiled. Drain them in a sieve, and mash them to a paste with a fork in a mixing bowl. Beat in the sugar, salt, lemon juice, a few sprinklings of MSG, and the rest of the raw egg yolk and continue to beat until smooth. Then rub the mixture with the back of a spoon through a fine sieve set over a bowl.

TO ASSEMBLE AND SERVE: Divide the seasoned egg filling into 6 equal parts and pack each part into the centre of a butterflied prawn. Seal the edges of each prawn by pressing them firmly together. Serve *ebi kimizushi* at room temperature to go with drinks, as part of a picnic box, or as a first course.

To make 10 to 12 *zensai*

6 slender young asparagus stalks,
    peeled
4 oz. *shiro miso* (white soya-bean
    paste)
2½ teaspoons powdered mustard

To make 6 *zensai*

A 3-inch square of *kombu* (dried kelp),
    cut from a sheet of packaged
    kombu and washed under cold
    running water
1½ oz. flour
24 large raw prawns (10 to 15 per
    pound), shelled and de-veined (*see
    page 168*)
¼ teaspoon salt
2½ teaspoons *mirin* (sweet *sake*), or
    substitute 1½ teaspoons pale dry
    sherry
1 egg white
6 small white turnips, peeled
3 oz. *somen* (Japanese noodles),
    or substitute any thin noodles,
    cut into 1-inch lengths
Vegetable oil
6 *kuri fukume-ni* (sweet chestnuts;
    page 123)

To make 6 chestnuts

6 peeled chestnuts (*page 123*)
2½ teaspoons green Japanese tea
    leaves
4 teaspoons sugar
1 scant teaspoon Japanese soya
    sauce

Karashi Zuke   辛子漬

MISO-MARINATED ASPARAGUS

TO COOK AND ASSEMBLE: 1. Snap the tips from the asparagus and save for future use. Slice the stalks lengthways into strips ½ inch wide, then cut these into 1½-inch lengths. Bring ¾ pint of water to the boil over a high heat. Add the asparagus, return to the boil, and drain immediately in a sieve. Run cold water over them to cool them quickly, and pat dry with kitchen paper.

Put the *miso* with the dry mustard into a small mixing bowl and mix until smooth. Spread half the mixture in a shallow baking dish or casserole and cover with a double thickness of cheesecloth the size of the dish. Place the asparagus in one layer on the cheesecloth and cover with another double thickness of cheesecloth. Top with the remaining *miso* and mustard mixture. Marinate for about 3 hours at room temperature, or refrigerate overnight.

Discard the marinade before serving the asparagus.

Igaguri   いが栗

THORNY PRAWN BALLS FILLED WITH SWEET CHESTNUTS

PREPARE IN ADVANCE: 1. Soak the *kombu* in 6 tablespoons of water for 30 minutes. Stir in 1½ oz. of flour, mix to a paste, and set aside.

2. Purée the prawns, a few at a time, in an electric blender or put them twice through a mincer, using the finest blade. Then, with an electric beater or wooden spoon, beat into the purée the salt, *mirin*, 1 egg white and 6 table-spoons of the flour and *kombu* liquid. Continue to beat until smooth.

3. Trim the turnips into ½-inch balls with a small, sharp knife. Divide the prawn mixture into 6 parts and, moistening your hands with cold water, shape into 6 balls. Make an indentation in the top of each ball and force the turnip into it. Pat into shape again, enclosing the turnip.

4. Spread the cut noodles out on a sheet of greaseproof paper. Then roll the prawn balls about in them until they adhere and protrude like thorns.

TO COOK: Pour enough oil into a deep-fat frying pan or deep frying pan to come 3 inches up the sides. Set over a high heat until the oil registers 375°F. on a deep-fat thermometer. Deep-fry the prawn balls 3 or 4 at a time for about 2 to 3 minutes, until they are golden brown. Remove and drain on kitchen paper.

Make a hole in the top of each ball with a chopstick or the point of a knife and spread it open gently. One by one, remove the turnips and insert sweet chestnuts in their places. Serve at room temperature.

Shibu Kawa-ni   澁皮煮

CHESTNUTS COOKED IN GREEN TEA

TO COOK: Cover the chestnuts with cold water and the tea leaves and bring to the boil in a small saucepan. Lower the heat and simmer uncovered for about 20 minutes until the chestnuts show no resistance when pierced with the tip of a sharp knife. Drain and wash under cold running water. Leave the brown membrane intact.

Put ⅜ pint of cold water, the sugar and the chestnuts into a saucepan and bring to the boil. Reduce the heat and simmer 20 minutes, then stir in the soya sauce. Simmer another 5 minutes, remove from the heat and cool to room temperature before draining and serving.

Begin with a small ball of puréed, seasoned prawns (*left*). Make a dent in it and press in a trimmed ½-inch turnip ball. Pat into shape again (*right*), enclosing the turnip.

Roll the prawn ball about in bits of thin noodle until the noodles adhere to the puréed prawn and stick out in all directions like thorns. Keep in the refrigerator until ready to cook.

Deep-fry the prawn balls until they are a golden brown. Then with chopsticks or the point of a knife, make a hole in the top of each ball and gently spread it open. Pluck out the turnip (*above, left*) and in its place insert a sweetened chestnut (*above, right*). The completed *igaguri* (*right*) now resembles a chestnut in its wild form, but its taste is highly sophisticated: first the diner encounters the crisp outer noodles, next the seasoned prawn, and last the sweet-cooked chestnut.

A tempting array of *zensai*, small portions of food
suitable as hors d'œuvre or as first courses, can
be made from recipes on pages 68 to 73 and
in the Recipe Booklet. They are, clock-wise from
upper right: prawns wrapped in seaweed; rolled
beef with spring onions; fried fluke seasoned with
vinegar sauce; *miso*-marinated asparagus; sliced
squid topped with pickled cod roe; sliced abalone
cooked in *sake* and soya sauce; soya-seasoned
Japanese snails cut into small pieces.

Awabi Sakani
鮑酒煮

SWEET-COOKED ABALONE

Empty the can of abalone in a small saucepan and add the water. Bring to the boil, then lower the heat and simmer uncovered 10 minutes. Add the *sake* and sugar and cook another 5 minutes, then stir in the soya sauce and cook 2 to 3 minutes longer. Cool to room temperature, then cut the abalone into slices $\frac{1}{2}$ inch thick and serve as an hors d'œuvre or first course.

To make 6 *zensai*

A 15-oz. can of abalone, packed in water
$\frac{1}{4}$ pint cold water
$2\frac{1}{2}$ tablespoons *sake* (rice wine)
1 oz. sugar
$2\frac{1}{2}$ teaspoons Japanese soya sauce

Hamaguri Shigure-ni
蛤しぐれ煮

SWEET-COOKED CLAMS

TO COOK: Put the *sake*, sugar and clams into a large frying pan and stir together thoroughly but gently. Bring to the boil over a high heat and cook for about 3 minutes uncovered. Stir in the soya sauce and cook briskly for another minute. Then remove the clams and set them aside in a bowl.

Boil the liquid in the frying pan over a high heat for about 10 minutes until it becomes syrupy. Add the clams and stir them gently in the sauce over a high heat for about 1 minute until they are thoroughly glazed.

Transfer the clams and their sauce to a deep bowl, and cool to room temperature. Serve cold, as part of a *bento*, or picnic box, or as an hors d'œuvre.

NOTE: Tiny shrimps, mussels or bits of fresh tunny fish may be substituted for the clams or cockles and prepared in precisely the same fashion.

To make 24 *zensai*

3 tablespoons *sake* (rice wine)
$1\frac{1}{2}$ oz. sugar
24 small little-neck clams, shelled, or substitute 24 cockles
$2\frac{1}{2}$ tablespoons Japanese soya sauce

Hamaguri Sakani
蛤酒煮

SAKE-SEASONED CLAMS

PREPARE IN ADVANCE: Have the clams shelled by your fishmonger and ask him to save the shells. Discard the shallower halves and scrub the deeper halves of the shells thoroughly. Drop them into boiling water, boil for 2 to 3 minutes, then drain. Rinse under running water and pat dry.

TO COOK AND SERVE: Bring the *sake* to the boil in a small saucepan over a high heat. Sprinkle with MSG, then drop in the clams, stir gently, and cover. Cook over a moderately high heat for 3 to 4 minutes, remove the clams with kitchen tongs and place one in each of the reserved shells. Garnish each clam with a half slice of lemon, and serve at room temperature.

To make 12 *zensai*

12 little-neck clams, or substitute 12 cockles
$1\frac{1}{2}$ pints boiling water
3 tablespoons *sake* (rice wine)
MSG
6 thin slices of lemon, cut in half

Gyuniku Negimaki
牛肉葱卷

STEAK AND SPRING-ONION ROLLS

PREPARE IN ADVANCE: Place the steak between sheets of greaseproof paper and pound it to a $\frac{1}{8}$-inch thickness with a meat pounder or the flat of a cleaver. Cut the steak in half crosswise. Arrange a strip of spring onions down the length of each piece of the meat, then, starting with the wide sides, roll the pieces into tight cylinders. Secure with toothpicks.

TO COOK: Preheat the grill—or light a charcoal grill or hibachi. Dip the rolls into the *teriyaki* sauce using chopsticks, and then grill them 3 inches from the heat for about 3 minutes. Dip them again into the sauce, and grill the other side for a minute. Remove the toothpicks, trim the ends of the rolls neatly with a sharp knife, and cut the rolls into 1-inch pieces. Stand each piece on end, to expose the spring onions, and serve at once.

To make 8 *zensai*

A 4-oz. slice (about $\frac{1}{4}$ inch thick) of rump steak
2 spring onions, including 3 inches of the green stalks, cut in half lengthways, then cut into 4-inch pieces
3 tablespoons *teriyaki* sauce (*page 175*)

IV

The World's Greatest Seafood

Long strands of *kombu* (kelp) are tied in sheaves with straw by the grandmother of a fishing family who live on the Inland Sea. The kelp, still damp after being washed up by the tide, is hung to dry. Eventually it will be used either to make a soup stock or it will be cooked as a vegetable to be eaten with fish.

The wealth that nature denied to the islands of Japan she seems to have lavished on the seas that surround them. No waters on earth are as generous as those that give Japan her astonishing variety of delectable ocean fare.

As any one who has eaten in Japan must have realized, if only vaguely, Japanese fish and shell-fish taste better than the same species anywhere else. This is not just a question of the way in which they are cooked, nor is it an illusion created by the bewitching colour and design of the exquisite presentation. The sea creatures themselves actually have a richer, deeper flavour—thanks to the Japan Current (like the Atlantic Gulf Stream), a mighty cornucopia of undersea life. Steep undersea escarpments outline this country of 3,620 islands and create a stirring action as the tropical tide mingles with colder waters from the north; this turbulence prevents the nourishing ocean minerals from settling to the bottom. It is these suspended minerals, prime food for marine life, that make Japanese sea products the best tasting in the world.

Since ancient times the Japanese have known the sea and what is in it. Their ancestors were seafarers—they had to be to make their way to the islands in the first place—and this primitive attachment to the ocean has never been lost. Although hemmed into narrow coastal plains by rugged mountains, and lacking grazing land, the Japanese are fortunate in their coastline, which is indented by thousands of shallow bays and sheltered inlets that make life easy for both fish and fishermen. So it was quite natural for the Japanese to forage seawards, first for sustenance, then, as they discovered the full extent of their marine treasure, to satisfy that craving for variety which distinguishes the civilized palate from the crude tastes of rustic peoples. Poor in many resources they may be, but no other people feast more richly on the ocean's bounty.

Every man, woman and child in Japan eats something from the sea every day, if not at every meal; some sea products, like *dashi*, a soup or cooking stock, or *katsuobushi*, processed dried bonito, are in so many dishes that the Japanese diner may not be aware, unless he is a cook, that he is eating seafood. Japanese reliance on the sea has created something so much more fundamental than that which the word "seafood" may signify to someone from the West that there is no Japanese equivalent to our seafood restaurants. In the great restaurants, a variety of seafood is essential to *every* carefully orchestrated meal, while smaller speciality houses produce symphonies with only one kind of fish, or one style of preparation. The gifts of the ocean are as basic to the Japanese diet as rice, and without them there would be no distinctive Japanese cuisine.

The ancient Shinto prayer, referred to earlier, lists the ocean foodstuffs of the early Japanese: "... things that dwell in the blue sea-plain, the broad of fin and the narrow of fin, seaweed from the offing, seaweed from the shore...". Broad fin and narrow, from shallow and deep, the Japanese have tried everything. There is probably nothing edible that swims or floats or scuttles across the ocean floor that they have not mastered. They eat whales that taste like beef and tiny clams that barely taste at all, pungent sea-urchins and sweetish sea bream, tunny fish that melts on the tongue and octopus tentacles that require good teeth. They have creamy sardines and juicy crabs and crisp squid and subtly flavoured prawns. There are aromas too delicate to name and flavours too rich to forget, globe-fish that could poison you if not properly cleaned, eels that hint at the murky fecundity of the ocean depths, and feathery-fleshed whitefish that suggest sunshine on a sparkling sea.

All told, the Japanese eat nine marine mammals, 63 species of sea fish, eight kinds of shell-fish, three different crabs, two kinds of prawns, and another half a dozen miscellaneous sea creatures. Six varieties of edible seaweed are plucked from the coastal waters, and 18 species of freshwater fish, particularly carp and *ayu*, a small trout-like fish, find their places in the contented stomachs of the Japanese. It adds up to 7,000 tons of seafood everyday, or, to take a more palatable statistic, nearly a pound of fish per head each week.

To gather this harvest, Japan's commercial fishing boats scour every ocean of the world. The Pacific, of course, is virtually a lake for Japanese fishermen. But efficient Japanese tunny clippers roam the Atlantic and Indian oceans, whale-killing fleets penetrate the Antarctic, and the Bering Sea is dragged for cod and halibut. Not even the Mediterranean is too far to roam for tunny fish. Equipped with loran navigation systems to guide them with precision to the best fishing grounds, with radar and sonar to locate the schools of fish, and with first-class canning, processing and deep-freeze devices, Japan's ocean-going fishermen take into their floating factories more fish than any other country—about one-sixth of the world's total catch. Sometimes these vessels remain at sea for six months, return to Japan briefly to unload their haul at the Tsukiji market in Tokyo, or the ports of Kobe or Hiroshima, and then are outward bound again without putting in at the small fishing towns which the fishermen call home.

But for every humming trawler far at sea there must be a hundred put-putting wooden cockle-shells no more than 20 feet long, trolling and seining and hand-lining the waters within sight of shore. They follow the tides and not the sun, and so, when the fish are running, I have often watched them as they leave at night, their yellow lanterns making the surface of a bay twinkle with stars like a sky turned upside down.

In many places, women play a vital role in community fishing operations. When the boats come home to the coast of Chiba, near Tokyo, the wives and daughters of the fishermen turn out in force and plunge up to their waists in the surf—even in the dead of winter—to haul the vessels on to the beach. In some Okinawa fishing communities the women take complete charge of the catch once it is landed, selling it, collecting the money, and paying their fishermen husbands' wages.

But it is the *ama*, the strapping diving girls, who are the real queens of the sea-coast, and who still provide most of the *awabi* (abalone, or sea-ear) and many other shell-fish for the *sushi* bars of Japan. Baby oysters can be grown in baskets, or can be raked up from sandy bottoms; clams can be dug up at low tide; octopus turn up regularly in fishing-nets and can be lured into earthenware pots on the sea floor and hauled out of the water before they know what's happening. But the *awabi*, single-shelled molluscs, live 40 feet down or deeper, and attach themselves like suction cups to the jagged undersea rocks. The only way to get them without destroying their young is to hack them off, one by one, with a heavy knife.

In Japan, diving for shell-fish like *awabi* has always been women's work, a calling and a skill passed on from *ama* mother to *ama* daughter for generations. The Japanese say a woman can better withstand the prolonged cold of the deep than a man. In hundreds of bays along Japan's coast the peculiar periodic whistle of the *ama* surfacing and letting out her breath is as familiar a sound as the cry of a gull or the roar of the waves.

Nowadays, most *ama* wear linen clothing from head to knee to protect them from the sun during the moments they are on the surface, to frighten away sharks—and as a concession to modern ideas of modesty. But in out-of-the-way corners of the country sturdy, sun-bronzed *ama* in nothing but loin-cloth and belt, and perhaps a diving mask, still prowl through an undersea world that they know as well as the lanes of their villages. Ordinary *ama* must go to the diving grounds in boat-loads of a dozen or more, and surface and dive under their own power. But an expert *ama* has her own boatman—usually her husband or a male relation in whom she has utter faith. With a lead weight to pull her down, and her boatman to haul her up, she can go deeper than her less-skilled sisters, and spend more time and breath on the bottom where the shell-fish are. During the season a champion *ama* may earn as much in a good day as the average Japanese factory girl makes in a month; not surprisingly, the *ama* rule matriarchal villages, and the best young divers can take their pick of husbands.

Nowadays the profession of *ama* is somehow considered old-fashioned and degrading—though how it can be more degrading than working at a factory bench is difficult for me to understand—and fewer and fewer *ama* village girls are following their mothers down to the sea. Consequently *awabi* prices are steadily rising. No matter how expensive they get, Japanese

Continued on page 80

77

Beyond the gleaming tunny-fish carcasses (*opposite*), each identified by bold red numbers, brokers signal their bids at one of the many noisy auctions that start the day's business at Tokyo's Tsukiji Central Market. The brokers have previously inspected the tuna, noted their weights—some weigh as much as 450 pounds—and judged the flesh for quality. The tails are slashed to reveal the freshness and fattiness of the meat, important in determining the price. When the auction begins, the rapid-fire barrage of bids reflects the brokers' appraisal of these factors. Lean tunny fish, brought all the way from the Indian Ocean, may go for only a couple of shillings a pound; firm, fatty tunny from near-by Pacific waters will bring in as much as 8 shillings. Some 90 other kinds of fish—unloaded only a few hours earlier—are sold at auctions. They include (*above*): bonito (*1*), *guji*, a type of sea bream (*2*), whitebait (*3*), squid (*4*), small sea bream (*5*), prawns (*6*), clams (*7*), sea bream (*8*), lobsters (*9*), a Japanese species of scorpion fish (*10*) and abalone (*11*).

A Spectacular Market for Fresh Fish by the Ton

Fish is as important in the Japanese diet as meat is in the West. However, the watery harvest of river, lake and sea offers a far greater range of choices to the Japanese than do the farms of the West. Fish shops offer everything from whale steaks, whose taste is remarkably similar to beef, to tiny molluscs. Large and small, sweet and tangy, tons of fish are delivered daily to sprawling markets in every large city. At the 50-acre Tsukiji Central Market in Tokyo alone, 2,000 tons of fish, most of it freshly caught, are sold each day. The sale starts at 5.45 a.m. when fiercely competitive brokers bid for a broad spectrum of finned and shelled sea food. These middlemen then display their wares in 1,500 market stalls where they sell the fish to the city's clamouring shopkeepers and restaurateurs.

lovers of shell-fish are not likely to give them up; whether raw, semi-raw and pickled in vinegar, steamed, or even dried and made chewy, the firm, mellow flesh of the *awabi* will always be regarded by the Japanese as one of the prizes of the ocean.

For a panoramic view of Japan's seafood empire, every visitor to the country should look in on the Tsukiji fish market in Tokyo, any morning before dawn. Here, in a scene of incredible congestion and seeming chaos, a few blocks from the Ginza, more than 70,000 people buy, sell and cart away all the sea products that the 20 million Japanese of the Tokyo metropolitan area require every day—and most of the fish will have been eaten before the next day's turmoil begins. Some of the fish is unloaded at Tsukiji straight from the ocean-going vessels which have just arrived from months at sea; most of it arrives in refrigerated carriages from other ports. But all of it is laid out under glaring light bulbs to be carefully inspected before it is sold. Somehow, the market smells of the sea, not of fish.

On one quay, row on row of gleaming, bulky tunny fish, tails chopped off and stuffed into mouths, identifying numbers painted on their sides, are laid out on wooden racks. Professional tunny buyers prod the carcasses, shine electric torches into the gills and examine the tail nubs to check the colour and condition of the meat. And then they bid for them, in a dozen or more frantic, noisy auctions all going on at the same time. Since many of these fish will be eaten uncooked either as *sushi* or *sashimi*, the buyers are very fussy, not only about their freshness but about their provenance. Tunny from the northern Pacific will fetch the highest prices because they will be fresher than from the Indian or Atlantic oceans and because they are fatter and contain more of the light pink, fatty *toro* flesh that *sashimi* fanciers prize.

From the auctions, hundreds of porters wheel the now-dismembered tunny fish into a vast maelstrom of activity where 1,500 wholesale stands display the full abundance of the sea. Here are silver sardines and mackerel, bright red *tai*, or sea bream, with enormous, reproachful eyes, quivering squid and cuttle-fish, blue-striped bonito, crates of pink Hokkaido crabs packed in ice, buckets of fresh oysters from Hiroshima on the Inland Sea, piles of iridescent *awabi*, boxes of prickly sea urchins—and fishes of all colours and sizes, some still flopping, some split, some already having lost their heads and tails.

To this heart of the market come the thousands of local fishmongers and restaurateurs, great and small, who insist on choosing everything fresh themselves. They look, they prod, they sniff and they buy, and then they cart their glistening purchases through clogged aisles into a seething traffic jam. As the sun rises, the flood of fish spreads out by lorry, motor cycle and bicycle, to every cranny of the world's biggest city and its suburbs.

Some of the best of the sea produce do not go far, for the finest fish eating in Japan can be had in the environs of Tsukiji and in near-by Ginza. This is especially true of *sashimi* and *sushi*, the two basic raw-fish dishes. In the days before refrigeration and fast transport, restaurants serving uncooked fish naturally set up near the docks to ensure their freshness. Nowadays delicious raw seafood is available far inland, but the excellent Tsukiji restaurants survive, patronised by thousands of people who know their fish.

Eating uncooked fish strikes many foreign visitors as barbaric and almost

indecent, but this attitude usually disappears with the first brave bite. Part of the instinctive Western uneasiness is due to the ugly word "raw", with its misleading suggestion of something coarse and tough. To overcome the initial reluctance of my friends, I remind them that *sashimi* is sometimes the first solid food served by Japanese hospitals to patients who have been on a liquid diet. The fact is that raw fish as the Japanese eat it does not taste or smell fishy. In a blindfold test the sceptic would not have the faintest idea he was eating fish; he would probably assume that his chunk of raw tunny was a cube of chilled rare roast beef.

Sashimi is the Japanese umbrella word for raw fillets of fish eaten alone, usually dipped in soya sauce and a special pungent horse-radish. *Sushi*—of which more will be said in Chapter 7—consists of balls of vinegared rice garnished either with a strip of raw seafood or with cooked prawns, cooked fish, vegetables, seaweed or egg.

Both *sashimi* and *sushi* are extremely popular. No formal menu in a good Japanese restaurant ever omits the *sashimi* course; but *sushi*, which is a meal in itself, as it includes rice, is not served at formal dinners, though there are more *sushi* restaurants in Japan than any other kind. *Sashimi* may also make up a meal by itself, and some restaurants serve nothing else, offering a dozen or more varieties of fish for a full dinner. Because so many sea animals can be eaten this way, an all-*sashimi* menu is never monotonous: it's more

Attracted by the flames of burning pine boughs, tasty, trout-like fish called *ayu* swim close to this skiff. There they are easy prey for trained cormorants, fish-catching birds that a boatman holds on 12-foot-long leashes. A ring around the cormorant's neck keeps it from swallowing, and when the bird is taken aboard, it surrenders its catch. *Ukai* (cormorant fishing) is more than 1,200 years old but flourishes today mainly on the Nagara river in Gifu Prefecture, where it has become a tourist attraction. The captured *ayu* are transferred to a restaurant boat where they are served raw or salt-grilled to the customers.

like a glorious binge. Of all their foods, I think the Japanese love *sashimi* best; certainly it is what they long for most when they are travelling abroad and can't eat as they do at home.

Everything concerned with the handling and preparation of *sashimi* is carried out with elaborate care. Not only must the fish be fresh—ideally between four and 12 hours out of the water, and refrigerated all the way from ship to table—but never frozen, for the drip of thawing leaches out all the flavour. The chef who cuts the *sashimi* into chunks just big enough for chopsticks to handle uses his knife to pick up the pieces so that the heat of his fingers won't be transferred to the fish. Nor is fish skinned, or shell-fish opened, until the moment of serving, for their natural "envelopes" preserve the flavour. Occasionally, to vary the taste and make a prettier presentation, the Japanese take their *sashimi* with the skin on. But fish skins are hard to chew when raw, so they have to be treated lightly with heat, either by pouring hot water over the skin through cheesecloth or by grilling the skin side for a few seconds.

By far the most popular *sashimi* fish is *maguro*, or tunny fish, both the fatty pink meat and the red lean, and the Japanese prefer it in spring or early summer. It is served to you in a shallow porcelain bowl: five or six juicy-looking, square-cut little red slabs, leaning on each other like fallen dominoes and decorated with slivers of green cabbage or white radish. Beside them, bedded on a tiny slice of radish, you find a dab of *wasabi*, the hot, green horse-radish paste. A separate small dipping bowl and a bottle of soya sauce complete the ensemble. Soya sauce goes into the dipping bowl, and *wasabi* is added with chopsticks. Pick up a chunk with the chopsticks, dip it in the sauce and pop the whole bit in your mouth. Chew slowly and roll it on your tongue: it is tender, meaty and succulent, a taste that can be compared to no other.

In winter, the Japanese are partial to white-meat *sashimi*, such as yellow-tail, *tai* (sea bream), flounder and squid. Squid is served in slabs, just like the red tunny, for squid is a rugged meat in spite of its colour. But the other white-meat *sashimi* usually arrives in slices so thin that you can see right through them to the pattern of the dish beneath. In this case, a dipping sauce called *pon-su*, half soya sauce and half a sour juice like our lime juice, imparts a slight tang, but the sea-sweet flavour of the fish always comes whispering through.

The Japanese hold that any fish or shell-fish that can be eaten cooked can also be eaten raw, but that doesn't mean that they consume raw seafood indiscriminately. For one thing, some fish just taste better raw than others. And fish that are excellent in one season may lack flavour in another; many are too fat just before the spawning period, for instance, and too lean right after it. Nor are all parts of the creature good raw; the thickest parts of the fish fillet are best; and only the main body of shell-fish, crustaceans and molluscs qualifies for *sashimi*. Another consideration is the degree of freshness. This is especially important for any one buying fish for *sashimi* in the West, where standards of freshness fall far short of those in Japan.

Although the Japanese dine gloriously on raw carp and other freshwater *sashimi*, Europeans preparing a *sashimi* meal would probably be wise to stick to salt-water species. In fact, only sea animals that spend all their lives in

82

the ocean should be used; salmon, shad or any other fish that moves up freshwater streams to spawn should be avoided. This is because our rivers are polluted and because freshwater fish sometimes have parasites that cannot exist in salt water. Lobsters and crabs must be bought alive to be eaten raw.

For many Japanese gourmets, all this attention to freshness and season and cut is not enough. They insist quite simply that a dead fish is not a fresh fish, and they prefer to eat them alive. The victim usually selected for this sacrifice is the prawn, and the ritual of eating it is called *odori*. *Odori* means dance, and that's what the prawn does as it is picked up, chewed and finally swallowed.

A Japanese doctor I know introduced me to *odori* at an excellent but unpretentious restaurant in the Shinjuku district of Tokyo. We sat at a bar and sipped *sake*. Then my host said something to the chef. Before my eyes the chef grabbed a live prawn from a squirming tankful, gutted and beheaded it with two quick flicks of his knife, stripped off the shell and rinsed the flesh, and placed the dancing prawn in front of me—all in about five seconds. Before I could react he did the same with another for my friend, who immediately captured it by the wriggling tail, dipped it in a sauce, and swallowed it down, making appreciative noises.

Determined not to be outdone I summoned all my resolve and reached for mine, but it squirmed violently—in agony, I was sure—and escaped from my trembling fingers. That was enough for one adventurous American. I waited patiently until the performance was over and then gingerly tasted the prawn. It was delicious, of course, although my host told me I had missed the best part. He insisted that the flavour is several times better while the *odori* is in progress—and I am willing to take his word for it.

Later I learned that most Japanese react to the experience much as I did. My friend is in a minority in his passion for *odori*; perhaps his being a surgeon has something to do with his tastes. But there is a restaurant in Tsukiji that cuts all its *sashimi* fillets out of living fish, and it is so busy that booking in advance is recommended.

A seafood even more dramatic than *odori*, or at least potentially so, is *fugu*, the blow-fish or globe-fish. This intriguing little creature, which can puff itself up to beach-ball size when threatened, is actually poisonous. That is, the liver and ovaries of the *fugu* contain a deadly toxic substance that spreads through the rest of the fish in an instant unless deftly removed in the first stage of cleaning. To the untrained eye, however, the liver looks just like the male fish's testes, a special delicacy highly prized by Japanese men as an aid to virility.

Dozens of times a year some cock-sure fisherman in Japan finds a mess of *fugu* in his nets, decides he knows how to clean them—and drops dead, chopsticks clattering from paralysed fingers. Duly reported in the Japanese press, these tragedies give the *fugu* connoisseur the heady feeling that he is playing a kind of Russian roulette—and winning. The danger of *fugu* has in fact inspired a homily on all kinds of risk. "Fugu wa kuitashii, inochi wa oshishii", says the Japanese who can't quite make up his mind on a bold course of action: "I would like to eat *fugu*, but I would like to live".

In fact, eating *fugu* prepared by a licensed *fugu* chef is perfectly safe. The chef has to pass oral, written and practical examinations in the techniques of

Continued on page 86

White, nearly transparent slices of raw *fugu* are often fashioned into fragile designs such as the sacred flying crane, Japan's noblest bird (*above*), garnished with a pine twig. The dark areas and the beak are made from grilled *fugu* skin, which also is edible, and the crest is grated *daikon* radish mixed with hot red pepper.

Eating "Fugu": A Thrill in Every Bite

From October 1 to March 31 each season, millions of Japanese put their lives at stake—some 200 lose—by eating *fugu*, a kind of blow-fish with a lethal poison in its liver and ovaries. But besides being esteemed as the most delicious of fish, carefully cleaned *fugu* are perfectly safe to eat. So restaurants, whose chefs must be specially licensed, serve it and the customers devour it.

A family trustingly dips into a beautifully designed crane fashioned from raw and grilled *fugu*. At Fukugen, a famous Tokyo restaurant devoted to serving "tiger" *fugu*, which is the tastiest and also the deadliest variety of the fish, the skilled and dedicated chefs reduce to zero the chances of accidental poisoning.

cleaning, and must demonstrate an infallible ability to distinguish testes from liver; his licence, with his photograph attached, is displayed prominently in his restaurant.

Thus safeguarded, the gourmets of Japan happily pay out more than £3 for a two-ounce portion of delicate "tiger" *fugu sashimi*, without doubt Japan's costliest food. In the best *fugu* restaurants they get it arranged in intricate patterns simulating chrysanthemum blossoms or birds in flight, and sliced so thin that the colours and design on the dish are visible through it. They eat it with an almost ritual awe, dipping the transparent slices in a special *pon-su* supercharged with chopped spring onions and radish, and welcoming the slight numbness of lips and tongue that results, it is said, from minute traces of the poison. Sophisticated *fugu* enthusiasts prefer the "noble" and "philosophical" flesh of *fugu* to all other *sashimi*, and they grow fretful during the summer months when it is not available; but unbelievers claim that the only thing they can taste is the sauce. To my taste buds, *fugu* does have a distinctive tang that is not present when the same sauce is applied to other fishes; but strangely, the tang is not always there when the *fugu* is tasted without the sauce. It seems to be another example of the Japanese genius for enhancing the natural flavour of their foods.

Fugu restaurants also produce a strong, pungent *fugu* stew served piping hot. And, of course, for hundreds of thousands of adventurous Japanese the high point of a *fugu* meal comes when the chef, with a comradely leer, offers them a cup of hot *sake* mixed with *fugu* testes. *Fugu* chefs and ageing businessmen swear by it, but what effect it may have I cannot say. Undoubtedly the theoretical danger in *fugu* enhances its popularity. Certainly the aesthetic and symbolic presentation of all foods makes them taste better to the Japanese. In the same way the very sounds of the names of certain fish increase their value in Japan.

The best example of this is the *tai*, a flat, bright pink fish. The *tai* has a distinguished flavour, and its red skin is considered lucky in itself, but it is the very name *tai* that ranks it as the finest fish in the sea. *Tai* sounds like *medetai*, meaning "felicitous", the root word for "congratulations", and so the *tai* has become the ceremonial fish served at weddings and other happy occasions. Sending a parcel of fish to a friend for a New Year's greeting may not sound like a good idea to us, but if the friend is Japanese and the fish is a *tai*, he will be delighted. The idea that *tai* is a noble fish has become so ingrained in Japanese minds that there is even a proverb that depends on the notion: "Kusattemo tai", meaning, "Even if it stinks, it's *tai*", conveys the thought that neither poverty nor age can destroy real quality.

This kind of symbolic pun, which may seem superstitious to foreigners, helps the Japanese in their quest for harmony with nature. To the Japanese, nothing on earth, not even a common fish, can exist in isolation; everything must be accorded its rightful place in the universal scheme of things. All aspects of a creature, its soul, its colour and character, even its name, are duly honoured. Take the carp: the Japanese admire its courage and perseverance in struggling upstream to spawn, and they make it a symbol of masculine strength, ambition and persistence. On Children's Day, early in May, every household with a son flies one or more gaily coloured windsock streamers, in the shape of a carp. When carp is eaten it is not just the flesh that is absorbed but in some way its noble attributes as well.

86

Through the centuries, water, fish and crab have figured prominently in Japanese folk-lore and art. Fish because of their suppleness and grace are considered to be one of nature's most beautiful creatures. A swimming fish is a favourite subject for picture scrolls to hang in the *tokonoma*, especially when these alcoves are in restaurants. In Buddhist temples the little gong that the priests beat while chanting their prayers more often than not turns out to be a hollow, carved wooden fish nestling on a silk pillow.

The Japanese respect for fish that is manifest in the way they catch, prepare and eat it even leads to solemn religious ceremonies. Every year, at the great temple of Sojiji, near Tokyo, priests chant their prayers to comfort the souls of fish that have died to feed the nation. On the following day the priests go out in boats to the middle of Tokyo Bay to perform the same service for fish that have died from natural causes. At Shimonoseki, on the straits between Honshu and Kyushu where most of the *fugu* are caught, yet another ceremony specifically honours the spirits of *fugu*. And throughout Japan fishermen toss a basketful of eels back into the sea once a year to atone for all the eels they have caught.

One of the most respected and symbolic fish products of all is *katsuobushi*, dried bonito, essential to all Japanese cookery. The ideographs for *katsuobushi* simply mean "bonito knot"—*katsuo* is bonito—but another set of ideographs pronounced the same way means "victorious warrior" Hence a stick of *katsuobushi* is a perfect gift on all congratulatory occasions, and it has become the most common and appropriate wedding present, significant, lucky and traditional.

But in a sense the real beauty of a *katsuobushi* wedding gift is that it is also eminently practical. The giver is never concerned as to whether his gift will be duplicated by others; every bride knows that the larger her army of victorious warriors, the better off she is: *katsuobushi* never spoils and it is used in almost everything. In fact, I think it is the most remarkable food product of Japan, a superb example of the adroit and sophisticated methods that the Japanese have devised for processing the harvest of their oceans.

From fresh bonito to finished *katsuobushi* is a transformation as complete as turning milk into cheese. The ancient, lengthy process is complex and scientifically sound, involving drying, smoking and mould fermentation. The result looks and feels like a mahogany boomerang, and it can be shaved into flakes only with a very sharp tool. Every Japanese kitchen is equipped with a special plane for doing this but it is available here pre-flaked. Although *katsuobushi* preserves all the protein value of the bonito, it doesn't even taste fishy—but it *is* delicious.

The Japanese love to sprinkle *katsuobushi* flakes on cooked vegetables, particularly spinach, on *tofu* dishes and even on rice; but the most important use for it is as a base for *dashi (Chapter 3)*, the remarkable soup stock that I consider the most sophisticated of all Japanese recipes.

The versatile *katsuobushi* represents only one of the many ways that the Japanese process their seafood. Seventy-six per cent of the 7-million-ton annual catch is preserved somehow: canned, frozen, salted, dried, preserved in soya sauce, or turned into sausages. Many of these methods are unique to Japan. For instance, a smooth, jelly-like fish paste, *kamaboko*, has been part of the Japanese diet for more than 400 years, and a fish sausage, developed

Looking like spiders squatting in a giant web, workers collect carefully cultivated *nori* (laver seaweed) while the tide is out. The vitamin-rich *nori* is picked off the hemp nets, then spread on coarse reed matting to dry in the sun. Sold in bundles of 10 sheets, the paper-thin *nori* is used as a garnish for wrapping round rice.

as a result of the food shortages of the Second World War, tastes like a traditional sausage and is consumed at the rate of 150,000 tons a year. A mixture of tiny fishes and slivers of kelp is preserved by being simmered in a salted, seasoned soya sauce until all the liquid is boiled away. The result, called *tsukudani*, makes a fine garnish for plain rice and other foods and is also served up to customers at *sake* shops and bars to keep them thirsty. Like peanuts or potato crisps, these insidious little snacks are difficult to resist.

Many Japanese get most of their high-quality protein from dried fish and prawns. One method of semi-drying fish that I have never encountered anywhere else keeps it for about eight or ten days without refrigeration and is very convenient for the housewife's lunch. Grilled, it tastes like a fresh fish though somewhat saltier. Its smell while cooking is marvellous, like unleavened bread baking just at the moment before it burns. As you walk along crowded residential streets at lunch time this delectable aroma wafts from many houses—and sends me scurrying to the nearest restaurant.

Of all the miracles of the sea to which the Japanese can guide us, none so inflames our prejudices yet offers so much for the future as the murky world of undersea vegetables. Again our English vocabulary leads us astray, and I do not know which word is worse: "seaweed", with its explicit meaning of uselessness and its dank evocation of sunken ships and drowned sailors, or "algae", the correct scientific term, which suggests to most people green scum on stagnant pools. When you think about it, of course, there is no reason why kelp or laver should be considered less appetizing than asparagus—in fact they are delicious—but the prejudice remains. Many visitors to Japan become queasy at the thought of seaweed but happily gobble up crisp sheets of pressed *nori* (laver) without a moment's hesitation.

In Japanese, the words for most seaweeds are as commonplace and respectable as "cabbage", and one of them even provides another of those homonymous symbols. Kelp, *katsuobushi*'s partner in *dashi*, is *kombu* and it sounds like *yorokobu*, the word for "happiness". Japanese department stores therefore offer vast arrays of elegantly packaged *kombu* assortments that a Japanese guest brings to his hostess as you or I might offer chocolates.

The six kinds of algae that the Japanese use account for about 10 per cent of their total food intake. Some of these sea vegetables are found wild in the ocean, but *nori* is painstakingly cultivated in sheltered inlets along the coast. Tokyo Bay itself produces excellent *nori*.

All these products are rich sources of minerals and vitamins, all are easily and quickly digestible. The basic good health of the Japanese people, despite their low consumption of foods like milk, meat and eggs that we consider essential, is generally credited to the seaweed as well as the fish in their diet. Most delightful of all, the seaweeds, especially *kombu* and *nori*, open up a whole new world—new for us, that is—of seasoning possibilities that have been fully exploited by the Japanese for centuries.

Nori, particularly rich in vitamins A, B_{12} and D, is pressed into paper-thin sheets and sun-dried on a smooth surface. Toasted to crispness and rolled neatly around rice and other ingredients, these purplish-black sheets make one standard kind of *sushi*; a clump of rice wrapped less elegantly in *nori* becomes *onigiri*, a plebeian snack that can be eaten with the fingers. Crumbled as a garnish over rice or *ochazuke*, the farmer's everyday mixture of rice and tea, *nori* gives it a salty flavour.

Besides its vital role in *dashi, kombu*—which is rich in iodine and vitamin C—provides a seasoning for root vegetables, a garnish for rice and another kind of *tsukudani*. Sometimes *kombu* is cut into tiny, oily strips and woven into miniature baskets about an inch high. Deep-fat-fried until crisp, these baskets are loaded with minute amounts of cooked vegetables and served on a tray; you eat the vegetables and then crunch the nourishing basket.

Wakame and *hijiki*, the other important sea vegetables, are used principally in salads and in soups. Sold dried, they are restored by soaking.

For years, population experts have been predicting that as man spreads over more and more of the earth's surface and exhausts its resources he will have to farm the sea extensively for sustenance. We need only to taste the seemingly infinite delights that Japan extracts from the animals and vegetables of the sea to discover how exciting this otherwise dismal future could be. Doctors assure us that such an ocean diet could be good for us as well. The Japanese suffer fewer heart attacks and have far less cholesterol in their veins than most Westerners; for example: comparative studies on Japanese-Americans have shown that this is not a racial quirk, but seems to be linked to a diet low in animal fats. Habits are changing, but the Japanese still take most of their protein from the sea.

Sashimi: SLICED RAW FISH

Sushi: VINEGARED RICE DISHES

Agemono: FRIED FOODS

Many foreigners who are disconcerted by the Japanese delight in eating raw fish think nothing themselves of eating raw oysters. Interestingly, "sashimi" neither tastes nor smells "fishy"; moreover, certain types of "sashimi", notably tunny fish, have the texture and the flavour of tender, rare beef.

Sashimi　　　　　　　　　　　　　　　　　鮨
SLICED RAW FISH

The most important factor in the preparation of "sashimi" is the absolute freshness of the fish. Frozen fish cannot be used. It is best to avoid freshwater fish since they can carry parasites. Keep the fish refrigerated, wrapped in cheesecloth, until ready to use. Handle the fish as little as possible; the warmth of your hands can spoil its freshness.

To serve 4 to 6

1 lb. fresh filleted sea bream, sea
  bass, red snapper, squid,
  abalone or tunny fish, in one
  piece

DIPPING SAUCE

3 to 5 tablespoons Japanese soya
  sauce, *chirizu* (*page 94*) or *tosa
  joyu* and its garnish (*page 94*)

GARNISH

A 2-inch section of *daikon* (Japanese
  white radish) or large icicle radish
  or white turnip, peeled, shredded
  and soaked in cold water until
  ready to use
1 carrot, peeled, shredded and soaked
  in cold water until ready to use
1 stick celery, cut in half lengthways,
  shredded and soaked in cold water
  until ready to use

CUTTING THE FISH: There are four basic fish-cutting methods for *sashimi* and a very sharp, heavy knife is indispensable to them all. (*See pages 92-93 for pictures and diagrams.*)

1. *Hira giri* (flat cut): This is the most popular shape, suitable for any filleted fish. Holding the fish firmly, cut straight down in slices about $\frac{1}{4}$ to $\frac{1}{2}$ inch thick and 1 inch wide, depending on the size of the fillet.

2. *Kaku giri* (cubic cut): This style of cutting is more often used for tunny fish. Cut the tunny fish as above (flat cut), then cut into $\frac{1}{2}$-inch cubes.

3. *Ito zukuri* (thread shape): Although this technique may be used with any small fish, it is especially suitable for squid. Cut the squid straight down into $\frac{1}{4}$-inch slices, then cut lengthways into $\frac{1}{4}$-inch-wide strips.

4. *Usu zukuri* (paper-thin slices): Place a fillet of bass or sea bream on a flat surface and, holding the fish firmly with one hand, slice it at an angle into almost transparent sheets.

TO SERVE: *Sashimi* may be composed of one fish or a variety of fish. To serve as part of a meal, arrange the fish attractively on individual serving plates. Garnish each plate with about $\frac{1}{2}$ teaspoon of *wasabi* (*see "tosa joyu" garnish, page 94*), and decorate with strips of *daikon*, carrot and/or celery. Cover with a sheet of plastic and refrigerate for no more than 1 hour before serving.

Pour the dipping sauce of your choice into tiny individual dishes and accompany each serving of *sashimi* with its own sauce. The *wasabi* may be mixed into the soya sauce or *tosa joyu* to taste.

NOTE: To serve as an hors d'œuvre, arrange two or more varieties or cuts of *sashimi* on a serving dish and accompany with dipping sauce.

The "petals" of this *sashimi* flower are of striped bass, sliced transparently thin. In the centre is red tunny fish, topped by a mound of *wasabi*. Alongside the soya sauce (*left*) is a garnish of *some oroshi* (*page 94*) in *pon-su*.

Here is an assortment of the most popular cuts and types of fish served as *sashimi*. At the top left is squid, for which cutting directions are given below. The dark red fish is tunny—sliced horizontally, straight and in cubes (*directions opposite, at the bottom*). The white-meat fish is striped bass, cut straight, paper thin, and mounded in strips (*opposite, centre*).

Transforming a Whole Fish or Fillets into "Sashimi"

Properly prepared *sashimi*—sliced raw fish—is one of the glories of the Japanese cuisine, and is steadily gaining in popularity throughout the Western world. To make *sashimi* takes little effort, but one rule must be remembered: always use fresh—never frozen—fish.

Sashimi is made from sea bream, sea bass, striped bass, red snapper, squid, abalone or tunny fish. While most of these fish are available throughout the British Isles, their absolute freshness is another matter and may be dictated by region and season.

Directions for cutting the various kinds of fillets are given on the right and opposite. You may, however, want to begin with a whole fish—either because you have caught one yourself, or because you plan to use the head and trimmings for fish stock. In that event, see the drawings (*top, opposite*) for filleting a whole fish. Instructions for serving *sashimi* are on pages 90 and 94.

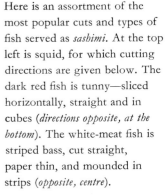

A DECORATIVE CUT FOR SQUID: With a sharp, heavy knife, make shallow cuts down the length of the fillet to within ⅛ inch of the other side. Then cut through the fillet crosswise, at ¼-inch intervals. Bend the ends of the strips slightly inwards to reveal the slits.

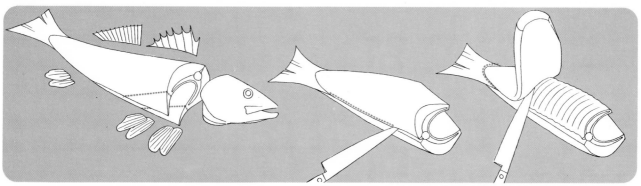

TO FILLET A FISH: First scale and wash the whole fish. Slit the fish open along its belly to gut it, then (*above, left*) cut off the fins, head and hard flaps near the head. Starting at the head, cut along the back (*above, centre*), freeing the top from the spine and radiating bones (*above, right*). Continue cutting until you reach the tail. Turn over and repeat the process on the other side, starting from the tail. Discard the spinal bones.

To skin (*right*), insert the tip of the knife at the pointed end of the fillet; holding firmly on to the skin, cut and push the flesh away with the side of the knife.

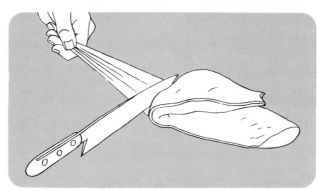

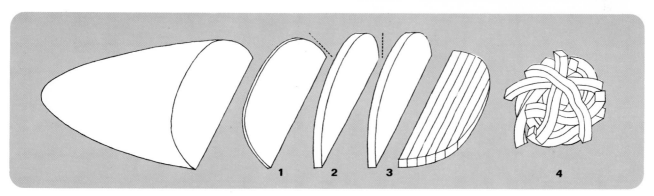

SLICING WHITE-MEAT FISH: Place the fish fillet (bass or sea bream) on a cutting surface and cut *usu zukuri* style into paper-thin slices (*1*). Or cut any filleted fish straight down *hira giri* style into ¼-inch-thick slices (*2*). A variation of this flat cut is known as the thread shape (*ito zukuri*), and is suitable for white-meat fish or squid: cut the ¼-inch-thick slices lengthways into ¼-inch-wide strips (*3*) and mound these (*4*) on top of one another.

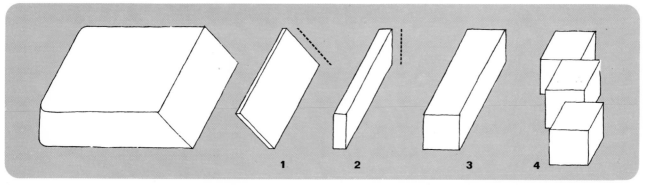

SLICING A FILLET OF TUNNY FISH: Begin with a section of the fillet, trimmed by you or your fishmonger into a rectangular loaf shape. The fish can be sliced *usu zukuri* style at an angle into paper-thin slices (*1*). Or it can be sliced in the *hira giri* style, suitable for any fish fillet, in which you cut straight down into slices ¼ inch thick (*2*). The cubic cut (*kaku giri*) is a style of cutting used almost exclusively for tunny because of its firm texture. First cut straight down, into slices ½ inch thick (*3*). Then cut these slices into ½-inch-wide cubes (*4*).

To serve 6 to 8

6 sheets of packaged *nori* (dried laver)

1 lb. fresh fish fillet (*see sashimi, page 90*)

DIPPING SAUCE

6 tablespoons *chirizu* or *tosa joyu* (below)

To make about ¼ pint

5 teaspoons *sake* (rice wine)

A 4 oz. section *daikon* (Japanese white radish), peeled and finely grated (3 tablespoons), or substitute 3 tablespoons finely grated icicle radish or white turnips

2 spring onions, including the green stalks, trimmed and sliced into thin rounds

3 tablespoons Japanese soya sauce

3 tablespoons fresh lemon juice

MSG

⅛ teaspoon *hichimi togarashi* (seven-pepper spice)

To make about ¼ pint

3 tablespoons Japanese soya sauce

2½ teaspoons *sake* (rice wine)

5 teaspoons pre-flaked *katsuobushi* (dried bonito)

MSG

GARNISH

2½ teaspoons *wasabi* (green horse-radish) powder, mixed with just enough cold water to make a thick paste and set aside to rest for 15 minutes

To make ¼ pint

A 3-inch round section of *daikon* (white radish), peeled

4 *takano tjume* (dried whole red peppers)

6 tablespoons *pon-su* (equal parts soya sauce and lemon or lime juice)

2 spring onions, including 3 inches of the green stalks, sliced into thin rounds

Isobe Zukuri 磯辺づくり
SASHIMI WRAPPED IN LAVER

PREPARE IN ADVANCE: 1. Select the fish according to directions on page 90. Cut the fillet into slices ½ inch thick and 6 or 7 inches long or as long as the sheet of *nori*.

TO ASSEMBLE AND SERVE: Pass the *nori*, a sheet at a time—and on one side only—over a gas flame or candle to intensify its flavour and colour. Lay the *nori* flat on a hard surface—the Japanese use a bamboo mat to facilitate the rolling—with the wide side of the mat facing toward you. Place a long slice of fish along the length of the *nori* and roll the *nori* into a long, thick, tight cylinder. Cut it crosswise into 1½-inch slices with a sharp knife. Roll and cut the remaining fish and *nori* in the same way. Serve with a dipping sauce, as part of a Japanese meal (*page 198*) or as a first course.

Chirizu ちり酢
SPICY DIPPING SAUCE FOR SASHIMI

PREPARE IN ADVANCE: 1. Warm the *sake* in a small saucepan. Then ignite it with a match, off the heat, and shake the pan gently until the flame dies out. Pour the *sake* into a small dish and cool.

2. Put the *sake* with the grated *daikon*, sliced spring onions, soya sauce, lemon juice, a sprinkling of MSG and ⅛ teaspoon of seven-pepper spice into a small mixing bowl. Mix well.

TO SERVE: Pour the dipping sauce into tiny individual dishes and serve with sea bass, sea bream or plaice *sashimi*.

Tosa Joyu 土佐醤油
DELICATE SOYA-BASED DIPPING SAUCE FOR SASHIMI

Put the soya sauce, *sake*, *katsuobushi* and a sprinkling of MSG into a small saucepan and bring to the boil uncovered, stirring constantly. Strain through a fine sieve set over a small bowl and cool to room temperature.

Divide the dipping sauce among 6 tiny individual dishes, and serve it with *sashimi* of any kind.

Garnish each plate of *sashimi* with about ½ teaspoon of *wasabi*, this to be mixed into the dipping sauce to individual taste.

Some Oroshi 漢字
WHITE-RADISH AND RED-PEPPER GARNISH

PREPARE IN ADVANCE: Make four openings in the flat side of the *daikon* with chopsticks or the tip of a sharp, pointed knife. Insert a dried red pepper deep into each opening, so that its tip is level with the surface of the *daikon*. Set aside for at least 4 hours, or refrigerate overnight. By then, the *daikon*'s moisture will have reconstituted the red peppers and the pepper will have spiced the *daikon*.

Grate the pepper-stuffed *daikon*, divide into 6 equal parts, and roll each part into a small ball.

TO SERVE: Pour the *pon-su* into 6 tiny dishes and add a grated *daikon*-and-pepper ball to each dish. Garnish with sliced spring onions and serve with *sashimi*.

94

"Sushi"—vinegared rice dishes—appear in many forms. All are based on vinegared rice, accompanied by slices of raw fish with or without omelette strips, sliced vegetables, "nori" seaweed, and a variety of colourful garnishes. These Japanese "sandwiches" may be prepared simply, by topping an oblong of vinegared rice with a dab of prepared horse-radish and slice of fish, or elaborately, by topping the rice with a wide variety of delicately seasoned ingredients, rolling them all in "nori", and cutting them into 1-inch-thick slices. The "sushi" recipes on the following pages can make unusual hors d'œuvre, first courses or satisfying lunches.

Sushi 鮨

RICE IN VINEGAR DRESSING

DRESSING: Put the rice vinegar, sugar, salt and *mirin* into a small enamelled or stainless-steel saucepan. Bring to the boil uncovered and stir in the MSG. Cool to room temperature.

NOTE: This dressing can be made in large quantities and stored unrefrigerated in a tightly covered jar for as long as 1 year.

RICE: Put 1 pint of cold water and the rice into a medium-sized stainless-steel or enamelled saucepan and let the rice soak for 30 minutes. Then add the square of *kombu* and bring to the boil over a high heat. Cover the pan, reduce the heat to moderate, and cook for about 10 minutes, until the rice has absorbed all of the water. Reduce the heat to its lowest point and simmer another 5 minutes. Let the rice rest off the heat for an additional 5 minutes before removing the cover and discarding the *kombu*.

Transfer the hot rice to a large non-metallic dish or tray—made of wood, enamel, ceramic, glass or plastic. Immediately pour on the vinegar dressing and mix thoroughly with a fork. The rice is ready to use when it has cooled to room temperature. Or it may be covered and left at room temperature for as long as 5 hours before serving.

To make about 2½ pints

VINEGAR DRESSING
3 tablespoons rice vinegar, or substitute 2½ tablespoons mild white vinegar
3 tablespoons sugar
2 teaspoons salt
1¼ tablespoons *mirin* (sweet *sake*), or substitute 2½ teaspoons pale dry sherry
½ teaspoon MSG
13 oz. Japanese rice or 13 oz. unconverted, short-grain white rice, washed thoroughly in cold running water and drained
A 2-inch square of *kombu* (dried kelp), cut with a heavy knife from a sheet of packaged *kombu* and washed under cold running water

Temarizushi 手鞠ずし

VINEGARED RICE AND FISH BALLS

PREPARE IN ADVANCE: 1. Sprinkle the fish liberally on both sides with salt and sparingly with MSG, and marinate at room temperature for 3 hours (or cover and refrigerate for 6 hours).

2. Heat a small frying pan over a high heat until a drop of water flicked across its surface instantly evaporates. Add the sesame seeds. Warm the seeds for about 2 to 3 minutes until they are lightly and evenly toasted, shaking the pan almost constantly. Set aside.

TO ASSEMBLE: Put the vinegar, sugar and 2½ tablespoons of cold water into a mixing bowl. Dip the fish, a slice at a time, in the mixture, moistening it well.

Lay a slice of fish in the centre of a strip of cheesecloth about 3 inches long and 2 inches wide. Place 1 teaspoon of *sushi* rice on the fish, then fold the ends of the fillet over it, enclosing the rice. Bring up the ends of the cheesecloth, and twist them tightly to squeeze the fish into a ball. Unwrap and repeat this process with the rest of the fish and rice, until all the balls are made. Sprinkle each ball with a few toasted sesame seeds and serve as an hors d'œuvre or a first course.

To make 10 balls

3 oz. plaice, flounder or other white-meat fish fillet, cut crosswise into paper-thin slices
2½ teaspoons salt
MSG
¼ teaspoon black sesame seeds
1¼ tablespoons rice vinegar or mild white vinegar
1 scant teaspoon sugar
3 tablespoons *sushi* rice (*above*)

Mazezushi
まぜずし

VINEGARED RICE MIXED WITH VEGETABLES AND SEAFOOD

2½ pints *sushi* rice (*page 95*)

2 rounds of canned sliced *renkon* (lotus root)

½ pint *niban dashi* (*page 54*)

1 scant teaspoon rice vinegar, or substitute 1 scant teaspoon mild white vinegar

2½ tablespoons plus 1¼ teaspoons sugar

½ teaspoon salt

MSG

1 medium-sized carrot, scraped and thinly sliced

1 whole canned *takenoko* (bamboo shoot), scraped, quartered and sliced thinly

1½ teaspoons *sake* (rice wine)

1 oz. (about 1½ tablespoons) shelled green peas

4 *shiitake* (dried Japanese mushrooms)

Vegetable oil

A 2-oz. piece of *gobo* (burdock), shredded and soaked in cold water

2½ tablespoons Japanese soya sauce

3 eggs

6 medium-sized prawns (16 to 20 per lb.)

3 oz. canned crab meat, picked over to remove any bones or cartilage, then flaked

GARNISH

1 sheet *nori* (dried laver)

1 to 2 pieces bottled *beni shoga* (red pickled ginger)

PREPARE IN ADVANCE: 1. Peel the lotus root rounds and cut them in half horizontally. Slice them crosswise into ⅛-inch-thick slices. Bring ⅜ pint of water to the boil in a small saucepan. Drop in the sliced lotus root, boil for 10 seconds, then transfer the lotus root to a sieve and drain.

Put 4 tablespoons of the *niban dashi*, 1 scant teaspoon vinegar, ¼ teaspoon sugar, ⅛ teaspoon salt and a few sprinklings of MSG into the saucepan. Bring to the boil over a high heat and add the lotus root. Boil for 1 minute, stirring constantly, then drain again and set the lotus root aside.

2. Bring ⅜ pint of water to the boil, add the thinly sliced carrot and bamboo shoot and boil briskly, uncovered, for 3 minutes. Transfer to a sieve and drain thoroughly.

Put 6 tablespoons of the *niban dashi*, 1 teaspoon sugar, ⅛ teaspoon salt, a few sprinklings of MSG and 1½ teaspoons of *sake* into the saucepan. Bring to the boil over a high heat and add the bamboo shoots and carrots. Boil uncovered for 3 minutes, and drain through a small sieve set over a mixing bowl. Set the bamboo shoot and carrot aside in a bowl. Reserve the liquid.

3. Bring ⅜ pint of lightly salted water to the boil and drop in the green peas. Boil for about 20 seconds, then drain in a sieve and add the peas to the reserved bamboo and carrot cooking liquid.

4. Place the *shiitake* in a bowl and cover with ¾ pint of cold water. Soak for at least 1 hour. Remove the *shiitake* from their soaking water, and reserve the water. Trim and discard the hard mushroom stalks, squeeze the mushrooms dry and chop them finely.

Heat about 1 tablespoon of vegetable oil over a moderately high heat in a small frying pan. Add the drained, shredded *gobo* and stir for about 1 minute, then add the mushrooms, 6 tablespoons of their soaking liquid, 6 tablespoons of the *niban dashi* and 2½ tablespoons of sugar. Cook for 5 minutes, stirring frequently, then stir in 2½ tablespoons of soya sauce. Reduce the heat to moderate and cook for about 15 minutes until all of the liquid in the pan evaporates. Remove and cool to room temperature.

5. The omelettes: Beat 3 eggs thoroughly in a mixing bowl with ⅛ teaspoon salt and a few sprinklings of MSG. Lightly grease the bottom and sides of a medium-sized frying pan with oil using a pastry brush or a sheet of kitchen paper. Heat the pan over a moderate heat until a drop of water flicked across its surface instantly evaporates. Pour in just enough of the eggs to coat the bottom of the pan lightly. Cook for about 30 seconds, then turn the omelette over—with chopsticks, a palette knife or the tips of your fingers—and cook for about another 10 seconds, until firm.

Slide the omelette onto a flat dish and cook 5 or 6 more omelettes in the same way, lightly oiling the pan each time. As the omelettes are done, pile them one on top of another. Then slice the omelettes into the thinnest possible shreds with a large, sharp knife.

6. Shell the prawns and de-vein them by making a shallow incision along the top with a small, sharp knife and lifting out the white or black intestinal vein with the tip of the knife. Wash the prawns quickly under cold running water and pat them dry with kitchen paper.

Bring ⅜ pint of lightly salted water to the boil and drop in the prawns. Bring back to the boil, uncovered, for 3 minutes. Drain and set aside.

7. Pass the sheet of *nori* over a flame, or a candle, on one side only, to intensify its colour and flavour, then slice into fine shreds.

8. Have the previously prepared *sushi* rice, *shiitake*, *gobo*, bamboo shoot, carrot, lotus root, shredded omelettes, peas, prawns, crab meat, pickled ginger and *nori* within easy reach.

TO ASSEMBLE AND SERVE: Thoroughly but gently stir the *shiitake*, *gobo*, carrot, lotus root, bamboo shoot and crab meat into the *sushi* rice with a wooden spoon or a fork. Divide the mixed *sushi* into 6 equal portions. Firmly pack them into 6 small, round bowls or small, square tins just large enough to hold them. Turn them out on to individual plates, and garnish each portion with strips of the egg pancake, a whole prawn, a few peas, a few slivers of *beni shoga*, and shredded *nori*.

TO MAKE FUKUSA ZUSHI, a variation of *mazezushi*: Chop all the prawns coarsely and add them, along with the peas, to the ingredients as described in the previous paragraph. Instead of shredding the omelettes, however, place them on a chopping board. Trim the omelettes into squares, and place a mound of the mixed *sushi* in the middle of each. Lift up the sides of each omelette and fold them into the middle to make a neat parcel. Then carefully turn the parcel over to conceal the seams. Lay a thin strip of the *nori* across the middle of each, thus decoratively "tying" the parcel, and decorate with small circles of *beni shoga*.

Serve *mazezushi* or the more elaborately presented *fukusa zushi* as a one-dish meal—for lunch or a light supper—perhaps with *miso* soup (*page 59*) and pickles.

Fukusa zushi, a parcel of vinegared rice, prawns, crab meat and vegetables, is made by first combining the ingredients in a bowl, then shaping the mixture in a small square or round mould. The mixed *sushi* is then wrapped in a thin, trimmed omelette. Tie the parcel with a strip of *nori*, and garnish with circles of red pickled ginger.

Colourful Variations on the Theme of "Sushi"

Sushi is, simply, vinegared rice plus, but the *sushi* devotee is faced with a difficult choice among the additions—the multitude of toppings and fillings. Above are *sushi* that have been rolled in *nori*—dried laver—and cut into rounds (*see sample recipe and pictures, page 100*). The *sushi* in the foreground are rice rolled up with strips of omelette, watercress, mushrooms and gourd shavings. Behind these are *sushi* filled with red tunny fish, and in the back, *sushi* filled with pickled yellow radish. To the right are *sushi* with mushrooms (*top*) and cucumbers. All are accompanied by soya dipping sauce and strips of pickled ginger.

Another type of *sushi* is *nigiri zushi*, in which an oblong of rice is topped with
fish (*page 101*). In the foreground the topping is of cooked, butterflied prawn.
Behind these are alternate rows of striped bass, partially surrounding a mound of
sushi rice topped with red caviar and encircled by *nori*. Behind the leaf fence on
the right is oily tunny fish; in front of the fence to the left is the lean dark-meat
tunny. The toppings in the back row are of omelette and squid, the omelette
decorated with a strip of *nori*. The cucumber *makizushi* (*above, right*) is a refreshing
change of pace, and the pickled ginger (*bottom left*) adds a touch of sharpness.

To serve 6

2½ pints *sushi* rice (*page 95*)

5 *shiitake* (dried Japanese
    mushrooms)

2 oz. sugar

5 teaspoons Japanese
    soya sauce

1 oz. *kanpyo* (dried gourd
    shavings)

⅜ pint *niban dashi* (*page 54*)

1 teaspoon salt

2 eggs

MSG

6 sheets packaged *nori* (dried laver)

12 sprigs watercress or Italian parsley
    or 12 young spinach leaves

18 very thin slices *beni shoga* (red
    pickled ginger)

Makizushi 巻ずし
VINEGARED RICE AND VEGETABLES ROLLED IN SEAWEED

PREPARE IN ADVANCE: 1. Soak the mushrooms in ¾ pint of cold water for 30 minutes in a large mixing bowl. Then cut off and discard the stalks and slice the mushrooms into ½-inch-wide strips. Place them in a small saucepan with ⅜ pint of their soaking liquid, 1 oz. of the sugar, and the soya sauce. Stir thoroughly and bring to the boil over a high heat. Then remove the mushrooms and continue to boil the liquid until it has reduced to 3 tablespoons. Replace the mushrooms in the liquid, and cool to room temperature.

2. Soak the *kanpyo* in cold water to cover for about 30 minutes, until very soft. Bring to the boil over a high heat, boil 3 minutes and drain.

Put the *kanpyo*, *niban dashi*, 1 oz. of the sugar and 1 scant teaspoon salt into another small pan and bring to the boil. Reduce the heat to moderate and cook uncovered until almost all the liquid evaporates. Be careful not to let it burn.

3. Beat 2 eggs with ⅛ teaspoon of salt in a small mixing bowl and sprinkle lightly with MSG. Lightly grease the bottom and sides of a large, heavy frying pan with vegetable oil using a pastry brush. Heat the pan over a moderate heat until a drop of water flicked onto its surface instantly evaporates. Pour in the eggs and tip the pan backwards and forwards to spread them evenly. Cook for a few seconds, or until the omelette is firm but still moist. Then tilt the pan above the heat. Roll the omelette into a compact cylinder with chopsticks or a fork and flip it on to the edge of a bamboo mat. Roll the omelette in the mat with one or two turns, and squeeze gently to make the roll firmer. Let it rest in the mat for 5 minutes, then unroll the omelette and cut it lengthways into 6 narrow strips.

TO ASSEMBLE AND SERVE: Pass the sheets of *nori* over a flame, on one side only, to intensify their colour and flavour. Place a sheet of *nori* on a bamboo mat or heavy cloth napkin. Divide the *sushi* rice into 6 portions and spread one portion over most of the *nori* sheet, leaving a 2-inch edge of the *nori* exposed. Place the *kanpyo* strips in a row across the middle of the rice, and

For *makizushi*, place a sheet of *nori* on a bamboo mat or cloth napkin and spread it within 2 inches of the edge with vinegared rice. Lay watercress and strips of *kanpyo*, mushrooms and omelette in rows across the middle of the rice (*left*). Use the mat to help roll the *nori* up, then roll the mat up one or two turns and squeeze gently (*centre*) to make it firmer. Unroll and slice (*right*) into 1-inch-wide rounds.

lay a row of mushrooms, watercress and a strip of egg along both sides. Roll the mixture up in the mat following the procedure described above. Let the *makizushi* rest 5 minutes, then unroll it and cut it into 1- to 1½-inch rounds. Assemble, roll and cut the remaining ingredients in the same way.

Serve the *makizushi*, garnished with slices of pickled ginger, to go with drinks, as a first course, or as a main luncheon course.

Nigiri Zushi にぎり鮨
VINEGARED RICE AND FISH "SANDWICHES"

PREPARE IN ADVANCE: 1. To prevent the prawns from curling when cooked, insert a toothpick lengthways along their inner curves. Bring ⅜ pint of water to the boil in a small saucepan and drop in the prawns. Cook for 3 minutes, then drain, remove the toothpicks and peel the prawns. De-vein them by making a shallow incision along the top of each prawn and removing the white or black intestinal vein with the point of a knife. Then cut the prawns three-quarters of the way through along their inner curves and gently spread them open, butterfly fashion. Flatten them slightly with the side of a cleaver or knife.

Put 4 tablespoons of cold water and 1½ tablespoons of the *sushi* dressing into a mixing bowl. Add the prawns, turn them about to coat them well, and marinate for 15 to 30 minutes.

2. Cut the filleted fish crosswise at an angle, into slices ¼ inch thick, with a sharp knife. (The thicker tunny-fish fillet should be cut crosswise into ½-inch-thick slices.) Arrange the fish on a dish and serve, or cover with a sheet of plastic and keep in a cool place (not the refrigerator) for no longer than ½ hour.

TO ASSEMBLE: Put the remaining tablespoon of *sushi* dressing with 2½ tablespoons of cold water into a small bowl. This mixture, called *tezu*, is used to moisten the hands to prevent the rice from becoming sticky. Dip your fingers in the *tezu* and lift up about 1 tablespoon of the rice. Shape it into an oblong. Smear a bit of the *wasabi* paste down the centre of a piece of fish and holding the rice in one hand and the fish in the other, press the two together. The fish should completely cover the top of the rice.

TO MAKE TEKKA MAKI, a variation of *nigiri zushi:* 1. Prepare the *sushi* rice, raw fish and prawns as directed above.

2. Pass the *nori* over a gas flame or candle on one side only to intensify the flavour and colour. Cut the *nori* in half and lay ½ sheet on the edge of a bamboo mat or sturdy cloth napkin. Spread about 3 tablespoons of rice over most of the *nori* sheet, leaving a 1-inch border of the *nori* exposed. Spread a streak of the *wasabi* paste crosswise through the middle of the rice and top with a row of raw fish. Use the mat or napkin to help you to roll the *nori* up tightly. Then roll up in the mat or napkin one or two turns, and let it rest 5 minutes. Remove the mat and slice crosswise into 1- to 1½-inch pieces. Make similar rolls with the remaining ingredients.

TO MAKE KAPPA MAKI, another variation: Substitute narrow strips of cucumber for the fish on one of the sheets of *nori*, omitting the *wasabi*.

TO SERVE: *Sushi* may be served, with soya sauce accompanying it, in many ways: on a large dish as cocktail food; 3 to 4 per person at the beginning of an elaborate Japanese dinner; 6 to 8 per person as a main luncheon course or on a tray at the end of a Japanese meal with *miso* soup (*page 59*).

To make about 4 dozen

1¼ pints *sushi* rice (*page 95*)
6 medium-sized raw prawns (16 to 20 per lb.) in their shells
2½ tablespoons *sushi* dressing (*page 95*)
2 lb. filleted sea bream, sea bass, red snapper, squid, abalone or tunny fish, in one piece (*see sashimi, page 90*)
2½ teaspoons *wasabi* (green horse-radish) powder, mixed to a paste with 2½ teaspoons of cold water and set aside to rest for 15 minutes

TEKKA AND KAPPA MAKI
2 sheets *nori* (dried laver)
1 cucumber, about 4 inches long, peeled, halved, seeded and cut lengthways into ¼-inch-wide strips
Japanese soya sauce

To make a rice and fish "sandwich", hold an oblong of vinegared rice in one hand and a slice of raw fish (tunny, here) dabbed with horse-radish in the other. Top the rice with the fish, and it is ready to eat.

101

Seafood and vegetables await immersion in batter and oil (*below, right*) and emerge (*left*) as delicately coated *tempura*.

The following recipes are called "agemono", literally, "fried things". Japanese frying techniques are not unlike ours, but because of the close attention paid to the batter with which the food is often coated and to the condition and temperature of the oil, Japanese fried foods are especially notable for their delicacy.

To deep-fry, fill a deep-fat frying pan or a large, heavy frying pan or casserole to a depth of 3 inches with vegetable oil (or a mixture of vegetable and sesame-seed oil). Heat the oil until it registers 375°F. on a deep-fat-frying thermometer.

To keep the oil clean during the frying, use a perforated spoon to remove food particles from the oil as they appear.

Tempura   天麩羅
DEEP-FRIED PRAWNS AND VEGETABLES IN BATTER

The "tempura" recipe below by no means encompasses all the ingredients that may be used. In addition to the ones listed on the right, substitutions or additions might include ¼-inch-thick slices of fish fillets; ¼-inch strips of carrot; blanched, quartered bamboo shoot; blanched French beans; ¼-inch strips of lotus root; skewered sections of spring onions; or small asparagus stalks.

To serve 6

PREPARE IN ADVANCE: 1. Peel the aubergine, but leave occasional ½-inch-wide strips of purple skin to add colour to the finished dish. Cut the aubergine in half lengthways, then cut into ¼-inch-thick slices. Wash in cold water, pat thoroughly dry with kitchen paper, and set aside.

2. Skewer 3 ginkgo nuts on each of 6 toothpicks.

3. Dip the prawns in the flour, and vigorously shake off the excess.

4. To prepare the batter, put 1 egg yolk with ¾ pint of ice-cold water and ⅛ teaspoon of bicarbonate of soda into a large mixing bowl. Sift in the flour and mix well with a wooden spoon. The batter should be somewhat thin and watery, and run easily off the spoon. If it is too thick, thin it with drops of cold water. Ideally, the batter should be used shortly after being made, but it may wait if necessary for no longer than 10 minutes.

TO COOK: Preheat the oven to Mark ¼: 250°F. Since *tempura* must be served hot, the most practical way to cook *tempura* is to divide the ingredients into individual portions, placing them on separate sheets of greaseproof paper so that a complete serving—composed of 3 prawns, 2 mange-tout, 2 mushroom halves, 3 ginkgo nuts, a slice of sweet potato—can be fried at one time and kept warm in the oven while the remaining portions are being fried.

Heat the oil as described in the introduction above, until it registers 375°F. on a deep-fat thermometer.

Dip one piece of food at a time into the batter, twirling it around to coat it, then drop it into the pan. Fry only 6 or 8 pieces of food at a time. Turn the pieces with chopsticks after one minute, and fry for about another minute, until they are a light gold. Drain on kitchen paper, arrange a serving of food on an individual plate or in a basket and keep warm in the oven for no longer than 5 minutes. Skim the oil, check the temperature of the oil, and fry the remaining portions.

TO SERVE: Each serving of *tempura* should be accompanied by a small dish of one of the *tempura* dipping sauces. Although this recipe will serve 6 as a main course, smaller amounts of *tempura* are often served as part of a 5-course Japanese dinner (*page 198*) or as a first course.

1 small aubergine (about ½ lb.)
18 canned *ginnan* (ginkgo nuts), drained
1 lb. raw prawns (16 to 20 per lb.), shelled and de-veined (*see page 168*)
12 mange-tout
6 white mushrooms, cut in half
1 medium-sized sweet potato (about ½ lb.) peeled and sliced into ¼-inch-thick rounds
Vegetable oil
2 oz. flour

BATTER (to make about 1¼ pints)
1 egg yolk
¾ pint ice-cold water
⅛ teaspoon bicarbonate of soda
6½ oz. flour

DIPPING SAUCE
⅝ pint *soba tsuyu* (*page 104*)
or 3 tablespoons *ajishio* (*page 104*)

103

To serve 8

2½ tablespoons salt
1½ teaspoons MSG
16 thin wedges of lemon

To serve 4 to 6

1 small carrot, scraped and cut into
  fine shreds (about 3 tablespoons)
A 2-inch piece *gobo* (burdock), cut
  into fine shreds (about 3
  tablespoons)
1½ tablespoons scraped fresh ginger
  root, cut into fine shreds
6 oz. fresh or frozen scallops or
  shelled prawns, cut in ¼-inch dice
3 oz. shelled green peas or 3 oz.
  frozen peas, thoroughly defrosted
⅜ pint *tempura* batter (*page 103*)
1 oz. flour
Vegetable oil

DIPPING SAUCE
⅜ pint *soba tsuyu* (*below*)

To make ⅝ pint

3 tablespoons *mirin* (sweet *sake*), or
  2½ tablespoons pale dry sherry
3 tablespoons Japanese soya
  sauce
⅜ pint *niban dashi* (*page 54*)
5 teaspoons pre-flaked *katsuobushi*
  (dried bonito)
Salt
MSG

TEN TSUYU
3 tablespoons *usukuchi* soya sauce, or
  substitute 2½ tablespoons Japanese
  soya sauce
3 tablespoons *mirin* (sweet *sake*), or
  2½ tablespoons pale dry sherry
⅜ pint *niban dashi* (*page 54*)
⅛ teaspoon salt
MSG
3 tablespoons pre-flaked *katsuobushi*
  (dried bonito)

GARNISH
2½ tablespoons finely grated *daikon*
  (Japanese white radish), or
  substitute 2½ tablespoons peeled,
  grated icicle radish or white turnip
1 tablespoon scraped, grated fresh
  ginger root

Ajishio 味鹽
LEMON AND SALT DIP

TO ASSEMBLE AND SERVE: Mix the 2½ tablespoons of salt and 1½ teaspoons of MSG together in a small bowl, then divide it into equal heaps in the centre of 8 very small plates. Garnish each portion with 2 thin lemon wedges.

Serve *ajishio* with *tempura* (*page 103*) or *domyoji age* (*opposite*). A little lemon juice is squeezed over the fish or shell-fish, which is then dipped into the salt and MSG mixture. Traditionally, this mixture is half-and-half, but that requires more MSG per serving than this book recommends (*page 48*).

Kaki Age かき揚
MIXED DEEP-FRIED PANCAKES

PREPARE IN ADVANCE: Mix together the shredded carrot, *gobo*, ginger, seafood and peas in a large bowl. Add the previously prepared *tempura* batter, sift the ounce of flour over it, and vigorously mix with a wooden spoon until the ingredients are well blended.

TO COOK: Place about 1½ tablespoons of the pancake mixture on a wide, flat metal slice and flatten it into 2½- to 3-inch rounds with the palm of your hand. With the aid of chopsticks or the side of a knife, carefully slide the pancake into the pan of hot oil and quickly repeat the procedure with 2 more pancakes. Fry the *kaki age* for about 1 minute on each side, until they are a golden brown, turning the pancakes carefully with chopsticks. Remove from the oil with a palette knife.

Drain the pancakes on kitchen paper. Carefully remove any food particles from the cooking oil with a fish slice or a perforated spoon, and shape and fry the remaining pancakes as described above, skimming the oil of food particles after each batch is fried.

TO SERVE: Place 3 or 4 pancakes on individual plates and serve, accompanied by the *soba tsuyu* dipping sauce, as part of a Japanese meal (*page 198*), for lunch or as a light supper.

A popular way of serving *kaki age* in Japan is as *domburi*—that is, a one-course meal: 2 pancakes are placed on top of individual servings of steamed rice (*page 124*), and the dipping sauce is poured over them.

Soba Tsuyu そばつゆ
MIRIN AND SOYA DIPPING SAUCE FOR TEMPURA AND NOODLES

TO COOK: Heat the *mirin* in a small saucepan over a moderate heat until lukewarm. Turn off the heat, ignite the *mirin* with a match, and shake the pan gently backwards and forwards until the flame dies out. Add soya sauce, *niban dashi*, *katsuobushi*, a pinch of salt, and sprinkle lightly with MSG. Bring to the boil over a high heat, then strain the sauce through a fine sieve set over a small bowl. Cool to room temperature and taste for seasoning, adding a little salt if necessary.

TO SERVE: Serve *soba tsuyu* or *ten tsuyu*, a variation, with *tempura* (*page 103*), *kaki age* (*above*) or *tatsuta age* (*Recipe Booklet*). The garnish of grated *daikon* and grated ginger root should be divided into separate portions and placed on the individual servings of food. The garnish is usually mixed into the dipping sauce to suit the individual taste.

104

Lacy *tempura* pancakes are made from morsels of seafood and vegetables. The food is twirled in batter, then scooped out with a spoon or fish slice. Chopsticks or the side of a knife are used to slide the food into the hot oil, where it instantly turns golden brown.

Domyoji Age 道明寺揚
DEEP-FRIED PRAWNS COATED WITH RICE

PREPARE IN ADVANCE: 1. Wash the rice in a strainer or colander under cold running water until its draining water runs clear. Then transfer it to a large mixing bowl, cover with cold water, and soak for 4 hours at room temperature. Drain and steam for 30 minutes in an oriental steamer, or steam the rice in an improvised steamer as described on page 180.

Spread the steamed rice out on a tray or large flat dish and cool to room temperature. Separate the grains by rubbing them gently through your fingers; then chop the rice coarsely, with a cleaver or large, sharp knife.

2. Make 3 cuts at ½-inch intervals across the inner curve of the prawns to prevent them from curling when fried.

3. Coat the prawns with flour and shake off any excess. Dip them into the bowl of egg whites, and roll them in the rice until the grains adhere firmly. Lay the prawns side by side on greaseproof paper and set aside.

TO COOK: Heat the oil in a deep-fat frying pan, casserole or frying pan, as described on page 103, until the oil registers 350°F. on a deep-fat thermometer. Fry the prawns 6 at a time for about 1 minute and drain on kitchen paper. Drop the green pepper into the oil and fry for 1 minute, until they are a delicate brown.

TO SERVE: Place 2 prawns and 1 or 2 strips of green pepper on each of 6 serving plates, and accompany each with a small, individual dish of *ajishio*. Serve as part of a Japanese meal (*page 198*), or as a first course.

Agedashi 揚げ出し
DEEP-FRIED TOFU IN SOYA SAUCE

TO COOK: Pat the *tofu* dry with kitchen paper and deep-fry them in the pan of hot oil for about 3 to 4 minutes, until they have turned a golden brown. Remove with a perforated spoon and drain on kitchen paper.

TO SERVE: Put the *soba tsuyu* and the soya sauce into a small mixing bowl and divide this dipping sauce among 6 individual serving bowls. Place 4 cubes of the fried *tofu* in each bowl and garnish each serving with about 1 tablespoon of grated *daikon*, ¾ teaspoon of grated ginger and about ½ teaspoon of *katsuobushi*. Mix these into the sauce to taste.

To serve 6

3 tablespoons *domyoji* (pre-cooked dried rice)
12 medium-sized raw prawns (16 to 20 per lb.), shelled and de-veined (*see page 168*)
2 oz. flour
2 egg whites, lightly beaten
1 medium-sized, green, sweet pepper, seeded, the white pith removed, and cut into strips 2 inches long and ½ inch wide
Vegetable oil

DIPPING SAUCE
3 tablespoons *ajishio* (*opposite*)

To serve 6

4 cakes *tofu* (soya-bean curd), fresh, canned or instant, and each cake cut into 6 equal parts
Vegetable oil
6 scant tablespoons *soba tsuyu* (*opposite*)
6 scant tablespoons Japanese soya sauce
6 scant tablespoons finely grated *daikon* (Japanese white radish), or substitute 6 scant tablespoons peeled, grated icicle radish or white turnip
1½ tablespoons scraped, grated fresh ginger root
2½ teaspoons flaked *katsuobushi* (dried bonito)

105

V

Simple, Satisfying Home Cooking

A steaming pot over a glowing hearth—a powerful symbol of home—contains boiling bamboo shoots that will be part of the meal Mrs. Fuji Horie (*background*) will serve her family. In her farmhouse about 100 miles south-west of Tokyo, this industrious housewife turns out a never-ending succession of meals with the aid of the jointed iron rod, said to be 500 years old, from which the pot is suspended.

One aspect of Japanese cuisine that remains a mystery to the foreign visitor is their home cooking. Even foreigners who have lived in Japan for years complain that "we have never been invited to a Japanese home". The simple explanation for this seeming stand-offishness is that the Japanese do far less entertaining at home than we do. For that matter, in the traditional Japanese manner, only a conceited husband would say that he thinks his home and his table are fit for an important guest, a category that includes many foreign visitors. Even if he is secretly proud of his house and of his wife's cooking, a well-bred man will assert, if pressed, that his home is too humble and his wife too unworldly to entertain—and he will therefore honour his guest by taking him to the best restaurant that he can afford.

Neither a broad hint that the visitor honestly wants to "see how the Japanese really eat and live" nor an insistence on informality is likely to carry much weight in these circumstances—the former might seem patronizing, and there is no such thing as informality where an important guest is concerned. Not only would it be rude to give a guest anything but the best that the host can manage, but it would be a blow to his pride because it would suggest that he did not know the proper way of doing things.

The only outsiders who eat at all frequently in Japanese homes are the very few who have built up long friendships with individuals and those, who have married into Japanese families. But even such privileged foreigners are not likely to have dined at homes other than those of their intimate friends or their relations. If the foreign gourmet tries very hard, he may be able to convince his Japanese acquaintance that he is truly interested in

Japanese-English Glossary

AEMONO: *mixed foods in a dressing*

DAIKON: *giant radish*

MIZUTAKI: *a simmered chicken dish*

MOCHI: *rice cake*

NABE: *a pot or saucepan*

SASHIMI: *slices of raw fish*

SHABU SHABU: *a simmered beef dish*

SUKIYAKI: *another type of simmered beef dish*

SUNOMONO: *vinegared salad*

SUSHI: *vinegared rice topped with raw fish or wrapped in laver*

TOFU: *soya-bean curd*

WASABI: *green horse-radish*

YUZU: *a citrus fruit very like a lime*

---

eating Japanese food; then, if he is lucky and if his host is daring, he will be taken to a Japanese restaurant instead of to a Western one.

When the Japanese insist that they can't entertain under their own roofs they do have a point. Many Japanese houses *are* small and crowded, especially in the cities, and the kitchens are tiny and poorly equipped. Only fairly wealthy Japanese can afford to have one uncluttered room with a *tokonoma*—or to own tasteful objects suitable for display in this alcove—and even possessors of mansions who do still entertain find it hard these days to obtain the regiments of maids who formerly took care of the kitchen work and the serving. A tremendous amount of work is implicit in the artistic and seasonally harmonious meals that constitute Japanese *grande cuisine* and that a guest deserves; nowadays only a fine restaurant is able to do this properly.

There is, finally, one more reason why so few outsiders, even Japanese, sit down at the family dinner table. Japanese men and women to a considerable extent still lead separate social lives. A woman has her circle of neighbours and friends whom she will occasionally invite to lunch when her husband and children are away—but in all probability she will never meet their husbands. A man's social life is centred round the people with whom he works; he will play golf and relax in bars, cabarets and restaurants with his colleagues and customers and never dream of including his wife in a party. On these bibulous occasions feminine companionship is provided by professional entertainers—geisha and bar hostesses; they are better trained in the witty and *risqué* repartee that is required for Japanese masculine enjoyment than are the proper housewives of Japan, whose traditional job is simply to take care of their houses and children, and not to amuse their menfolk.

Consequently a Japanese husband rarely brings home casual acquaintances or important guests. When a Japanese family does entertain, the visitors are likely to be relations, or very old and long-standing friends, school friends, perhaps, whose tastes and preferences are known and who can be fed without undue fuss. Even when an old friend comes for a visit, he is likely to leave his wife at home unless she happens to be a close friend of his host's wife.

Despite the fact that the Japanese housewife has few people to admire her culinary skill, the meals she provides her family are delectable, varied and nourishing. For one thing, she has probably studied home economics at school and then attended cookery classes—as well as lessons in flower arranging and the tea ceremony—in that period after leaving school when a Japanese girl is formally prepared for marriage. Even after marriage she will probably be enrolled in one of the many flourishing cookery schools that can be found in every town and city in Japan. Some of these schools are so successful that they own big buildings in town centres, publish exquisitely illustrated cookery books, run their own television programmes, teach Chinese and Western cooking as well as Japanese, and even sponsor correspondence courses.

Many housewives belong to cooking clubs that invite a different chef to lecture and demonstrate every week, and still others eagerly follow the recipes and cooking hints that come to them regularly in a steady barrage, from women's magazines, television and radio, and local women's organizations. It is safe to say that the Japanese *ok'san* ("honourable interior one", or housewife) spends more time and thought on food than does her Western counterpart. Part of this is necessity; her kitchen and refrigerator are so small that she must shop every day. And part is due to the ready availability of fresh foods in season.

The more sophisticated Japanese housewife strives to attain the same skilful presentation of food in season that the great chefs have mastered and keeps to the same basic principle of emphasizing natural tastes. But she knows that she has neither the equipment nor the many hands needed to achieve perfection, and so she readily compromises. Her cooking reflects the pragmatic, rather than the artistic, side of the Japanese character, which can be summed up in the Japanese proverb, "hana yori dango", which means, roughly, that dumplings are better than flowers if you are hungry.

Certainly there is nothing very artistic or refined about *umeboshi*, the first item on the traditional morning menu. *Umeboshi* is a tiny red pickled plum so sour that just one nibble will lift your scalp, shoot lightning down your spine, and shrivel your toes—an inner cold shower that will wake you up if it doesn't knock you out. Those Japanese who start their day with *umeboshi* —nature's own mouth-wash—find that it clears the fuzzy night tastes from their tongues. Country families, and even some city households, still pickle their own *umeboshi* and keep them in tubs for years. *Umeboshi* is not only a family standby; it is served with morning tea in all Japanese inns, so beware.

Umeboshi also turns up in Japanese *bento*—the little lunch boxes sometimes packed by housewives, but more frequently sold to railway passengers, picnickers and theatre audiences—where it fulfills a double purpose: set in the middle of a field of white rice the little red plum provides a pretty representation of the Japanese flag and it also helps preserve the rice.

The classic breakfast dish at home is rice, a heaped bowl of it often sprinkled with flakes of *nori*, dried laver, or other garnishes. Mama or the maid will have set out the *nori* in a pile of toasted, crispy sheets, giving everyone a choice of crumbling it over his bowl or constructing an impromptu *maki-zushi* by rolling a wad of rice in a sheet of *nori* and eating it in the fingers.

The rice bowl with *nori* may be considered the Japanese approximation to eggs, buttered toast, cornflakes, and pancakes—all of which are gaining popularity in Japan. But the nourishing soup called *misoshiru* (*page 59*) is the equivalent of bacon and eggs. *Misoshiru* is also eaten at other meals, and it is encountered in many varieties in all kinds of restaurants, but at the first meal of the day it seems to be a necessity. To the majority of Japanese, breakfast is not breakfast without this thick, aromatic soup.

Essentially, *misoshiru* is merely *dashi*, the soup stock, plus about a tablespoonful per serving of *miso*, the fermented paste of soya beans and rice that has so many uses in Japan. To these basic ingredients are added a few cubes of *tofu* and possibly some *wakame*, seaweed, and sliced or chopped vegetables such as spring onions or *daikon*. Often, particularly in farm households where everyone eats every meal at home, a huge pot of *miso-shiru* will be cooked in the morning and reheated for each meal, and it seems to get better as the day goes on. In large families the *ok'san* keeps the *misoshiru* pot beside her at the table, next to the tub of rice, and ladles out second helpings to her hungry brood.

You never use a spoon for *misoshiru*—or for any Japanese soup. You pick up the lacquered wooden bowl, pluck out the *tofu* and chunks of vegetable with your chopsticks, and then sip down the steamy liquid.

Misoshiru comes in a bowl with a lid to keep it warm until you are ready for it. But unlike the exquisite colour combinations and symbolic patterns of *suimono*, a clear soup, *misoshiru* makes about as much appeal to the eye as a bowl of porridge. All it offers is filling, low-calorie warmth, tremendous nourishment and a distinctive mellow-pungent flavour. It is not a taste that makes new friends right away, especially when *wakame* is included, but once you've adjusted to it, you can't get enough. One American I know, long resident in Tokyo, who always stayed at Japanese-style inns when travelling through Japan, says it took many months before he could face *misoshiru* on an empty stomach. At length he found it tastier than the cold fried eggs, sometimes cooked the night before, that a good many inns inflict on foreign guests at breakfast. Now, back in the United States, he insists on his Japanese wife giving him *misoshiru* every morning. She americanizes it occasionally by dropping in an egg, and when they've run out of *tofu* he substitutes cottage cheese, but the pure taste of *misoshiru* remains.

The Japanese who can afford to do so eat eggs for breakfast, too, but not usually in their bean-paste soup. One favourite dish is a frothy whip of raw egg poured over hot rice, which cooks the egg, sprinkled with *nori*. Then there is *tamago dashimaki* (*page 178*), the sweetened, flaky, many-layered omelette described in Chapter 3; this dish, however, requires considerable time to make and is often bought already prepared. A similar egg concoction turns up, with vinegared rice, as one kind of *sushi*.

With husband and children gone for the day, and assuming that no neighbours or relations are expected to drop in, the frugal *ok'san* will probably put together a lunch from left-overs. The first step will be to reheat the breakfast rice in a rice cooker. Unheard of a generation ago, the electric rice cooker is now standard equipment in just about every Japanese kitchen, and it is such an amazing appliance that it has become one of Japan's most successful exports to rice-eating nations all over Asia. Anyone who can measure cupfuls of rice and water can cook rice to perfection with this thinking kitchen machine. Provided the measurements are accurate, the rice cooker will turn itself off when the rice is done and will keep it hot until served. And for making cold rice seem like new, the cooker is ideal.

Although the Japanese love their white rice plain after other foods, when they are making a meal of rice itself they usually combine it with something else or garnish it before serving. The housewife preparing her midday meal of cooked rice can choose from a variety of ways of dressing it up to improve the taste and make it more nourishing.

The simplest of these is to sprinkle salty *furikake* over the rice. Years ago, housewives made their own mixtures, but now *furikake* is bought bottled with a sprinkler top. Every bottle has a combination of two or more contrasting ingredients, dried and chopped into tiny bits that expand and develop their taste when they come into contact with the hot, moist rice. There are dozens of combinations: *katsuobushi* (dried bonito) flakes, sesame and seaweed; or seaweed, egg, fish, sesame, salt, tea and monosodium glutamate; or dried sea bream, ground sesame seed, toasted *nori* and salt.

Opposite: The Japanese belief that "man eats with his eyes as well as his mouth" is demonstrated by the method of serving a typical five-course family dinner. The portions are delicate, and the colours, shapes and textures are as carefully balanced as the flavours. On the black lacquer tray is a bowl of *botan wan*, a clear soup with sea bass, wild vegetables and lime. Above it is a light second course, *kani kyuri ikomi*—cucumber rounds encircling crab meat, watercress and red pickled ginger. The third course, presented on the folded napkin on the red tray at the right on the top, is a fried dish —*domyoji age*—deep-fried prawns encrusted with dried rice and served with green pepper, aubergine and lemon. Below it, in the round pottery bowl, are *nimono*, or simmered dishes—taro potatoes, duck and chrysanthemum leaves. The picked vegetables on the square plate below traditionally end the meal, providing a refreshing, palate-cleansing taste. With the pickles comes rice, on the left on the black tray. The tea service at the left on the top—like the hot *oshibori* (the folded napkin in a basket) at the bottom on the right—is an integral part of a Japanese meal. Recipes for all the dishes illustrated may be located by using the Recipe Index.

Although the best Japanese cooking is found in the great restaurants, there are a number of fine amateur chefs. One of them is Mitsugoro Bando, a leading actor who has enjoyed cooking since he was 16 years old. In the two pictures on the right Mr. Bando prepares a meal and then plays host to his daughter and son-in-law, Mr. and Mrs. Masaki Sano. On the near right, he is dipping pieces of pork, for grilling, into a sauce of his own concoction which includes soya sauce, vinegar, a sweet rice wine, called *mirin*, and seasoned salt. On the table in the foreground are a steamed lobster and a raw *sayori*, snipe fish.

If cooked fish or meat or vegetables are left over from the previous evening, the housewife may reheat these, with dipping sauces, and pour the whole thing over her rice bowl. This is a casual version of *domburi*—the word merely means bowl—a cheap but delicious dish found in ordinary restaurants with many different kinds of ingredients. Probably one of the most popular is *oyako domburi* (*page 124*). *Oyako* means mother and child; it is a poetic reference to the chicken and egg spread over the rice.

Still another common rice lunch is *chazuke*, literally, "soaked in tea". A long time ago, *chazuke* was simply the quickest way to finish a bowl of rice: you poured a little tea in the bowl and drank it down, tea and rice grains together. This is still done at home, although it is considered bad manners in public. A more elaborate *chazuke* is as an interesting dish in its own right; there are many restaurants well known for their *chazuke* recipes and every housewife has her favourite recipe. Generally, slices of *sashimi*, slivers of salted fish, and *nori*, *katsuobushi* or pickles of various kinds are placed on top of the rice, and boiling tea is poured over it and allowed to soak for a few minutes. It is eaten with chopsticks, not drunk. Frequently the tea is omitted and replaced by *dashi*, opening up another whole realm of flavours.

The family evening meal is much more complicated. For one thing, the Japanese housewife is often uncertain when her husband will arrive home, or whether he will show up tiddly or sober, well-fed or famished. In working-class households this often depends on how long it has been since pay day and whether Papa still has cash to throw away. But on the expense-account level, the *ok'san* has no such guide to her husband's probable condition. Nevertheless, it is considered her wifely duty to wait up for him with a hot meal at the ready, no matter how late he returns. Some modern wives rebel at this vestige of feudalism and insist that their husbands at least inform them of their plans; but the loyal wife who sits patiently until the early hours, with her pots simmering instead of her temper, is still an ideal example of connubial virtue, and, believe it or not, she still exists.

The task of the patient *ok'san* is further complicated by the fact that the Japanese distinguish to a greater extent than we do between the tastes of children and adults. The recipes in this book are designed to suit the adult palate, but there are also children's versions of many of the dishes, and so Mama must prepare both. For example, the *tare* sauce, a kind of Japanese barbecue sauce, used by adults is considered too "hot" for children; they

will get a sweeter edition. In *kushizashi*—skewer-grilled meats, fowl and vegetables—adults will find hot peppers on their bamboo skewers while children get milder spring onions instead. Even *sushi* mellows a bit for young taste buds: no hot *wasabi* in the rice, more bland items like egg instead of the pungent sea urchin, a greater number of pretty, bright-coloured attractions. On the other hand—and this is a contradiction I cannot explain—Tokyo children love the strong-smelling cheesy *natto*, the fermented soya bean, which, frankly, repels every adult foreigner I have ever asked about it—and it is not sought after by many Japanese from other parts of the country either.

To cope with both of these problems at once, the Japanese housewife will probably feed her children first. When the *danna-san*, the master, arrives, he will be able to take a leisurely bath and change into his kimono without having to feel guilty about delaying the children's supper; he may then join his wife over a relaxing bottle of hot *sake* before starting dinner.

Every course of the meal will probably be served at the same time, enabling one to pick and choose from each dish as one pleases. What we would call the main course—the Japanese don't think of it in this way—will vary, but there are three additional dishes that are absolutely indispensable: rice, soup (clear or *misoshiru*) and *tsukemono*.

Tsukemono, soaked things, are lightly pickled and slightly sour *daikon*, cucumber, miniature aubergines, melons, and other vegetables, which the Japanese eat with their plain rice towards the end of a meal. This rice and pickles combination is a basic element in the traditional Japanese diet. Regardless of what else is on the menu, many Japanese still crave for their rice and *tsukemono*—and some poor people eat nothing else. The most common type is *takuan*, which is *daikon* pickled for months in rice bran and salt, and the phrase "rice and *takuan*" is an everyday expression to describe a frugal meal, though even the wealthy eat *takuan* as well as other pickles following other dishes.

City dwellers now buy their *tsukemono* ready-made, but in the old days—and this is still true in some rural areas—the most important test for a bride was her skill at making *tsukemono*. Of the many varieties of *tsukemono* my favourites are *nara zuke*, melons pickled in the residue of *sake* manufacture, and *wasabi zuke*, vegetables, such as miniature aubergines, pickled in *wasabi* and mustard—a kind of unsweetened Japanese piccalilli.

Although a dish of rice and pickles is the most important part of the meal to many Japanese, it usually follows what we would regard as the main course. Generally this consists of fish or shell-fish, either grilled, steamed or deep-fried as *tempura*.

For the *ok'san*, steaming (see Recipe Index for *mushimono*) is the easiest of these methods, for she simply puts such ingredients as fish, mushrooms, onions, ginkgo nuts and slivered carrots into a covered pot. This is a popular technique, and delicious enough, but not one to tempt a husband who is already over-fond of eating out. As these steamed dishes include many foods, the only side dish served with them is *sunomono*, the Japanese version of salad, already discussed in Chapter 3.

With a little more effort and essentially the same ingredients, the housewife can probably offer her family more taste and variety by grilling her

Opposite: The Watanabe family enjoys a very special picnic under a cherry tree in the garden of the famous Heian shrine in Kyoto. Prepared by a caterer, their repast is far more elaborate than the lunch most housewives would prepare. In each of the individual half-moon boxes, called *hangetsu*, there is a selection of appetizing morsels and a ball of rice. The contents of the three round bowls in the foreground, which fit together to become a lidded box called a *koban*, consist mainly of pieces of roast duck and various kinds of fish.

115

fish; she will then fill out the menu with other dishes besides *sunomono*, particularly *aemono* (*pages 62ff.*). At this point, with grilled fish, *sunomono*, *aemono*, soup, rice, pickles and tea, our cosy home dinner begins to look like a modest feast, and the *danna-san* may decide to eat at home more often.

If the *ok'san* is really eager to please her family she may produce a dinner of *tempura* (*page 103*). The diners dip the cooked *tempura* into salt unless she has made a special sauce to mark the occasion. Afterwards, of course, comes the soup, rice and pickles.

On those happy evenings when a housewife knows for certain that the whole family will be able to eat together, with perhaps some relations or old friends contributing to the festive mood, she might plan a dinner where everyone does his own cooking, right at the table. This technique, called *nabemono*, not only saves work for the housewife but gives her the rare chance to sit down with everyone else and enjoy the party.

Among the popular *nabemono* dishes are the *sukiyaki* and *mizutaki* already described. In *nabe* cooking (*page 132*) the ingredients are all pre-cut into bite-sized pieces and cooked in a broth that is bubbling in a pot on a brazier or hot plate in the centre of the table. The diners either pick up the raw ingredients from a plate with their chopsticks and hold them in the broth until cooked—as in *shabu shabu*—or they simply pluck the titbits from the communal broth, one by one. The broth may be *dashi* alone, or *dashi* seasoned with soya sauce and *sake*; it may also be a "self-stock" made from the meat to be used—chicken broth, with the fat removed, for chicken; beef broth for beef; fish stock, made from heads and bones, for seafood *nabe*. More often than not this broth is eaten as a soup at the end of the meal.

One of the most common *nabe* dishes is *yosenabe* (*page 132*), a Japanese bouillabaisse of many kinds of fish cooked with vegetables, *kombu* and *dashi*. It can also be prepared in the kitchen and brought to the table when ready. Most *nabe* cooking is not strongly seasoned, and *yosenabe*, no exception, is rather bland in taste, but a dipping sauce based on *yuzu* juice, soya sauce and *sake* imparts a tangy flavour to the juicy chunks of tender fish.

Another, even simpler, communal dish is *yudofu* (*page 132*), steaming *tofu*. The cubes of *tofu* are boiled at the table in a pan of water often with *kombu* added, and dipped with chopsticks into a mixture of soya sauce, chopped spring onions and *katsuobushi* flakes. Since *tofu* retains a remarkable amount of heat, like melted cheese in a fondue, it is easy to burn one's lips on it, so everyone gently waves his cube in the air to cool it before gobbling it down. *Yudofu* is a very homely dish, superb on a cold winter's night.

No one, least of all the *ok'san*, pretends that this cookery on the table is on the level of *haute cuisine*. But for the Japanese there is some special magic about it. Perhaps the sight and aroma of the steaming cauldron stimulates the appetite, perhaps it is the conviviality and spirit of togetherness that automatically spring up when a group of people eat from the same pot, perhaps it is merely the warmth of the fire or the rare presence of both parents enjoying themselves at the same table at the same time.

On an ordinary day, Mama might put almost anything into the pot so long as it will taste good and is nourishing. But on occasions of special significance, such as holidays, weddings, funerals and the baby's first visit to a shrine, the menu is fixed by tradition and not even a modern young house-

116   *Continued on page 120*

Shinto Rituals for Marriage Vows

Japanese marriages are seldom made in heaven. More often than not, the parents of the young people arrange the union with the aid of a go-between, usually a trusted family friend. No religious sanction is required; formerly the ceremony was conducted in the home of the bridegroom. In recent years, however, an increasing number of weddings, such as the one seen below, have been held in Shinto shrines, the centres of the ancient and still venerated rituals of nature and ancestor worship. In contrast to weddings at home, where the only outsiders were serving girls, the ceremony at the shrine includes white-robed priests and black-hatted musicians who play ancient music composed centuries ago for the imperial court.

A solemn moment in the Shinto wedding ceremony occurs when the groom promises the gods to assume the responsibility of marriage. In this ceremony at the Toshogu shrine in Nikko, the bride kneels beside her husband before an altar laden with offerings. She is resplendent in a costly silk robe; over her heavy wig, a white silk *tsunokakushi*, or "concealer of horns", symbolizes her promise to avoid the fault of jealousy.

The culmination of the ceremony is called the *sansankudo*, literally "three, three, nine times". The custom requires that the bride and groom take three sips of cold *sake* from each of three lacquered cups. A smiling attendant (*above*) pours *sake* into the first cup. The bride drinks the *sake* in three sips; the cup is refilled and passed to the bridegroom, who does the same. When the second cup is offered, it is the groom who sips before the bride. But the bride again drinks first from the third cup. Since three is considered a lucky number and nine the luckiest, the felicitous combination helps to explain why, with this rite, the marriage is finally solemnized. Shortly after the ceremony, the wedding party joins relatives and friends at a banquet (*above, right*) which includes entertainment. On either side of the bride and groom (*behind the dancers*) are the go-between and his wife; next to them, parents, relations, guests.

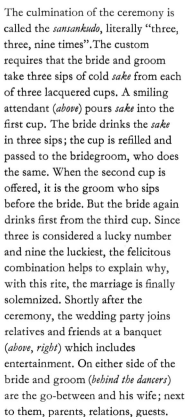

For the banquet, the bride (*centre*) exchanges her bridal robe for a vivid kimono and dons a different wig which indicates matronly status. The bride accepts warm *sake* from a geisha, one of many cups that will flow freely. The lavish meal includes a clam soup, *hamaguri*, whose coupled shells symbolize the union. To make it clear who the principal characters are, the napkins in front of the trays have on them the words "bride" and "groom".

This kind of sweet, called *kyogashi*, which is made to order for special events such as birthdays and weddings, varies in colour and design according to the seasons. The flowery blossom shapes and the predominantly pastel shades of these assortments from Kyoto mark the sweets as spring-time confections. The octagonal box on the left at the top was designed to commemorate the birth of the emperor's grandson.

wife would ignore the culinary requirements of each particular ceremony.

In their devotion to ritual and form the Japanese have invented dozens of these special ceremonial dishes. Each one symbolizes in some way the meaning of the event. I have already mentioned (Chapter 4) that *tai* (sea bream) and *kombu* (kelp) are considered felicitous foods because of their names; they are eaten on almost all happy days. Another happy food is *sekihan*, red rice (*page 126*), made by steaming a glutinous species of rice together with *azuki*, red beans; it comes out a bright pinkish red, and, for the simple reason that red is considered a joyous and lucky colour, *sekihan* is the correct fare at shrine and children's festivals, and at every wedding.

For a reason that seems strange to us, the lobster is also an essential food for a festive occasion, particularly on birthdays. The lobster's body is bent, like those of many old people in Japan, and the Japanese regard it not as a reminder of infirmity, as we might, but as a symbol of the ripe old age that those who partake of lobster may hope to achieve.

On Children's Day, May 5, a sweet cake wrapped in oak leaves is offered; oak leaves stand for a long life and family continuity as they do not fall until new leaves come out in the spring. Girls' Day, March 3, also known as the Doll Festival, invariably calls for a green cake called *kusamochi*, probably because the green suggests the new innocent buds of spring-time, and therefore girlhood. There is even a special funeral cake, impressed with a design of the leaf of the lotus, a plant sacred to Buddhism.

Tai, sekihan and *kombu* are of course essential to the traditional wedding feast. *Kombu* in this case carries a double meaning: the word can mean a fertile woman and is also a pun on happiness. And the wedding *tai* is always served whole, because there is joy and hope in wholeness and to cut it implies separation. Then there is sure to be *kazunoko*, herring roe, which sounds like the words for "many children", and *mame* beans, which can also mean good health. The wedding *suimono* will usually contain a clam in the shell, the two shells of the clam signifying the two partners in marriage.

On New Year's Day, Japan's biggest holiday, families gather at the ancestral home and partake of the most elaborately symbolic menu of all. Many of the foods that are considered felicitous all the year round are included in the feast, but in addition there is a long list of special foods and of eating customs varying from region to region. *Mirin*, the sweet *sake*, for example, is used only for cooking during the rest of the year, but on the four or five days of the New Year holiday it is lightly flavoured with pepper and other spices and sipped from a set of three ritual cups.

The main New Year's meal, traditionally served from a special four-tiered set of nesting boxes, includes *kombu*, lobster, *mame*, slices of *kamaboko* (fish loaf) and *tai*, plus *daidai*, a Japanese orange, which also means "generation after generation"; leaves of chrysanthemum, the imperial flower; chestnuts, from a pun on part of the written character meaning "mastery"; carp, for its indomitable spirit; and a good-luck fern called *urajiro*, which is white on its underside and therefore stands for honesty and purity of motive.

The most important New Year food is *mochi*, a rice cake made by pounding hot, steamed rice into a sticky dough. *Mochi-tsuki*, the rice-pounding ceremony, takes place a few days before the New Year and is a festive occasion at the rural homes that still observe it. Only men, working in pairs, are permitted to wield the big mallets that pulverize the mass of steamed rice in a wooden tub, while the agile housewife, ducking in between the blows, turns the hot paste. When finished, the dough is formed into round cakes, symbolizing a mirror, one of the three ancient imperial treasures, and which are used as Shinto offerings, or into square cakes for eating.

Mochi can also mean "to have", so it symbolizes wealth. The cakes are very practical as well: they can be kept for days and prepared for eating merely by toasting over a fire, so during the New Year season, which is supposed to be a time of rest for all, the *ok'san* never has to bother to cook rice for her family. This enables her to accompany the family to the shrine on New Year's morning with her husband and children.

The fun and emotional satisfaction that the Japanese get out of the appearance and symbolism of their ceremonial foods is difficult to translate into other cultures. The Japanese chef of an American family in Tokyo was confronted, one December day, with unexpected guests. He had no time to shop, but he did his best. One dish, a layer of ketchup adorned with a few green peas, puzzled the lady of the house. "Like Christmas?" he later asked her, hopefully. "No", she thought to herself, "like Japan."

Nimono: <small>FOODS COOKED IN SEASONED LIQUID</small>

Gohan: <small>RICE</small>

Menrui: <small>NOODLES</small>

Nabemono: <small>ONE-POT COOKERY</small>

The following recipes are for "nimono"—foods simmered in liquid. Although a few "nimono" dishes do serve as main courses, for the most part they are delicately seasoned small dishes, usually meant to accompany other courses in a meal.

Kimini 黄身煮

SAKE-FLAVOURED PRAWNS WITH EGG-YOLK GLAZE

PREPARE IN ADVANCE: 1. Salt the prawns lightly and dip them into cornflour to coat them well on all sides, then shake off any excess. Bring ¾ pint of water to the boil in a small saucepan and add the prawns. Boil for about 10 seconds, remove with a perforated spoon, and rinse under cold running water. Drain and set aside.

2. Sprinkle the beans or mange-tout liberally with salt before dropping them into ¾ pint of boiling water. Boil briskly, uncovered, for about 8 to 10 minutes, until tender but still slightly resistant to the bite. Drain the beans in a sieve and cool them quickly under cold running water.

3. Put ⅜ pint *niban dashi*, 1 scant teaspoon sugar, ¼ teaspoon salt, 1½ teaspoons *sake* and ¼ teaspoon soya sauce into a small saucepan. Bring to the boil over a moderate heat and add the green vegetables. When the liquid returns to the boil remove the pan from the heat and set aside to cool.

TO COOK AND ASSEMBLE: Put 3 tablespoons *sake*, 5 tablespoons *niban dashi*, 1 scant teaspoon sugar, ½ teaspoon of salt and ½ teaspoon of MSG into a medium-sized saucepan. Bring to the boil, drop in the prawns and return to the boil. Slowly pour the beaten egg yolks over the prawns, do not stir, but cover the pan immediately. Then lower the heat and simmer for 2 minutes. Turn off the heat and let the prawns rest still covered for a minute before serving.

Drain the cooled French beans or mange-tout and serve with *kimini* as part of a Japanese dinner (*page 198*).

Nitsuke 煮付け

FRESH SARDINES COOKED IN SAKE-FLAVOURED SAUCE

TO COOK: Put the *sake*, sugar and soya sauce into a fairly large saucepan, add the ginger and bring to the boil over a high heat. Drop in the fish, return to the boil, then reduce the heat to its lowest point. Set a small, heavy pan lid inside the pan directly on top of the fish to keep them intact. Simmer for 20 to 30 minutes, until the liquid has almost completely evaporated.

To serve 6

18 medium-sized raw prawns, 16 to 20 per lb., shelled and de-veined (*see page 168*)
Cornflour
3 tablespoons *sake* (rice wine)
5 tablespoons *niban dashi* (*page 54*)
1 scant teaspoon sugar
½ teaspoon salt
½ teaspoon MSG
4 egg yolks, well beaten

GARNISH

1 lb. French beans, trimmed and cut into ½-inch pieces, or fresh or frozen mange-tout
Salt
⅜ pint *niban dashi* (*page 54*)
1 scant teaspoon sugar
¼ teaspoon salt
1½ teaspoons *sake* (rice wine)
¼ teaspoon Japanese soya sauce

To serve 6

¼ pint *sake* (rice wine)
2 oz. sugar
4 tablespoons Japanese soya sauce
2 teaspoons scraped, finely sliced fresh ginger root
2 to 2½ lb. fresh sardines, or substitute 2½ lb. mackerel or sea bream, cleaned and with head removed

TO SERVE: *Nitsuke* may be served either hot or at room temperature, with any remaining sauce poured over the fish. Serve as part of a Japanese dinner (*page 198*) or as a luncheon dish.

Nitsuke may be refrigerated and kept for two or three days. When ready to serve, reheat, moistened with a tablespoon or so of *sake*.

Kuri Fukume-ni   栗ふくめ煮
SWEET CHESTNUTS

To serve 4 to 6

20 chestnuts
2½ oz. sugar

PREPARE IN ADVANCE: Cut a long gash in the flat, softer side of each of the 20 chestnuts with a small, sharp knife. Put the chestnuts into a medium-sized saucepan, cover them completely with cold water and bring to the boil. Cook briskly for 2 or 3 minutes, then remove the chestnuts from the pan and peel off their shells.

TO COOK AND SERVE: Bring ¾ pint of water to the boil in a small saucepan and drop in the peeled chestnuts. Simmer uncovered for about 20 minutes, then drain and set aside.

Put ⅜ pint of cold water and 1½ oz. of sugar into a small saucepan. Bring to the boil, add the chestnuts, and cook uncovered over a moderate heat for about 20 minutes, until the chestnuts are tender but not falling apart. Stir in 1 more ounce of sugar and cook for another 5 minutes. Cool to room temperature in the cooking liquid.

Drain the chestnuts and serve as a sweet course, towards the end of a Japanese meal or as the filling for *igaguri* (*page 70*).

Umani   うま煮
CHICKEN AND VEGETABLES SIMMERED IN SEASONED BROTH

To serve 6

2 *gobo* (burdock), washed and cut into 1-inch-long pieces
3 *shiitake* (Japanese dried mushrooms)
2 oz. shelled green peas or 2 oz. frozen peas, thoroughly defrosted
1½ tablespoons vegetable oil
1 whole chicken breast, boned but with skin left on (*see pages 176-177*), and cut into strips ½ inch wide by 1 inch long
1 canned *konnyaku* (gelatinous root vegetable), cut into ½-inch dice
2 carrots, scraped and cut into ½-inch pieces
2 whole canned *takenoko* (bamboo shoots), cut into ½-inch pieces
⅜ pint *niban dashi* (*page 54*), or substitute ⅜ pint chicken stock
1½ oz. sugar
1¼ teaspoons salt
1 scant teaspoon Japanese soya sauce
MSG

PREPARE IN ADVANCE: 1. Bring ¾ pint of water to the boil in a small saucepan, drop in the *gobo* and boil briskly, uncovered, for 5 minutes. Drain and set them aside.

2. Soak the mushrooms in cold water for 2 hours. Then cut off and discard their stalks, and slice the mushrooms into ½-inch pieces. Discard their soaking liquid.

3. Bring ⅜ pint of water to the boil in a small saucepan, drop in the peas, and cook briskly for 2 minutes. Drain the peas in a sieve and cool them quickly under cold running water.

TO COOK: Heat 1½ tablespoons of oil over a high heat in a large, heavy frying pan until a light haze forms above it. Add the strips of chicken and cook for about 2 to 3 minutes, stirring frequently, until the chicken is golden brown. Add the *konnyaku*, carrots, bamboo shoots and *gobo*, and stir thoroughly. Then pour in the *dashi* or chicken stock, and 1½ oz. of sugar. Stir again, cover the pan and cook for 5 minutes over a moderately high heat.

Now add the mushrooms, salt, soya sauce and a few sprinklings of MSG and re-cover the pan. Lower the heat and simmer an additional 8 to 10 minutes. Stir in the fresh or defrosted frozen green peas, and simmer for about another 2 to 3 minutes, just long enough to heat them through.

TO SERVE: Serve hot or at room temperature as part of a Japanese meal (*page 198*) or as a luncheon dish.

123

Rice is so essential to Japan—as it is to all Asia—that it has come to have a symbolic meaning: a bowl of steamed, unadorned rice always appears at the end of even the most sumptuous dinner, so that the host can ensure that the diner has indeed had enough to eat. Of course, rice is also served more elaborately—in a bowl as a one-dish meal topped or mixed with fish, meat, poultry, eggs or vegetables.

Gohan　御飯
STEAMED RICE

To make 1¼ pints

7 oz. Japanese rice, or substitute 7 oz. unconverted short-grain white rice
⅝ pint cold water

TO COOK: Pour the rice into a sieve. Run cold water over the rice until the draining water is clear, stirring with a wooden spoon. Drain thoroughly and transfer the rice to a heavy, medium-sized saucepan. Add ⅝ pint of cold water and let the rice soak undisturbed for 30 minutes. Then bring to the boil over a moderate heat, cover the pan tightly and cook for about 10 minutes, until all the water has been absorbed. Reduce the heat to its lowest point and simmer the rice undisturbed for 5 minutes. Remove from the heat and let the rice rest, still in its covered pan, for 5 more minutes. Remove the lid from the pan and fluff the rice gently with chopsticks or a fork to separate the grains. Serve the hot rice at once.

To reheat left-over rice, place it in a colander and set the colander over 1½ inches of boiling water in a large, heavy pan. Cover the pan tightly, and steam the rice for about 5 minutes.

Oyako Domburi　親子丼
CHICKEN OMELETTE ON RICE

To serve 2

½ chicken breast (about 4 oz.), skinned and boned (*see pages 176-177*), cut into ¼-inch dice
2 spring onions, including about 2 inches of the green stalks, cut in half lengthways, then into 1½-inch-long pieces
6 tablespoons *domburi ni shiru* (*opposite*)
1¼ pints *gohan* (steamed rice, *above*)
4 eggs
A pinch of *kona sansho* (Japanese pepper)
1 sheet *nori* (dried laver), crumbled

PREPARE IN ADVANCE: 1. Divide the chicken and spring onions in half and place them in separate bowls. Mix 3 tablespoons of *domburi ni shiru* into each bowl, and place the bowls within easy reach of the stove.

2. Put ⅝ pint of hot steamed rice into each of 2 serving bowls, cover, and keep warm in a Mark ¼: 250°F. oven while you prepare the omelettes.

TO COOK AND SERVE: Pour the entire contents of one of the bowls of chicken, spring onions and sauce into a small frying pan. Bring to the boil over a high heat, reduce the heat to moderate, and cover the pan. Cook for 2 minutes.

Meanwhile, break 2 eggs in a small bowl and stir together just long enough to mix the yolks and whites using chopsticks or a spoon. Stir in the *kona sansho* and pour the eggs into the pan. Cover the pan again and cook for about another 2 to 3 minutes, until the eggs are lightly set.

Slide the omelette on top of one of the bowls of rice and garnish with the crumbled *nori*. Quickly make the second omelette with the rest of the ingredients and serve at once.

VARIATIONS ON OYAKO DOMBURI: To make *tanin domburi*, follow the procedure above precisely, but substitute 6 oz. of very thinly sliced beef for the chicken. In other variations, the omelette is omitted. Instead, 4 or 6 prawns *tempura* (*page 103*) are placed over the rice in a bowl and served with 3 tablespoons *domburi ni shiru* poured over the top (*tendon domburi*). To make *yakitori domburi*, prepare chicken and spring onions as for *yakitori* (*page 175*), then, after arranging a serving on the steamed rice, pour 3 tablespoons *domburi ni shiru* over it. Sprinkle with *kona sansho*.

Domburi Ni Shiru
どんぶり煮汁
DIPPING SAUCE FOR DOMBURI

TO COOK: Bring the *mirin* to the boil in a small saucepan over a moderate heat. Remove the pan from the heat and set the *mirin* alight with a match. Shake the pan gently until the flame dies out, then stir in the soya sauce and *dashi*, and sprinkle lightly with MSG. Bring to the boil over a high heat, then cool to room temperature.

Serve with *oyako domburi*, *tendon domburi* and *tanin domburi* (*opposite*).

To make about ⅝ pint

4 tablespoons *mirin* (sweet *sake*), or substitute 3 tablespoons pale dry sherry
4 tablespoons Japanese soya sauce
⅜ pint *niban dashi* (*page 54*)
MSG

Tori Gohan
鶏御飯
CHICKEN AND RICE WITH MUSHROOMS

PREPARE IN ADVANCE: 1. Cut the chicken breast into shreds approximately 1 inch long and ⅛ inch wide.

2. Steam the *shiitake* for 1 minute in an oriental steamer or in the improvised steamer described on page 180. Remove from the pan and shred the mushrooms as finely as possible while they are still hot.

TO COOK: Drain the rice and mix it with the *dashi*, *mirin*, salt, a few sprinklings of MSG and the soya sauce in a large saucepan. Add the *gobo* and *shiitake*, then the chicken. Bring to the boil over a high heat, stir once or twice and cover tightly. Reduce the heat to moderate and cook for 3 minutes, then lower the heat again and simmer about 4 minutes longer. Turn off the heat, and let the *tori gohan* rest covered for 2 minutes before serving.

TO SERVE: Divide equally among 4 serving bowls and garnish each portion with a sprinkling of the chopped parsley. Serve as a luncheon dish, accompanied perhaps by *miso* soup (*page 59*) and bottled Japanese pickles; or serve in smaller portions at the end of a 5- or 7-course Japanese dinner (*page 198*). Shredded uncooked prawns, clams or lobster may be substituted for the chicken and cooked in precisely the same way.

To serve 4

1 whole chicken breast (about ½ lb.), skinned and boned (*see pages 176-177*)
4 medium-sized *shiitake* (dried Japanese mushrooms)
1 lb. 10 oz. white Japanese rice, or substitute 1 lb. 12 oz. unconverted short-grain rice, washed and soaked in water to cover for 3 hours
1½ pints *niban dashi* (*page 54*), or substitute 1½ pints chicken broth
1 tablespoon *mirin* (sweet *sake*), or substitute 2½ teaspoons pale dry sherry
1 scant teaspoon salt
MSG
1 scant teaspoon Japanese soya sauce
2 oz. (about 4 inches) *gobo* (burdock), washed and very thinly slivered
1 tablespoon finely chopped parsley

The automatic electric rice cooker is a comparatively recent Japanese invention that can ensure perfectly steamed rice every time. It works on the principle of the double saucepan. Thermostatic controls reduce the heat at precisely the right moment, and then keep the rice warm.
The cooker is imported into England by Cydilda (*page 207*).

Sekihan 赤飯
RED-COOKED FESTIVAL RICE

To serve 6

14 oz. *azuki* (red beans)
1 lb. *mochi gome* (Japanese sweet rice)
1 teaspoon black sesame seeds
1 teaspoon salt
¼ teaspoon MSG

PREPARE IN ADVANCE: 1. A day before you plan to serve *sekihan*, place the beans in a colander or sieve and wash them under cold running water. Then transfer them to a medium-sized pan, cover them with 3 pints of cold water, and bring to the boil over a high heat. Reduce the heat to its lowest point and simmer the beans uncovered for 45 minutes, until they are tender.

Drain the beans through a large sieve or colander set over a large mixing bowl. Reserve the bean liquid and cover the beans with cold water in another bowl. Cool to room temperature.

2. Wash the rice in a large colander or strainer under cold running water, stirring with a wooden spoon, until the draining water runs clear. Drain thoroughly and add the rice to the bowl of bean liquid. Soak for 8 hours or overnight, covered, in the refrigerator.

3. Drain the rice, discard the soaking liquid and mix the rice and 6 oz. of the soaked beans in a bowl.

NOTE: The remaining beans, which were used to give added flavour to the *sekihan*, can be drained and refrigerated in plastic bags, then cooked with sugar as a sweet dish (*mizuyokan*, *Recipe Booklet*).

Steam the rice and beans in an oriental steamer, or place them in a colander and set the colander in a large pan filled with 1½ inches of water. Bring the water to the boil over a high heat, cover the pan tightly, and steam for 40 minutes, replenishing the water in the pan if it boils away.

4. Meanwhile, heat a small frying pan over a high heat until a drop of water flicked across its surface evaporates instantly. Add the sesame seeds and, shaking the pan gently, cook 2 to 3 minutes, until the seeds are lightly toasted. Transfer the seeds to a small bowl and toss with 1 teaspoon of salt and ¼ teaspoon of MSG.

TO SERVE: Transfer the steamed rice and beans to a large serving bowl or individual bowls. Serve either hot or at room temperature with baked fish or as a sweet course with *kuri fukume-ni* (*page 123*). In either case sprinkle the *sekihan* with the sesame seeds before serving.

In Japan *sekihan* is a festive dish, served at weddings or on birthdays.

Maze Gohan まぜ御飯
MIXED RICE AND VEGETABLES

To serve 3

1 *shiitake* (dried Japanese mushroom)
A 4-oz. loaf of canned *konnyaku* (gelatinous root vegetable), sliced thin and shredded
1¼ pints *niban dashi* (*page 54*)
5 teaspoons *mirin* (sweet *sake*), or substitute 4 teaspoons pale dry sherry
1 teaspoon salt
1 scant teaspoon Japanese soya sauce
1¼ lb. Japanese rice, or substitute 1¼ lb. unconverted short-grain white rice, soaked 3 hours in water to cover
1 carrot, scraped, cut in half lengthways and shredded fine
12 canned *ginnan* (ginkgo) nuts
A 3-oz. piece of canned *kamaboko* (fish cake), sliced thinly
2½ oz. fresh green peas or 2½ oz. frozen peas, thoroughly defrosted

PREPARE IN ADVANCE: 1. Soften the *shiitake* by steaming it for 1 minute in an oriental steamer or the substitute described on page 180. While it is still hot, cut off and discard its hard stalk, and shred the cap finely.

2. Bring ⅜ pint of water to the boil in a small saucepan. Add the shredded *konnyaku* and return the water to the boil. Drain the *konnyaku* in a sieve and run cold water over it to cool it quickly. Drain again and set aside.

3. Put the *dashi*, *mirin*, salt and soya sauce into a large mixing bowl.

TO COOK: Put the rice, *dashi* mixture, *shiitake*, *konnyaku*, carrot, nuts and fish cake into a medium-sized saucepan. Stir together gently, and bring to the boil over a high heat. Then reduce the heat to low, cover the pan, and simmer undisturbed for about 4 to 6 minutes, until the liquid is completely absorbed by the rice. Stir in the green peas, cover again and simmer for 2 minutes. Serve as a main course, accompanied perhaps by soup.

126

"Menrui"—almost as important an element in the Japanese cuisine as rice—are available as thin noodles, wide noodles and buckwheat noodles. They are served simply—with a dipping sauce—or are mixed with other ingredients in a broth as a one dish meal. The following recipes include not only hot noodle dishes but also those served ice cold as delicate summer meals.

Kitsune Udon きつねうどん
FOX NOODLES

Because legend has it that the Japanese fox has a passion for fried "tofu"—how he managed to first taste it is never explained—this slightly sweet "tofu" and noodle dish is fancifully called "kitsune udon", or fox noodles.

To serve 6

A 6-oz. cake of *tofu* (soya-bean curd), fresh, canned or instant, sliced in ¼-inch-thick pieces
Vegetable oil
A 14-oz. packet *udon* (wide noodles), or substitute
1 lb. medium-thick spaghetti
4½ teaspoons salt
⅜ pint *niban dashi* (*page 54*)
2½ tablespoons sugar
5 teaspoons Japanese soya sauce
MSG
2½ pints *ichiban dashi* (*page 54*)
2 spring onions, including at least 3 inches of the green stalks, sliced into thin rounds

PREPARE IN ADVANCE: 1. If you want to rid the *tofu* of excess moisture, thus making it firmer, place the slices side by side on a flat plate. Cover with foil and place a 1-lb pan, casserole or small chopping board on top. Tilt the plate so that the water drains off. Set aside for at least 30 minutes, then pour off the accumulated water and pat the *tofu* dry with kitchen paper.

2. Pour enough vegetable oil into a large, heavy frying pan to come about 1½ inches up the sides of the pan. Set over a high heat until the oil registers 350°F. on a deep-fat thermometer. Drop in 6 or 8 slices of *tofu* at a time and fry them for about 1 minute, turning them over until they are brown on all sides.

Drain the fried *tofu* on kitchen paper. Then with the chopsticks, dip them one at a time in a bowl of hot water to rid them of any remaining oil, and drain again on kitchen paper.

3. Bring 3¼ pints of water to the boil in a large saucepan. Drop in the noodles, return the water to the boil, and cook them uncovered for about 20 minutes, stirring occasionally, until they are very soft. Stir in 2¼ teaspoons of salt, cover the pan, and turn off the heat. Let the noodles rest covered for 5 minutes, then drain them in a colander, and run cold water over them for 5 minutes. Drain again and set aside.

4. Put ⅜ pint of *niban dashi* with 5 teaspoons of the sugar and 2½ teaspoons of the soya sauce into a small saucepan. Stir thoroughly and bring to the boil over a high heat. Then salt lightly and add a sprinkling of MSG. Drop in the *tofu* and boil over a high heat for about 5 to 8 minutes, until the liquid has been reduced to about 4 tablespoons. Set the *tofu* and its liquid aside off the heat.

TO COOK AND SERVE: Put 2½ pints of *ichiban dashi* with 2½ teaspoons sugar, 2 teaspoons salt and 2½ teaspoons soya sauce into a medium-sized saucepan. Stir thoroughly, bring to the boil, and add the noodles. Return to the boil and serve at once. Pour the broth and noodles into 6 serving bowls, top each serving with a few pieces of the sweetened *tofu* and garnish with the sliced spring onions.

NOTE: If you prefer a more subtle flavour, omit cooking the *tofu* in the sweet sauce (*step 4*). Instead, cut both the *tofu* and spring onions lengthways into long, narrow strips. After the noodles have been reheated in the broth, transfer them to serving bowls, and leave the broth in the pan. Add the spring onions and *tofu* and bring back to the boil, then divide the contents of the pan equally among the bowls of noodles.

DIPPING SAUCE FOR NOODLES

To make ⅝ pint

3 tablespoons *mirin* (sweet *sake*), or
    substitute 2½ tablespoons pale dry
    sherry
3 tablespoons Japanese soya sauce
⅜ pint *niban dashi* (*page 54*)
5 teaspoons pre-flaked *katsuobushi*
    (dried bonito)
½ teaspoon salt
MSG

TO COOK: Quickly heat the *mirin* until it is lukewarm in a small saucepan, then remove the pan from the heat and set the *mirin* alight with a match. Shake the pan gently until the flame dies out.

Stir in the soya sauce, the *dashi*, *katsuobushi*, salt and a few sprinklings of MSG. Bring to the boil over a high heat, and strain the sauce into a bowl. Let it cool to room temperature.

Serve as the dipping sauce for *hiyamugi* (*below*), *zarusoba* (*page 131*) or *hiyashi somen* (*Recipe Booklet*).

Hiyamugi ひやむぎ

COLD NOODLES WITH PRAWNS AND MUSHROOMS

To serve 6

6 medium-sized prawns in their
    shells (16 to 20 per lb.)
12 sprigs watercress or young
    spinach leaves
3 *shiitake* (dried Japanese
    mushrooms)
½ teaspoon sugar
2½ teaspoons Japanese soya
    sauce
Vegetable oil
2 eggs, well beaten
A 1-lb. packet of *hiyamugi*
    (thin Japanese noodles), or
    substitute 1 lb. Italian
    vermicelli

DIPPING SAUCE
⅝ pint *menrui no dashi* (*above*)
1¼ teaspoons grated lime rind

PREPARE IN ADVANCE: 1. Drop the prawns into ¾ pint of boiling water and boil for about 3 minutes, until they turn pink and are firm to the touch. Drain in a colander and run cold water over them.

Peel the prawns and de-vein them by making a shallow incision down their backs with a small, sharp knife and lifting out the black or white intestinal veins with the point of the knife.

2. Blanch the watercress or spinach by plunging it into a small pan of boiling water for 10 seconds, then drain it. Let it rest in a bowl of cold water until ready to use.

3. Soak the *shiitake* in 1½ pints of cold water for 1 hour, then transfer the mushrooms and their soaking liquid to a medium-sized saucepan and bring to the boil over a high heat. Add ½ teaspoon of sugar and 2½ teaspoons of soya sauce, lower the heat to moderate, and cook the *shiitake* uncovered for about 20 minutes, until the liquid is a rich brown and has been reduced to about 4 tablespoons. Set the pan aside off the heat. You will use the *shiitake* later, but the liquid can be discarded.

4. Lightly grease a large frying pan or omelette pan with vegetable oil using a pastry brush or kitchen paper. Heat the pan over a moderate heat until a drop of cold water flicked on its surface evaporates instantly. Pour in the eggs and cook without stirring for about 20 seconds, until the omelette is set, then turn it out on a dish in one piece.

Trim the rounded edges of the omelette with a knife to form a rectangle, and cut into 1-inch squares. Holding the squares with chopsticks, dip them one at a time into a bowl of hot water for 1 second to remove any remaining oil, and drain on kitchen paper.

TO COOK AND SERVE: Bring 3½ pints of water to the boil in a large saucepan. Drop in the noodles, return to the boil and, stirring occasionally, cook uncovered for about 10 minutes, until they are very soft. Drain the noodles in a colander, run cold water over them for 5 minutes, and drain again.

Divide the noodles among 6 individual serving bowls and put 2 or 3 ice cubes in each bowl. Garnish each with a prawn, 2 sprigs of watercress or with spinach leaves, ½ *shiitake*, and a few squares of the omelette. Accompany with *menrui no dashi*, flavoured with grated lime rind.

A light summer dish of *hiyamugi*—cold noodles
with a prawn, watercress stems, egg, and a mushroom,
—is encircled by a section of bamboo and accompanied
by a delicate dipping sauce (*top right*) and warm *sake*.

To serve 6

A 14-oz. packet *udon* (wide noodles),
    or substitute 1 lb. medium-thick
    spaghetti
4½ teaspoons salt
1 whole ½-lb. chicken breast or
    duck breast, skinned and boned
    (*pages 176-177*)
2½ pints *ichiban dashi* (*page 54*)
2½ teaspoons sugar
2½ teaspoons Japanese soya
    sauce
2 spring onions, including at least
    3 inches of the green stalks,
    halved and sliced thinly lengthways

Tori Nanban とりなんばん

HOT NOODLES AND CHICKEN IN BROTH

PREPARE IN ADVANCE: 1. Bring 3¼ pints of water to the boil in a large saucepan. Drop in the noodles, return to the boil and cook uncovered for about 20 minutes, until the noodles are very soft, stirring occasionally. Stir in 2½ teaspoons of the salt, cover the pan tightly, and turn off the heat. Let the noodles rest covered for 5 minutes. Then drain them in a colander, and run cold water over them for 5 minutes. Drain again and set aside.

2. Cut each boned chicken breast in half horizontally, then into strips about ¼ inch wide by 2 inches long.

TO COOK AND SERVE: Put the *dashi*, sugar, the remaining 2 teaspoons of salt and the soya sauce into a medium-sized saucepan, stir and bring to the boil, uncovered. Add the noodles, return to the boil, and remove from the heat. Remove the noodles from the soup with a perforated spoon and divide them among 6 deep bowls.

The delicate flavour of noodles served in broth with duck and spring onions is accented by *suzuko mizore-ae*—red caviar and radish (*page 64*).

Drop the strips of chicken and the spring onions into the soup. Bring the soup to the boil again over a high heat, boil for 2 minutes, then pour the contents of the pan over the noodles and serve at once.

Zarusoba ざるそば
BUCKWHEAT NOODLES WITH LAVER

Bring 3¼ pints of water to the boil in a large saucepan. Add the *soba* and, stirring occasionally, cook for 6 to 7 minutes, until very soft. Drain the noodles in a colander and quickly run cold water over them. Drain again and divide the noodles among 6 serving bowls (the Japanese would use *zaru*, which are round, curved bamboo baskets), and top with crumbled *nori*. Garnish each bowl with spring onions and a teaspoon of *wasabi* paste. Serve the dipping sauce separately, in individual small bowls or dishes. Traditionally, the *wasabi* and spring onions are mixed into the dipping sauce to the taste of each diner.

To serve 6

A 16-oz. packet of *soba* (buckwheat noodles)
3 sheets packaged *nori* (dried laver), passed over a flame on one side only and coarsely crumbled
2 spring onions, including at least 3 inches of the green stalks, sliced into thin rounds
3 teaspoons *wasabi* (horse-radish) powder, mixed with just enough cold water to make a thick paste, then set aside to rest for 15 minutes

DIPPING SAUCE
⅝ pint *soba tsuyu* (*page 104*)

Buckwheat noodles, topped with bits of *nori*, are shown with dipping sauce (*top right*) and hot water to make soup from left-over noodles.

In all "nabe"—one-pot, do-it-yourself—cooking, the actual cooking is done at the dinner table, although the uncooked food is sliced and arranged in advance. An electric frying pan or casserole is most effective in preparing "nabemono", but a heavy, shallow casserole or frying pan set over a methylated-spirits burner, charcoal-burning hibachi, or gas ring does almost as well.

Set the heating unit and its cooking pot in the centre of the dining table and pre-heat, or bring the specified liquid to the boil. Adjust the heat so that the liquid simmers throughout the cooking. Provide each diner with a plate, a small dish of dipping sauce, when appropriate, and chopsticks or a long-handled fork with heatproof handle such as a fondue fork. Traditionally, each diner selects his own food from the dish of ingredients and cooks it himself in the simmering liquid.

Yosenabe 寄鍋
SEAFOOD AND VEGETABLES IN BROTH

"Yosenabe" means "a gathering of everything", and as in all "nabe" cooking, vegetables other than those specified may be used—among them cabbage rolls (see "tori mizutaki" and "shabu shabu", pages 134-135) bamboo shoots, and mushrooms.

PREPARE IN ADVANCE: 1. Chop off the tail section of the lobster at the point where it joins the body with a cleaver or large, heavy knife. Twist or cut off the large claws. Split the body of the lobster in half and remove and discard the gelatinous sac (stomach) in the head and the long intestinal vein attached to it. Cut the tail crosswise into 1-inch-wide slices and chop the lobster halves crosswise into quarters.

2. Cut the carrots obliquely, by making a diagonal slice, then rolling the carrot a quarter turn and slicing again.

Bring $\frac{3}{8}$ pint of water to the boil in a small saucepan, drop in the carrots and return to the boil. Drain the carrots in a sieve and run cold water over them. Set aside.

3. Soak the *harusame* in a bowl of cold water for about 30 minutes, until soft. Drain and cut into 4-inch lengths.

4. Bring $\frac{3}{8}$ pint of water to the boil in a small saucepan and drop in the fish. Cook briskly for about 10 seconds, drain in a sieve and run cold water over the fish to cool it quickly.

5. Arrange the clams or cockles, lobster or prawns, carrots, spring onions, noodles and fish chunks attractively on a large dish.

TO COOK: Put $1\frac{1}{4}$ pints of chicken broth and the piece of *kombu* into the cooking utensil, following the directions in the introduction (*above*), and bring to the boil. Lower the heat so that the broth simmers constantly throughout the meal. Traditionally, each diner selects and cooks his own food to taste. None of the ingredients in *yosenabe* needs be cooked longer than a moment, two at the most. Serve with small dishes of dipping sauce.

Yudofu 湯豆腐
BUBBLING TOFU

PREPARE IN ADVANCE: 1. Put 6 tablespoons soya sauce with 5 teaspoons of *mirin* (or the dry sherry) into a small saucepan and sprinkle lightly with MSG. Bring to the boil, stirring constantly, then pour into individual serving bowls.

To serve 6

A $1\frac{1}{2}$-lb. live lobster cut into serving pieces, or substitute 12 large raw prawns (10 to 15 per lb.), peeled and de-veined (*see page 168*)

2 medium-sized carrots, scraped

3 oz. *harusame* (transparent noodles)

$\frac{1}{2}$ lb. fillet of sea bream or any other white-meat fish, cut into 1-inch pieces

12 cherrystone clams, shelled, or substitute 12 cockles, shelled

8 spring onions, including at least 3 inches of the green stalks, cut into 2-inch pieces

$1\frac{1}{4}$ pints chicken broth or $1\frac{1}{4}$ pints *ichiban dashi* (*page 54*)

A 4-inch piece of *kombu* (dried kelp), cut with a heavy knife from a sheet of packaged *kombu* and washed under cold water

DIPPING SAUCE
1 recipe *chirizu* (*page 94*)

To serve 4

$2\frac{1}{2}$ pints cold water

A 4-inch square of *kombu* (dried kelp), cut with a heavy knife from a sheet of packaged *kombu* and washed under cold running water

4 cakes *tofu* (soya-bean curd), fresh or canned

DIPPING SAUCE
6 tablespoons Japanese soya sauce

5 teaspoons *mirin* (sweet *sake*), or substitute 4 teaspoons pale dry sherry

MSG

132

A colourful *yosenabe*—"gathering of everything"—includes lobster, prawns, red snapper, carrots, spring onions, *tofu* and noodles.

2. Slice the 4 spring onions crosswise into very thin rounds.

3. Garnish the sauce with spring onions, ginger, *hanakatsuo* and *nori*, and then set it aside.

4. Cut the 4 cakes of *tofu* into 1-inch cubes.

5. Pass the sheet of *nori* over a flame on one side only and cut it into ½-inch-square pieces.

TO COOK AND SERVE: Following the *nabe* procedure described in the introduction on the opposite page, place the cooking pot of your choice on the dining table. Pour in the 2½ pints of cold water, add the square of *kombu*, and bring to the boil.

Drop in the *tofu* and simmer gently for 2 to 3 minutes—if cooked too rapidly or too long, the *tofu* will harden.

Scoop the *tofu* out of the broth with a perforated slice or spoon and place in individual bowls. Ladle a little of the broth into each bowl, and serve with the dipping sauce and garnishes.

GARNISH

4 spring onions, including 3 inches of the green stalks

2½ teaspoons grated, scraped fresh ginger

2½ teaspoons *hanakatsuo* (finely flaked dried bonito)

1 sheet packaged *nori* (dried laver)

133

To serve 4

1 lb. boneless lean beef,
  preferably fillet or rump

An 8-oz. can *shirataki* (long
  noodle-like threads), drained

1 whole canned *takenoko* (bamboo
  shoot)

A 2-inch-long strip of beef fat,
  folded into a square packet

6 spring onions, including 3 inches of
  the stem, cut into 1½-inch pieces

1 medium-sized yellow onion, peeled
  and sliced ½ inch thick

4 to 6 small white mushrooms, cut
  into ¼-inch-thick slices

2 cakes *tofu* (soya-bean curd), fresh,
  canned or instant, cut into 1-inch
  cubes

2 oz. Chinese chrysanthemum
  leaves, watercress or Chinese
  cabbage

SAUCE

3 tablespoons to ¼ pint Japanese
  soya sauce

1½ to 3 oz. sugar

3 to 9 tablespoons *sake* (rice wine)

To serve 6

2 whole chicken breasts, boned (*see
  pages 176-177*) and cut into
  1-inch pieces

2 lb. Chinese cabbage

5 teaspoons salt

4 large scraped carrots, cut
  lengthways into ¼-inch-wide strips

8 spring onions, including 3 inches of
  the green stalks, cut lengthways
  into narrow strips

2 cakes *tofu* (soya-bean curd), fresh,
  canned or instant, cut into 1-inch
  cubes

12 small white mushrooms

12 to 14 sprigs watercress

1½ pints chicken stock

A 4-inch square of *kombu* (dried
  kelp), cut with a heavy knife from
  a sheet of packaged *kombu* and
  washed under cold running water

Sukiyaki すき燒

BEEF AND VEGETABLES SIMMERED IN SOYA SAUCE AND SAKE

PREPARE IN ADVANCE: 1. Place the beef in your freezer, or in the freezing compartment of your refrigerator, for about 30 minutes, or just long enough to stiffen it slightly for easier slicing. Then cut the beef against the grain into slices ⅛ inch thick, and cut the slices in half crosswise using a heavy, sharp knife.

2. Bring ⅜ pint of water to the boil and drop in the *shirataki*; then return to the boil. Drain and cut the noodles into thirds.

3. Scrape the bamboo shoot at the base, cut it in half lengthways, and slice it thinly crosswise. Run cold running water over the slices and drain.

4. Arrange the meat, *shirataki* and vegetables attractively in separate rows on a large dish.

TO COOK AND SERVE: If you are using an electric frying pan, preheat to 425°F. If not, substitute a large frying pan set over a table burner and preheat for several minutes.

Hold the folded strip of fat with chopsticks and rub it over the bottom of the hot frying pan. Add 6 to 8 slices of meat to the pan, pour in 3 table-spoons of soya sauce, and sprinkle the meat with 2½ tablespoons of sugar. Cook for a minute, stir, and turn the meat over. Push the meat to one side of the pan. Add about ⅓ of the spring onions, onion, mushrooms, *tofu*, *shirataki*, greens and bamboo shoot in more or less equal amounts, sprinkle them with 3 tablespoons *sake* and cook for an additional 4 to 5 minutes.

Transfer the contents of the pan to individual plates using chopsticks or long-handled forks, such as fondue forks, and serve. Continue cooking the remaining *sukiyaki* batch by batch as described above, checking the tem-perature of the pan from time to time. If it seems too hot and the food be-gins to stick or burn, lower the heat or cool the pan more quickly by adding a drop or two of cold water to the sauce.

Tori Mizutaki 鶏水炒

CHICKEN AND VEGETABLES COOKED IN BROTH WITH PON-SU DIPPING SAUCE

PREPARE IN ADVANCE: 1. Bring ¾ pint of water to the boil in a small saucepan. Drop in the pieces of chicken and boil briskly for about 10 seconds, then drain and rinse under cold running water.

2. Cut off the base of the cabbage and separate the leaves. Discard the inner core.

Bring ¾ pint of water to the boil with 5 teaspoons of salt in a medium-sized saucepan. Drop in the cabbage and boil for about 1 minute, until the leaves wilt and shrink. Then cover the pan and boil 1 minute longer. Drain in a colander and cool the cabbage under cold running water. Drain again.

Arrange the cabbage leaves one on top of another in the centre of a bam-boo mat or heavy cloth napkin. Starting with the wide end, use the mat or napkin to roll the cabbage into a tight cylinder. Unwrap and cut the roll crosswise into sections 1 inch wide.

3. Bring ⅜ pint of water to the boil in a small saucepan and drop in the carrot strips. Return to the boil, drain, and cool under cold running water.

4. Arrange the chicken, cabbage rolls, carrots, spring onions, *tofu*, mush-rooms and watercress in concentric circles or long rows on a large dish.

134

5. To make the sauce and garnish, put the lemon or lime juice and soya sauce into a mixing bowl, then pour into individual small bowls. Put the grated *daikon* and sliced spring onions into other small, separate bowls or dishes. Set a bowl of sauce and garnish beside each serving plate. Traditionally they are then mixed together to the taste of each diner.

TO COOK AND SERVE: Following the procedures described on page 132, prepare the cooking pot of your choice at the table and pour in the chicken stock. Add the *kombu* and bring the stock to the boil. Then lower the heat so that the stock keeps simmering throughout the meal. Instruct each diner to dip the food of his choice into the broth, cook it for 2 or 3 minutes, then drop it into the sauce.

When all the food has been consumed, remove and discard the *kombu*. Ladle the broth into individual bowls and serve as a soup course.

NOTE: Warm *sake* is particularly suitable for this winter *nabe*. In Japan, for an intimate home dinner, the ceramic *sake* bottle is often placed directly in the broth to keep it warm during the meal.

TO MAKE CHIRINABE: Substitute white-meat fish chunks for the chicken. In this case, use water instead of stock and serve with *chirizu* (*page 94*).

Shabu Shabu　　　しゃぶしゃぶ

BEEF AND VEGETABLES COOKED IN BROTH WITH DIPPING SAUCE

PREPARE IN ADVANCE: 1. Cut each slice of meat in half crosswise.

2. Trim the base of the cabbage and separate the leaves. Discard the inner core. Bring ¾ pint of water to the boil with 5 teaspoons of salt in a small saucepan. Drop in the cabbage and boil for about a minute, until the leaves wilt and shrink. Then cover the pan and boil 1 minute longer. Drain in a colander and run cold water over the cabbage to cool it quickly.

3. Bring ⅜ pint of water to the boil in a small saucepan and drop in the spinach. Return to the boil, drain and cool under cold water. Bring another ⅜ pint of water to the boil and add the carrot strips. Return to the boil, then drain and cool in the same way.

4. Arrange the cabbage leaves one on top of another in the centre of a bamboo mat or heavy cloth napkin. Lay the spinach leaves in a neat row down the centre of the top leaf. Starting with the wide side of the mat or napkin, use it to roll the cabbage into a tight cylinder. Unwrap and cut the roll into 1-inch-long sections.

5. Arrange the beef, cabbage rolls, carrots, spring onions, *tofu* and mushrooms in concentric circles or rows on a large serving dish.

TO COOK AND SERVE: Pour the chicken broth into the cooking pot of your choice, following the directions on page 132, and add the square of *kombu*. Bring to the boil, then adjust the heat so that the stock simmers throughout the meal. Each guest selects a piece of food from the dish with chopsticks or a fork and swishes it about in the simmering broth until it is cooked to taste. It is this swishing that sounds to the Japanese like *shabu shabu*, hence the name of the dish.

The cooking procedure is as follows: First cook the meat in the broth for 2 to 3 seconds, then add the vegetables. Simmer another minute and remove the food with chopsticks or a fork. When all the food has been cooked, the *kombu* is removed and the broth is ladled into bowls and drunk as soup.

PON-SU DIPPING SAUCE

5 tablespoons fresh lemon or lime juice

5 tablespoons Japanese soya sauce

GARNISH

2½ tablespoons finely grated *daikon* (Japanese white radish), or substitute 2½ tablespoons peeled, grated icicle radish or white turnip

2 spring onions, including 3 inches of the green stalks, sliced into thin rounds

To serve 6

1½ lb. boneless sirloin or rump steak, sliced ⅛ inch thick

2 lb. Chinese cabbage

5 teaspoons salt

12 to 14 young spinach leaves, stripped from their stalks

8 carrots, scraped and cut lengthways into strips ¼ inch wide by 2 inches long

8 spring onions, including at least 3 inches of the green stalk, cut lengthways into narrow strips

2 cakes *tofu* (soya-bean curd), fresh, canned or instant, cut into 1-inch cubes

12 small white mushrooms

2½ pints chicken broth

A 4-inch square of *kombu* (dried kelp), cut with a heavy knife from a sheet of packaged *kombu* and washed under cold running water

DIPPING SAUCE

⅜ pint *goma joyu* dressing (*page 62*) or *pon-su* (equal parts soya sauce and lemon or lime juice)

135

VI

A Ceremony That Begot a Cuisine

A Japanese hostess
conducting the unique
social and artistic ritual
of the tea ceremony,
graciously offers a bowl of
tea to a guest. Evolved by
Zen Buddhist monks
centuries ago as an aesthetic
experience, the ceremony
strongly influenced Japan's
culture and gave rise to a
highly refined cuisine.

The best food in Japan goes by the name of *kaiseki*, a word that comes
from a curious and beautiful Japanese social custom called the tea ceremony. The tea ceremony, in its simplest terms, is a way of getting the most
out of drinking tea—not tea as we know it or even as the Japanese know it
every day, but a special kind of tea made from green tea leaves ground
to a fine powder, then reverently served according to rules laid down centuries ago and still faithfully followed. The food that accompanies the tea is
special too: *kaiseki ryori*, "tea cooking", is food prepared and eaten under
the most refined circumstances possible. Many of the best restaurants in
Japan call their cooking *kaiseki*, and the dishes they offer may indeed be
identical to those one would find at a tea ceremony. But unless the food is
served as an accompaniment to the tea ceremony it will not add up to the
complete aesthetic experience that the Japanese know and love. No one
can understand Japan and its food without having *kaiseki*, and no one
can appreciate the nuances and rituals of *kaiseki* without some understanding of the origins of the tea ceremony. It is unique.

The roots of these rituals go back to the 13th century, when Zen Buddhist monks in China drank tea ceremonially during their devotions—
partly to keep themselves alert, partly as a gesture of fraternity, like the
passing of a loving cup. In the 15th and 16th centuries, these rituals were
brought to a fine art by Japanese tea masters, Zen priests and monks appointed to prepare the ceremonial teas of the rulers and their courts. There
were several great tea masters, most notably one called Sen Rikyu, and the
manner in which these great masters conducted the tea ceremony—their

*Japanese-English
Glossary*

MISO: *fermented soya-bean paste*
MISOSHIRU: *soya-bean-paste soup*
SASHIMI: *slices of raw fish*

deportment, dress, conversation and level of aesthetic appreciation—set the standards for patterns of behaviour throughout Japanese society. They were in effect Japan's arbiters of taste.

The rules laid down by the great masters for the tea ceremony are, in large measure, still observed by the Japanese. These rules embraced everything from the ideal dimensions for the tea hut to the ideal number of guests, three to five. There were rules for the order in which dishes should be presented, so that each dish would appear at the precise moment in the meal when its texture, flavour and temperature would be best appreciated. Most of all there were rules for the heart of the ceremony, the preparation of the tea. The water had to be boiled in an iron kettle over a charcoal fire; the tea had to be whipped in the cup, or tea bowl, with a bamboo whisk until the froth on the top was exactly the right depth; the bowl was offered and sipped from with gestures as carefully choreographed as those of a dance.

The tea ceremony remains to this day a cultural ideal that has to do with how people live and what they consider important. It is concerned with tea, of course, and with food, but it is also concerned with the setting in which the two are served—the room, the plates, the utensils—and with the manners and conversation of the participants. In short, it is the Japanese idea of a truly pleasant social occasion. Because its standards of beauty and deportment profoundly influence the whole of Japanese life, the tea ceremony is sometimes treated as a cult and sometimes is conducted with a good deal of display. But in fact this ceremony, which was evolved by men who combined virility with sensitivity, is a search for harmony with nature and with one's self; it may also serve as a kind of entertainment.

Not everyone, to be sure, is entertained by it. Foreigners are apt to admire it extravagantly or consider it a complete bore. Frank Lloyd Wright, the great American architect, spent four years in Japan supervising the construction of the Imperial Hotel in Tokyo, now, sadly, torn down, and came to admire "this science or art of most gracefully. . . .getting a cup of tea made". None the less he confessed that its fine points somewhat eluded him and that he eventually became bored by its severity and discipline.

To the Japanese, however, the tea ceremony is no less entertaining for being disciplined and severe. Take, for example, the demands of *kaiseki*, which of all the cuisines of the world puts the most emphasis upon harmonious combinations of colour—not only in the food itself, but between the food and the dishes. That is to say, the food must delight the eye delicately, as a Japanese painting does, or a flower. Similarly, it must give off a fragrance that does not leap up and startle the nose, but is elusive and hard to place. If the eye and the nose are not charmed, then—to a Japanese of any breeding whatsoever—the food simply does not taste good. A Japanese is not merely taking in food, he is taking in a complete sensory experience. To do so he must "pay attention" in a special way, and paying attention is what the tea ceremony is all about.

One can begin to learn about this special attentiveness by putting oneself in the role of the host—although properly speaking, no one can be a tea-ceremony host without years of intensive study. To start with, the host may have got up at dawn to pluck mushrooms or wild herbs from the near-by woods or to pick out a fish at the morning market. In any case, he will have

chosen all the food himself, selecting only what is in season and available locally. He will also have swept and prepared his tea-house and his garden, sprinkling each stepping stone in the garden path, being sure that a few leaves or a few pine needles remain in order to present an appearance of natural, seasonal charm. For the tea hut itself, which is made of the simplest but most exquisite materials, he will have chosen a hanging scroll and arranged a few seasonal flowers to please the tastes of his particular guests.

In the same way he will prepare the food with great care, according to the season, decorating the rice in the springtime with tiny cherry blossoms and flavouring bits of squid with the leaf buds of little fresh Japanese peppers. The food will also be appropriate to the time of day—often the tea ceremony starts at midday, but dawn and evening also make beautiful settings —and the food will look well in the dishes he has chosen to use. He is, in other words, creating a mood, and every part of the meal, even the timing with which he serves it, must further that mood.

The essence of the tea ceremony is harmony—harmony between host and guest, between the meal and the season, between the food and its con-

In a corner of her home, a Kyoto matron instructs her two daughters in the tea ceremony. The purpose of such lessons is to help the girls reach the level of proficiency required of refined and capable Japanese hostesses. The mother, seated in the position prescribed for a hostess, watches as one daughter sips tea. Then the cup will be set down, refilled and offered to her sister.

tainers, between the flavour and texture of one food and another. The host may, for instance, decide to create a tea ceremony around a particularly tasty mushroom, the *matsutake*, which is found under pine trees in October, when the frost has turned the leaves to splendid colours on the forest hillsides. Since the *matsutake* is available for only a short time, he will serve it in as many ways as he can. He may start by offering his guests—on an orange and yellow tray that matches the autumnal colours of the season—a lacquer box of rice cooked with chestnuts, a lacquer dish holding pieces of *horenso* (Japanese spinach) boiled with sliced *matsutake* caps, and a soup garnished with more *matsutake* caps combined with small pieces of raw sea eel. To further enhance the taste of the mushrooms he may follow these dishes with one of cooked chicken in which the *matsutake* caps are combined with *togarashi*, a small, pungent red pepper, and with *zuiki*, the crisp white stem of the taro plant.

This still leaves the *matsutake* stems unused, a waste that would be considered bad form. Being less delicate, they are not cooked with the caps, but instead are served separately. First they are sliced longitudinally. Then they are chopped and placed inside a circle of cooked sea eel, and arranged on fresh fern leaves in a shallow basket, a countrified container more in keeping with the relative coarseness of the stems than fine lacquer would be. Into the basket also goes a bit of grated red carrot called *momiji oroshi*—literally "maple leaves", because that's what they look like—along with a few richly flavoured leaves of the beef-steak plant *shiso*, cooked *tempura* style.

In this meal the *matsutake* mushroom has been used in many ways—in a soup, with a green vegetable, with chicken and pungent peppers, with fish and aromatic leaves—yet no guest could possibly feel that he had had too much of it. For one thing, the mushrooms are in season too briefly for anyone to become tired of their taste; for another, the host has used them sparingly, adding only a few to each dish. The whole effect is very simple and very subtle, and this is what *kaiseki* is meant to be. It would not be considered proper, for instance, to serve something out of season, unless the host did so for the sheer joy of pleasing one particular guest, a friend known to have a passion for that food—and even then, that passion should be known to the rest of the guests.

Neither would it be considered proper to go out of the way to get a *kaiseki* ingredient, to send to another city for a certain fish, for example, or an unusual variety of chestnut. This confuses expense with imagination, and *kaiseki* is not based on extravagance. Rather it is something of a game, an exercise in style, in which the host seeks to create the most beautiful effects from the simplest possible means. Thus for flavouring one turns to wild leaves rather than cultivated ones—to the crisp green leaves of the *shiso* plant, for instance, which when chopped up add colour to a dish and when used whole add texture. And if the meal is based on one star ingredient—on the sweet fish called *ayu*, for instance—then every part of the fish will be used, but in different guises: the flesh may be roasted, the skin and head served with boiled vegetables, the rest put into the soup. From this it follows, in theory at least, that a poor man can put on as fine a *kaiseki* as a rich man, since what is essentially required of the cook is inventiveness and imagination.

140

Continued on page 145

A Time-Hallowed Ceremony
That Nourishes the Japanese Soul

The simplest definition of the traditional tea ceremony is that it is an occasion when tea is made, served and sipped with graceful patterns of motion, as pictured on the following pages. Presiding over it are tea masters or their students, more than half of whom today are women. The ceremony may take place in the principal room of any home, but ideally it is held in a rustic tea hut, decorated only by a simple wall scroll and a flower arrangement. A subtle fragrance of incense fills the room. The guests inspect the objects of the tea service, often of great antiquity, and comment on their history and beauty. In sum, then, the tea ceremony is far more than the social occasion it appears to be. To the Japanese, it serves as an island of serenity where they can refresh their senses and nourish their souls.

TEA CEREMONY UTENSILS
Listed below are the Japanese objects in this photograph.

1 *Kensui*—bowl for waste water
2 *Hishaku*—water dipper
3 *Futaoki*—rest for kettle lid or dipper
4 *Kobukusa*—small silk napkin
5 *Fukusa*—another silk napkin
6 *Sensu*—fan
7 *Fukusa bassami*—silk bag
8 *Chawan*—tea bowl
9 *Chakin*—linen tea cloth
10 *Natsume*—tea caddy
11 *Chashaku*—bamboo teaspoon
12 *Chasen*—bamboo whisk
13 *Mizusashi*—cold-water jar
14 *Shikiita*—protective tile on which brazier stands
15 *Furo*—brazier
16 *Okama*—tea-kettle

After the guests have arrived, the host—the hostess in this case—brings in all the utensils needed for the tea ceremony, except for the brazier and kettle, which are already in place. The various objects are then arranged in a harmonious and artistic pattern, and the hostess proceeds ritually to clean the already immaculate teaspoon, tea caddy and tea bowl. One at a time she wipes the teaspoon and tea caddy with the silk napkin called the *fukusa*. Now she picks up the bamboo dipper— a brand-new dipper is used each time a tea ceremony is performed—and transfers a small quantity of hot water from the tea-kettle to the tea bowl. To wipe and dry the bowl, she folds a small oblong piece of pure linen cloth called a *chakin*, also brand-new, over the sides of the bowl, and turns it round and round in her hands. Done in a deliberate manner, the rotation of the bowl is meant to steady her hands and clear her mind. Thus the hostess's public washing of these objects not only ensures absolute cleanliness but also shows the thoroughness of her concern for her guests and helps to concentrate her attention on the demands of the ceremony to come.

When the tea bowl has been wiped dry, the hostess places the tea cloth on the rim of the kettle lid (*background*) and sets the bowl directly before her. Next, from its perch on the lacquered tea caddy, she lifts the teaspoon, a slender piece of bamboo curved at one tip and no more than eight inches long, and with gentle, careful motions she opens the caddy, trying not to disturb the slightly mounded shape of the tea, brilliant in its golden setting. Like all Japanese foods, the finely ground tea is a visual delight. Various blends of tea are used, depending upon the degree of formality of the occasion. The hostess measures two or three small scoops of tea into the bowl, delicately pouring the powder to form a minuscule mound that repeats the shape of the tea in the caddy. When the last scoop has been tipped into the bowl, she taps the spoon against the bowl's inside rim to shake off any specks that might still cling to the spoon. The tea masters say that the soft tap of the bamboo against the bowl—neither too sharp nor too muffled—helps to focus the minds of the hostess and her guests on the ordered procession of the ritual.

Now ready to add the water—the freshest, purest available—the hostess lowers the bamboo dipper open side down into the kettle. With a graceful, continuous motion, she rotates the dipper as it sinks into the water and so avoids disconcerting gurgles as the dipper fills. Then she lifts it out, places it over the centre of the tea bowl and tips the dipper just enough to pour about one third of the boiling water over the tea. To make sure that the water boils at just the right temperature, she takes great care beforehand to prepare a bed of ashes, either in a square sunken fire-box or in a movable brazier, that will create just the right amount of draught necessary for a glowing charcoal fire. This ensures an even heat under the singing tea-kettle. Guests listen appreciatively to this melodious sound, often likened to the wind sighing through pine trees or the plashing of a gentle stream. For the hostess, the kettle's song shows whether the water has reached the proper temperature. If the bubbles should roll and surge excessively, the hostess will dip cold water from the chinaware jar (*right foreground*) into the hot kettle to "restore the youth of the water".

The final step in preparing the tea involves an object perfectly formed for its function. This is the *chasen*, a hand-made whisk whose shape, developed many centuries ago, has defied improvement. The whisk whips the tea and water together into what one tea master has described as a "liquid jade froth". More than 50 steps are required to turn a single piece of bamboo into a whisk, formed at one end into a handle and curved at the other to form small prongs, and the best whisks come from a town near Kyoto called Chasenmura, which literally means the tea-whisk village. Despite their beauty and utility, whisks are often used only once and then discarded. Since each guest drinks the entire contents of the bowl, the hostess whips a relatively small amount of tea and water for each serving. Her guests watch attentively, for to attain the technique required to whip the tea with a vigorous but graceful motion demands long hours of practice and years of experience. A simple ceremony like this one lasts about 40 minutes, but ceremonies that include the elegant meal called *kaiseki* may last for four hours.

When she has whisked the tea, the hostess places the tea bowl on the silk *kobukusa*; the guest picks up both in the manner illustrated below and raises it in thanks. Then the guest turns the cup to a suitable spot—dictated by the bowl's shape and decoration—and sips slowly, appreciatively noting the tea's froth and colour as well as its taste and aroma.

Theory does not always accord with practice. While emphasis is primarily on simplicity of form, it does not follow that the content of the meal is inexpensive. As a matter of fact, the ingredients used are often the most expensive foods available. And while to the untutored eye the utensils, the trays and the bowls may seem simple and unassuming, there is a simplicity and lack of ostentation that may cost many hundreds of pounds to achieve. A single tea bowl that has the combined attributes of having been made by one of the great artists of the past, and of having pleased one of the legendary tea masters sufficiently for him to deign to sign it, can cost more than £40,000. From the Western point of view, there are no art objects on earth that are less pretentious and more expensive than these.

However, the ceremony can be performed with bowls and kettles that are well within the reach of people of ordinary means. Good contemporary bowls are available for about £10, and better ones can be bought at prices of up to about £850. Some of these objects may even have been made by craftsmen whose work is so fine that the government has conferred upon certain of these brilliant artists the title of "Living National Treasure".

Despite the inroads that increasing industrialization has made on tradition, the tea ceremony remains a national institution in Japan. Literally millions of men and women are enrolled in one or other of the schools of tea-making. The largest of the schools, Urasenke, also has a televised programme, and now has even extended its activities to a branch in New York City. Intense rivalry characterizes the relationship of the major schools, and each claims to transmit the purest traditions of simplicity and beauty.

Sometimes the simplicity of *kaiseki* is dictated not only by style, but by an exquisite concern for the occasion. Here, for example, is a menu for a September *otsukimi*, or moon viewing, when the moon is especially luminous and the fronds of the pampas grass are at their best. Because the guests' attention will be focused elsewhere—on looking at the moon—the meal has been chosen to enhance that experience and at the same time remain unobtrusive. It consists of a small heap of *shiso*-flavoured rice in a lacquer bucket; two glowing halves of hard-boiled egg, which suggest the moon, on a pale, stemmed dish, set off by a few soya beans cooked in their pods; a small dish of stewed *ayu* and a similar dish of chopped mackerel lightly cooked in vinegar. Bringing magic to this quiet feast is a bowl of *misoshiru*, brown as the earth, in which is floating a white circle of fish cake, or *shinjo* —another echo of the moon—decorated with a few Chinese pea pods and brown beans arranged to look like a spray of flowering bush clover.

The desire to make everything in *kaiseki* absolutely perfect for the occasion extends, of course, to the perfect pleasure of the guests. Nothing should startle their eyes; nothing should make them gasp. One of the host's first considerations should be what his guests are used to, what they can appreciate and enjoy. He is supposed to cater for their tastes rather than for his own—an excellent principle for entertaining—and he should make sure beforehand that they all like what he plans to serve. He should not, for instance, offer some extremely refined dish to people who would find it more impressive than good to eat. And he should manage the meal so subtly that no one really notices how marvellously it has been planned.

To a foreigner unfamiliar with *kaiseki*, its delicacy is sometimes too overwhelming for him to appreciate. He may not see, for instance, that the colours of the dishes placed before him pick up the colours of the garden he has just walked through. Nor may he realize that the vegetables he is eating in early spring are the young shoots of bamboo and butterbur and fiddle fern, all of them picked wild. But in summer, when it is almost too hot to eat, even an untutored guest can appreciate the light *kaiseki*, almost a picnic, placed before him by a thoughtful host. On a simple black tray, accompanied by a clear-glass *sake* cup that looks like a piece of sculptured ice, there may be a little china dish with a few pale slices of *sashimi*, slightly cooked and cooled to make it more tender; the *sashimi* will be set off by tiny cucumbers, still carrying their tender yellow blossoms. The main dish will make him think—as it was meant to—of a feast in a cool hill-side grove. It will consist of delicious morsels of various foods, very lightly cooked, then cooled and arranged on the freshest green bamboo section obtainable: rice balls with fresh red ginger stems; golden eggs with green bell peppers; pale pink prawns; tiny aubergines roasted in *miso*. As a pungent garnish to this soothing snack, there may be a few green leaves of *shiso*.

Such a meal invites nibbling, but in fact *kaiseki* food is not meant to be nibbled at. The economy practised in its cooking extends to the eating as well; everything put before the guest is meant to be consumed. To make this simpler, the portions are kept small and very few things are served with bones or other inedible parts. Only rarely, and then only for certain special occasions, is lobster served in its shell.

Behind this cleanliness is a principle—to be immaculate in one's surroundings contributes to purity of heart—and this principle, like all the others associated with *kaiseki*, comes from the ritual of the tea ceremony.

When the tea ceremony was evolving, the patrons of the great tea masters were men of wealth and power, and the tea ceremony came to be surrounded by an aura of luxury. Every ingredient, every utensil, everything seen or touched or tasted was the finest obtainable. At the same time the ceremony was never ostentatious, for the great tea masters were followers of Zen and subscribed to the Zen ideals of simplicity, serenity, withdrawal and contemplation. We know, for instance, that the greatest of the tea masters, Sen Rikyu, always stressed the principle of "less is more", and served his noble guests meals of the utmost simplicity. There is a record, in a 16th-century diary, of one of Sen Rikyu's *kaiseki* menus for a tea ceremony given in the autumn of the year 1556.

Sen Rikyu's *kaiseki* began with a group of four dishes in black lacquer bowls on a black lacquer tray: one contained raw carp and vegetables, another contained asparagus, a third contained a soup of crushed duck and vegetable, and the fourth was a bowl of rice. This was followed by a plate of sweets served on a table or a tray on legs. The meal was concluded with skewered quail and pepper in an earthenware bowl, accompanied by two pieces of raw sea bream on a plate and a few pickles. Today a typical meal would offer a much greater variety of taste sensations. The fish, possibly sea-bass *sashimi*, would be served with needle-cut cucumber prepared with *wasabi* (horse-radish) and vinegar. The bean-paste soup would contain rice-flour dumplings and a garnish of *shiso* leaves and pungent green pepper.

The soup and fish would be followed by a plate of cooked foods of various kinds—boiled egg, salted duck meat and citron-flavoured broth. After this would come something grilled or baked, perhaps a grilled fish such as *ayu* accompanied by its roe. A clear soup would follow, possibly of jelly-fish with needle-cut ginger for seasoning, and this would be served with side dishes of plain-fried lobster and plain-boiled taro, a potato-like root vegetable. And all this would be accompanied from time to time by rice and *sake*.

Whatever the menu, a good *kaiseki* meal should offer the same range of sensations to the eyes and nose as it does to the palate: this is the essence of *kaiseki*. And beyond that it should also offer the body nourishment appropriate to the season. There is a wonderful *kaiseki* menu devised to be served in late December around the turning of the year, a time rich in associations for the Japanese. The New Year is one of their most important festivals, and during the celebrations they also commemorate the death of a band of heroes, 47 faithful samurai who gave their lives to avenge a terrible wrong done their lord in the year 1701. Both these events, along with December's cold weather, are taken into account in a meal hearty enough to ward off the chill and delicate enough to tempt the sternest warrior from his duties.

This December menu begins with one of the most carefully contrived soups imaginable. It is made of *miso*—but a white *miso* rather than the common red variety. Floating in the snowy soup is a piece of *tofu*, bean-curd cake, that has been frozen out of doors and thawed so that it has acquired a special texture and flavour. The first frozen *tofu* came from a snow-bound temple on Mount Koya, where its freezing—perhaps unavoidable—became the occasion for a new experience in taste.

Since there are few fresh vegetables in December, the giant radish, *daikon*, comes into its own and is served boiled, with a sauce of *miso* paste, as a side dish to the soup. After this there follows a dish that ingeniously commemorates the encirclement and death of the ancient heroes. A slice of red snapper has been salted in the morning, and by evening it has contracted into a circle. Into its centre goes a small mound of boiled noodles, *soba*, because this is what the heroes are said to have eaten before attacking their lord's enemies—and also because *soba* is one of Japan's favourite winter foods. On top of the pale yellow *soba* is a little piece of dark-brown seaweed and a few slivers of spring onions. Looking at this little composition one thinks, aha, the moon crossed by clouds—and remembers that the heroes set out on a moonlit night. Then, lest this allusion be carried too far, the final dish is a sturdy combination of octopus and sweet potatoes served on rough, country plates.

The effect of this meal, with its tones of brown and white—like snow on the roof of a wooden house—is quite extraordinary. Yet the ingredients that compose it are not in the least unusual in Japan—all of them are simple, seasonal, local and fresh. What transforms them into a memorable gastronomic experience is the spirit and the thought. *Kaiseki*, they say, takes the right materials, the right flavourings and seasonings, and the right heart. Without the right heart there can be no true *kaiseki*. To think out a menu perfectly, to choose exactly the right dishes, to arrange the food with perfect artistry, to serve the meal with smoothness and finesse, to make every moment one of happy refinement—this is true *kaiseki*. No wonder so few people become great tea hosts. And no wonder so many keep trying.

Tea-Ceremony Cooking

Overleaf: A meal like the one shown on the next two pages is an example of *kaiseki ryori* (tea-ceremony cooking), in which Japanese formal dining reaches its pinnacle. Following the rules laid down by the great tea masters of old, the host tries —under ideal conditions—to use only locally obtained, seasonal foods. The trays, bowls and serving dishes are chosen with the same care as the tea ceremony utensils (*see pages 141-144*) and each food must be perfectly complemented by its container. The *kaiseki* illustrated is, by the choice of foods, an appropriate one for late spring or early summer. The courses, numbered in the order of serving, are as follows:

1 Rice in a black lacquer bowl comes with soup flavoured with soya-bean paste, and above these is salted raw fluke garnished with asparagus.
2 A clear soup is dominated by a square of white *tofu* (soya-bean curd) with slivers of fish paste and crab meat and is garnished with *warabi*, a fern.
3 Grilled sea bream is in a precious pottery bowl and steamed rice in the large black lacquer bowl.
4 In an antique china bowl, bamboo shoots and *fuki*, a Japanese vegetable, are garnished with *sansho* (pepper) leaf.
5 A clear kelp broth is served in a covered bowl.
6 Broad beans, from the fields, are coupled with prawns from the sea, stuffed with egg yolks.
7 Pickles made from marrow accompany white Chinese cabbage.
8 *Yuto*, a soup made from burned rice, is served from a red lacquer jug.
9 *Sake* pot and cups: the drink is served throughout the meal.

147

VII

Eating Out as
a Way of Life

The Kawataro restaurant, in Fukuoka in the island of Kyushu, serves only the freshest seafood. Caught in the near-by Inland Sea, the fish and shell-fish are stored alive in the large pool directly behind the counter (*background*). As the owner serves Ise lobster and sea bream to customers, an assistant nets another sea bream to fill a new order.

The husband who takes six hours or so to make his way home from the office several times a week, and who often turns up somewhat unsteady on his feet, may automatically be suspected by Westerners of philandering. Not so in Japan, for it is just as likely, as we have seen in Chapter 5, that he has merely been eating and drinking and enjoying himself, and perhaps flirting harmlessly with a bar hostess. Far from bringing shame on himself and his wife, the man who habitually dines out earns a reputation as an important fellow, someone who is tuned in to the affairs of the world and who knows how to live well. For in Japan good living means restaurant eating; in variety, in taste and in the aesthetics of food presentation, restaurant meals are very much better than anything the average housewife can produce. And this generalization applies not only to the lofty establishments that serve as the guardians and exemplars of Japanese *grande cuisine* but also to thousands and thousands of tiny workaday eating places crammed together in the narrow beehive streets of urban Japan.

I have eaten thousands of restaurant meals in Japan—either delivered to my inn or at the restaurants themselves, and because my wife is Japanese I have eaten at innumerable places where the presence of a foreigner would ordinarily create a stir. Only twice has the food been disappointing, and never have I encountered a Japanese version of the workman's café. Moreover, I doubt that Japan's consistently high restaurant standards will ever decline—as those of the French, for instance, have done—for restaurants and drinking places play a crucial role in Japan's social and business life, serving many needs that are met in other countries by different institutions.

Japanese-English Glossary

DASHI: *all-purpose soup stock*

FUGU: *globe-fish*

KATSUOBUSHI: *dried bonito*

MIRIN: *sweet rice wine*

NORI: *laver seaweed*

PON-SU: *soya-sauce and citrus-juice dressing*

SASHIMI: *slices of raw fish*

SUKIYAKI: *a simmered beef dish*

TATAMI: *straw matting*

TEMPURA: *deep-fried food*

TERIYAKI: *a grilling method using a "mirin" and soya-sauce marinade*

TOFU: *soya-bean curd*

TOKONOMA: *an alcove for displaying decorative objects*

TORO: *belly flesh of tunny fish*

TSUKEMONO: *pickled things*

WASABI: *green horse-radish*

For example, the grandest restaurants are in effect private domains for the affluent and powerful, the equivalent—but with much more grace and beauty—of the stuffy and exclusive London clubs in Pall Mall or the private dining rooms maintained by large business corporations. In the isolated rooms of Japan's most elegant eating places, over *sake* cups and *sashimi* and a full array of meticulously presented formal dishes, cabinet ministers, bureaucrats and members of parliament and their financial backers reach most of the political and economic decisions that govern Japan. While the geisha keep the *sake* flowing and artfully sustain the mood of harmony and good cheer through any arguments that might develop, political compromises are worked out, candidates for office selected, alliances forged, influence peddled and—occasionally—officials corrupted. Leading political figures hold court nearly every night at their favourite restaurants, and everyone in the political world knows which restaurant "belongs" to which party faction. In some cases the powerful politician may actually share the ownership of the restaurant, having set up a favourite geisha as its proprietress.

At a different place in the scale there are restaurants that are forums for the stylish and fashionable. Restaurants provide the setting for reunions, parties and banquets, for testimonial dinners honouring champions of judo or professors of history, and for receptions to launch a new film or a new and mammoth oil tanker.

Entertaining in Japan is virtually synonymous with going to a restaurant. Most modern Japanese houses and apartments lack the uncluttered natural grace of the Japanese architectural ideal. Therefore they cannot provide the atmosphere that the Japanese consider necessary for the full aesthetic enjoyment of a meal. But restaurants, even ordinary ones, specialize in atmosphere, for their proprietors realize that they are supposed to fulfill the average person's yearning for the beautiful, uncrowded and harmonious— the better things of life that he cannot afford at home but for which he hungers deeply.

Conjuring up this atmosphere requires careful—and expensive—attention to every detail, not only to the food itself. Just as the articles that adorn the *tokonoma* are precisely arranged, so must a dish and tray be of the right colour and material to bring out the hue and texture of the food upon it. Equal care and expense are lavished on what will be seen beyond the tray and dishes: the room, the garden, the view.

Even in the modest restaurants squeezed together like so many hand-made doll houses in the narrow alleys of the big cities, considerable effort is make to provide some kind of natural view, often when a space of only five or ten square feet is available. In Kyoto, where attention to nature and atmosphere is at its peak, customers at one small restaurant can rinse their fingers in a perfect miniature stream that babbles along the bar in front of them, landscaped with rocks and moss and dwarf trees. A near-by shop seats its clientele in booths around a Lilliputian pond, fitted out with tiny bridges and tea-houses and swarming with live and very active carp. Pond and dining area together take up an area of less than 20 square feet, and traffic roars by just 50 feet away, but seated in that cameo garden, watching the carp and savouring the food, you feel as if you had stumbled on Eden.

Japanese restaurants could not provide so elaborate an atmosphere if the customers had to pay for it out of their meagre salaries. Fortunately, the restaurant business can depend on the huge patronage of the *sha yo zoku*, the "company business tribe", or, as we would say, the expense-account executives. Expense-account eating and drinking is a much bigger enterprise in Japan than anywhere else; 90 per cent of the food and drink consumed in the better restaurants in Tokyo is paid for directly by one business firm or another, and not by the customers. The diner simply signs the bill, leaving his card if he is not well-known to the manager, and at the end of the month his firm's cashier will pay it.

It is safe to say that no deal is ever signed in Japan, no big sale ever concluded, unless the individuals concerned have eaten and drunk together at a restaurant or bar. The Japanese do not like dealing with strangers, and in order to avoid this necessity Japanese businessmen spend vast sums and long hours establishing and maintaining good personal relationships in every direction, with everyone in business or government whose affairs are likely to concern them in any fashion. The best way to do this is to take the other fellow to a bar or restaurant or cabaret—or preferably to all three; he will reciprocate later, and a good time will be had by all. Once the Japanese have dined and wined together they are friends, and business can then proceed on a basis of mutual personal obligation. To the Japanese an agreement confirmed personally is much more binding than the iron-clad clauses of a contract; failure to meet a promise made to someone with whom you have exchanged *sake* cups and sung old songs is a breach of honour, but a written contract with a stranger is merely a piece of paper with no such binding moral force. Many foreigners, trying to deal with the Japanese in a no-nonsense, business-is-business manner, have discovered to their dismay that without restaurant entertaining nothing gets done.

The recipients of expense-account entertainment are not only officials of the government or of companies whose good will is important; Japanese executives may use tax-free company money to entertain heads of departments within their own companies, the departmental heads may do the same for heads of sections, and so on down the line until the lowliest clerk can on occasion expect to be given his night out—all in the name of personnel relations and business efficiency.

The government tax office makes no effort to ensure that business matters are discussed at any of these great or small affairs: that would destroy the whole purpose of the exercise. The only limitation is on the over-all amount spent. Every year each company is entitled to deduct from taxable income all "social expenses" up to one-quarter of one per cent of its total capital, and half of any such expenses over that. This unofficial subsidy to Japan's bars and restaurants adds up to nearly £670 million a year, a sum equal to one-tenth of the national budget.

Important politicians and captains of industry are more or less obliged, because of their status, to take their guests to the great restaurants where dinner, drinks and entertainment can cost over £20 a head. The lower echelons of the *sha yo zoku*, and those unfortunates who must bring their wallets with them, may rarely dine on the gastronomic peaks, but what they miss in elegance and perfection they can more than make up for in the variety offered by everyday restaurant fare. For a couple of shillings hungry

Many proprietors of Japanese restaurants entice customers inside by displaying remarkably realistic plastic facsimiles of their specialities outside the front door. Small labels give the names and prices of the dishes and, in the larger cities, the English translations. For example, on the top right in this display case is *kanisu*, boiled crab, at 400 yen (about 9s.).

Continued on page 161

NOODLES TWO WAYS
At the Yabuizu noodle restaurant, customers enjoy *zarusoba*, noodles and soup served separately (*above, right*), and *tempura soba*, noodle soup topped with a fried prawn (*above, left*).

A SAMPLING OF *SUSHI*
The chef (*opposite*) at the Isogen restaurant rolls up *sushi* (vinegared rice) in a sheath of seaweed to make cylindrical *makizushi*. In the centre of the large bowl are slices of similar rolls, stuffed with tunny fish or cucumber. The other *sushi* morsels are mostly mounds of rice topped with a slice of raw fish. The small, round box on the left contains *chirashi*, loose rice covered with fish. The block-like boxes, stacked upside down, contain wooden *sake* cups.

Sampling the Speciality Restaurants

The Japanese like to eat out—and they do, with a fervour and a frequency that are unmatched in the West. As a consequence, not only do restaurants flourish by the thousands but they are also found in every size and description. They range from the elegant and expensive preserves of the wealthy and influential to tiny cubby-holes and mobile food bars. Of all the eating establishments, the public most often patronizes those restaurants which specialize in one way or another—perhaps in a distinctive cooking technique or in serving a single kind of food or in making the dishes associated with a particular region of Japan. On this and the following pages are shown some of Tokyo's most popular types of speciality restaurants. There are countless others as well, but despite their diversity, they share several qualities: the food is uniformly good both in its preparation and presentation, the restaurants are immaculately clean, and the prices are fair and often quite low.

154

TEMPURA, PIECE BY PIECE
The chef at the Ten-ichi serves each *tempura* item as it reaches deep-fried perfection, and is ready with a new piece when the customer finishes eating the previous one. Shown below are vegetables, ginkgo nuts and seafoods awaiting *tempura* frying.

SLICES OF RAW FISH
A cheerful chef at the Otomo *sashimi* restaurant poses proudly with a few of the many raw fish dishes advertised on the long, handwritten menu that lies on his counter. The fish used for *sashimi* not only must be as fresh as possible but also must be expertly sliced to make the most of its flavour.

GRILLS FROM THE WEST
The French chef's hat on a cook at the Ginsen, an expensive steak house (*below*), is worn because this sort of restaurant was originally designed to cater for foreigners. But these establishments quickly attracted many Japanese. The principal dish is steak and vegetables grilled on the large stainless-steel *teppan*.

BROCHETTES, JAPANESE STYLE

Yakitori—food grilled on skewers over a charcoal fire—sends up a tantalizing
aroma that has customers waiting eagerly for service at the Torishige restaurant. On
the skewers (*from the left*) are chicken, duck liver and minced-chicken patties.

SNACKS AND *SAKE* ON WHEELS
A late-night sight on Japanese streets is the food wagon. From its sizzling grill come fish, potatoes, eggs, giant radish and fried soya-bean curd. Hunched on stools, customers savour the *sake* and the snacks provided by this mobile grill.

ONE-POT COOKING
The Junidanya restaurant specializes in *shabu shabu*, one kind of *nabemono* (one-pot) dish made with thinly sliced beef and vegetables. The ingredients are first stirred in a bubbling broth. Then they are dipped in sauces, garnished with red pepper, salt and sesame seeds and eaten with assorted pickles.

159

Japanese can fill up with a tasty bowl of *ramen*, Chinese-style noodles; for £4 or so they may treat their palates to an epicurean masterpiece of raw *fugu* and *tempura*; in between those extremes stretches a bewildering choice of restaurants for every budget, every taste, every mood. Someone has calculated that in Tokyo alone there are 105,000 licensed restaurants not counting bars and coffee shops, or more than one for every 100 persons. However, that figure only proves that Tokyo is big, its restaurants small, and that the Japanese like to eat out. For the gourmet, a more interesting statistic would be the number of different *kinds* of restaurants—which no one to my knowledge has ever totted up. My guess would be that you could go to a different type of eating place every day for many months. Perhaps that is what we really mean when we call them "everyday" restaurants.

There are restaurants that serve a six- or seven-course meal in which the main ingredient of every dish is *tofu*—and it is not monotonous at all. Some restaurants handle only whale meat offered both as *sukiyaki* and raw *sashimi*, some specialize in crab, grilled, or vinegared, or boiled with vegetables and noodles, and some do all kinds of things with all parts of the turtle. One excellent Ginza eating house offers nothing but sardines—raw, fried, salt-grilled, soya-grilled, mashed, curried or steeped in broth. And up in the mountains, near the resort of Nikko, is an unpretentious country restaurant offering only carp in dozens of styles ranging from *arai*, a kind of *sashimi*, to a thick-sauce melange resembling Chinese sweet-and-sour fish. Other seafood restaurants concentrate not on one species but on a single method of preparation such as grilling, cooking at the table or, of course, *sashimi*.

One of the most common restaurant foods is *yakitori*, skewered bits of chicken, chicken liver and spring onions grilled over a charcoal fire (*page 175*). Four or five little chunks are impaled on each slim bamboo *kushi* and brushed with a *teriyaki* sauce before grilling. To eat, you pick up the skewer and bite off the titbits one by one. Tiny quail eggs, ginkgo nuts, green peppers and other delicacies get the same treatment. Many *yakitori* shops are little more than open-air stalls, and you can easily find them by following your nose: their charcoal stoves face the street and the smoky, appetizing aroma of grilling chicken pervades the neighbourhood. Fancier establishments do their grilling in a pit set in the middle of a *tatami*-carpeted room. They usually offer a complete and graduated meal, starting with tiny sparrows, grilled whole on the skewer—the bones are fine enough to chew—and then quail, chicken, duck livers and finally pieces of duck.

Then there is *teppanyaki*, a plain and hearty method of grilling meat and chicken on a metal plate. There are numerous ways of doing it, and one can find restaurants specializing in each: *okonomiyaki*, in which you get your own little gas or charcoal grill and a plate of meats and vegetables and then do it all yourself; *karibayaki*, or "hunters' grill", where your kimonoed waitress manages things on a perforated metal dome that lets just enough juices run off to keep the meat dry but tender; *ishiyaki*, in which a sizzling stone takes the place of the hot plate; and *batayaki*, *bata* being the nearest Japanese approximation to "butter": meats grilled in butter. Similar to these, and very popular in Japan, are restaurants offering "Genghis Khan barbecue", which is mutton grilled over charcoal, and a Korean beef barbecue, with a hot sauce, cooked in the same way. In recent years the

Restaurants like the Sasagayuki in Tokyo (*opposite*) serve entire meals of *tofu* (soya-bean curd), one of the most versatile of Japanese foods. Although it has little flavour of its own, it absorbs other flavours easily, so *tofu* is used in innumerable dishes both for its soft, comforting texture and for the different tastes it adopts. Spread before three diners is an assortment of *tofu* dishes which includes: *giseidofu*, uncooked *tofu* topped by strips of deep-fried *tofu* (*1*); *namashoyu dofu*, *tofu* boiled in weak soya sauce flavoured with lemon and ginger (*2*); *hiyayako dofu*, another uncooked but chilled *tofu*, this time with a spicy soya sauce (*3*); *iridofu*, or *tofu* scrambled with chicken and peas (*4*); *koyadofu*, dried *tofu* boiled in soya-sauce soup with mushrooms (*5*).

161

Japanese have adapted *teppanyaki* to Western-style steak, using the superb Matsuzaka and Kobe beef. At these "Japanese steak houses", originally developed for the tourist trade but now popular with the Japanese as well, the customers sit round a huge grill on which a chef deftly manipulates sizzling chunks of tender beef and parcels them out, done to order, with bean sprouts and *pon-su* sauce.

Many Tokyo restaurants serve food Osaka style, and Tokyo-style establishments can be found in Osaka, so that expatriates from both cities can eat happily far from home. The two cuisines are fundamentally the same but differences do exist—Osaka food is richer and sweeter, for instance—and despite rapid modern transport which has reduced the distance between the two cities, there has been little blending of the two styles. In Tokyo, moreover, one can find a seemingly endless yet ever increasing number of restaurants specializing in foods from one region of the country or another. These regional restaurants cater primarily for the hundreds of thousands of home-sick young men from the country who have come to the big city to make their fortunes. These places just ooze nostalgia: the excellent food is authentic, imported waitresses in traditional regional costume speak the local dialect and sing local folk songs, and the dishes and décor reflect the regional cultures and crafts. The dreamy expression in the eyes of the customers is a sure indication that the restaurant has evoked memories of their native villages. By eating at a few of these places a foreigner can simulate a tour of Japan cheaply, quickly and without ever leaving Tokyo.

Coming a little way down the epicurean scale to simpler fare, but still within the range of good eating, there are restaurants specializing in *chazuke*, in which tea or *dashi* is poured over the rice after it is cooked, and others devoted to *chameshi*, rice cooked with other ingredients. *Chameshi*—the word means "tea rice"—originated several centuries ago with Buddhist priests who cooked their rice with brewed tea instead of plain water, but nowadays soya sauce and *mirin* are used instead of tea, and in the fancier versions, usually called *kamameshi*, or "pot rice", many kinds of finely chopped seafood, meats, vegetables and mushrooms may be added. The better *kamameshi* restaurants offer a staggering selection of ingredients and combinations, and cook each portion to order in an individual pot that is then set before the customer in a scooped-out block of wood. Some Tokyo restaurants, like the crowded and boisterous Tori-gin in the Ginza, serve both *yakitori* and *kamameshi*, and with *sake* or beer it's a wonderful combination.

Other rice restaurants include those concentrating on *nigiri meshi*, which is a ball of rice pressed together around *katsuobushi* flakes or some kind of fish paste or *tsukemono*, and sometimes wrapped in a sheet of *nori*, and shops specializing in any of a number of kinds of *domburi*, the bowl of rice with sauces and meat or chicken that housewives sometimes make for lunch out of left-overs. *Domburi* is often topped with a piece of prawn *tempura*, in which case it is called *tendon*, or with a pork cutlet: *tonkatsu*.

The lowly pork cutlet, *tonkatsu*—*ton* is pork, *katsu* is the Japanese pronunciation of "cutlet"—is a standard working man's meal available in many cheap cafés, but there are restaurants that specialize in this dish. Dipped in breadcrumbs and fried lightly in oil, *tonkatsu* is commonly served with a thick, pungent sauce on a bed of shredded cabbage spiced with *shiso*, the beef-steak plant; the cabbage and the *shiso* help to cut the oiliness.

Over the doorway of every restaurant hangs a short curtain, a *noren*, which the customers have to duck under or brush through in order to enter. It is hung at a tantalizing height, its bottom hem just below eye level, so that a passer-by cannot see anything but the floor of the restaurant without ducking his head or holding aside the curtain and peering in. Once he does that, he will be greeted by a chorus of "irasshai"—"welcome"—from the staff and will find it embarrassing to turn away.

To the proprietor of a restaurant his *noren* symbolizes the reputation of his establishment. Moreover, the *noren*, usually made of strips of heavy blue cloth, carries the insignia of the shop in bold white characters. Anywhere in Japan you can tell at a glance what kind of food the place serves from a glance at the curtain. Even a foreigner can soon learn to spot the particular lettering which signifies an eel restaurant or a noodle shop. And if he sees a *noren* made of strands of rope instead of cloth, he will know that behind it lies a humble, inexpensive eating house catering for workmen.

Most of Japan's eating places, and many of those I have been talking about, are snack bars. In Western countries these restaurants usually provide fast service and so-so food at best, but the food served over the counters of Japan is almost invariably excellent, and for certain foods—the rice and seafood titbits called *sushi* and *tempura* for example—you simply have to eat at the bar if you want to get the best.

The foodstuffs and the preparations must be of the highest quality at bars like these because the customer can watch almost every step of the cooking. Seated at the gleaming, scrubbed wooden bar with room in some places for only half a dozen people, the customer can examine the food closely, talk directly to the chef to tell him what is wanted and then watch—and learn—as it is prepared. He will see the care, the reverence almost, with which each dish is cooked, arranged and garnished, and how the head chef, usually the owner, examines every portion before it is served.

A *tempura* chef usually works inside a horseshoe-shaped bar with up to 15 customers sitting around it. The menu will consist of about a dozen ingredients as well as prawns: squid, shell-fish and various other kinds of fish, an assortment of vegetables including green pepper, lotus root, carrots, spring onions, aubergines, ginger and mushrooms. An expert *tempura* chef will toss his batter-coated prawns and leafy vegetables into the pan with a peculiar twist of the wrist; this prevents them from curling up and absorbing too much oil, which would make them soggy. At the critical moment for each ingredient he plucks the pieces out with a pair of long chopsticks, puts the food into a flat basket covered with absorbent paper and places it in front of the guest, who dips the morsels in salt or soya and *mirin*.

When two or three guests come in together, the chef can easily remember who has had what, as he serves them simultaneously. But his memory is taxed when he has five or six groups of people who are at different stages of his long menu; 15 customers at a time seems to be the limit for one chef. Large *tempura* restaurants like the Ten-ichi in Tokyo therefore divide their premises into many small rooms, with a chef and his circular bar in each. This preserves the intimate relationship between the chef and his customer that is so essential to this kind of eating. As Isao Yabuki, the owner of the

Ten-ichi, points out, this relationship is just as important to the chef as to the customer. "The good cook is the flattered cook," he says in his book on Tokyo food, "and what more flattering to a man than those murmurs of mm—mm—mm as the eager guests regale themselves?"

Another advantage of this type of restaurant, particularly for the nervous foreigner who suspects that cleanliness is non-existent outside his own kitchen, is that it lets one see just how clean Japan's restaurants actually are. Even in very small places the floors are sloshed down several times an hour, the workers wearing wooden clogs that keep their feet several inches above the wet floor. Wooden cutting blocks are washed after every use and grills scraped down immediately. Chopsticks are used once and thrown away and counters scrubbed repeatedly until the wood gleams white. No employee who touches the food will handle money, and since every Japanese bathes at least once a day, staff hygiene is never a problem. The kitchens of restaurants with private dining rooms are not open to public view, but having inspected many of them and found them just as spotless as the snack bars, I can say without reservation that the standards of hygiene in Japan are the highest in the world.

Stepping from the grimy street into one of these spick-and-span restaurants, the customer himself may feel unclean, or at least bedraggled. The Japanese have an answer for this, too: *oshibori*. These are small, damp towels —nowadays sterilized and rolled up in cellophane—which every Japanese restaurant and bar sets before each customer as soon as he sits down. *Oshibori* come steaming hot for most of the year and provide a refreshing and highly civilized way to wipe the casual dust from your hands and make you feel ready to handle your food. A man—or a woman without make-up— can get even more refreshment out of the *oshibori* by rubbing it over the face and neck, especially in the summer when *oshibori* are handed out ice cold.

No other counter restaurants of this type have as much to offer the adventurous gourmet as Japan's *sushi* shops. Some people consider that the cold snacks collectively called *sushi* (*pages 95-101*) are the national dish of Japan; there is nothing remotely like it anywhere else in the world. You can find it in one form or another in every corner of Japan and I have yet to meet a native who says he doesn't like it. Even foreigners, once they have overcome their prejudice against raw fish, rave about *sushi* and argue with each other over the merits of their favourite *sushi* place.

The typical *sushi* restaurant is small, cheerful and sparkling with scrubbed wood. The bar runs the length of the room, presided over by one or more white-clad chefs, hands red from constant washing, towels knotted around their foreheads. "Irasshai", they shout as you duck under the *noren* and slide open the door, and as soon as you have sat down at the bar a huge cup of tea, an *oshibori* and a little mound of sliced ginger are set before you—the ginger is to cleanse your palate before starting and between courses. You wipe your hands with the *oshibori*, sip your tea and examine the offerings of the day spread out in a refrigerated glass case running along the back of the bar. There will be the dark-red lean tunny fish, the marbled fatty *toro*, little slabs of snow-white squid, chunks of fish shiny and speckled like herring, blood-red *akagai* clams, mounds of caviar glistening like jewels, octopus tentacles, abalone still in the shell, pale fingers of prawn and, in the midst of all this seafood, little yellow rectangles of omelette, in which certain *sushi* are wrapped and eaten. Take your time; no one will rush you.

When you are ready you point to what you want, or order it by name. The chef's hands flash like a magician's, quicker than the eye; he has been trained and has practised for years before he is allowed to serve the customers. Out comes the delicacy you have indicated. If it needs cutting, the long knife smoothly slices off two even pieces. From a large tub beside him the chef grabs a handful of vinegared rice; deftly he kneads it, squeezing in a bit of *wasabi*. Two fingers of one hand press the rice in the palm of the other: one tiny loaf-shaped rice ball is ready. Then another. The flashing hands slow down. Gently the two slices of fish or whatever it may be are pressed on the two mounds of rice. Then, with a proud flourish, the chef picks them up in one hand and whisks them on to a slanted, shelf-like part of the counter, where they await your pleasure. The whole process has taken perhaps 30 seconds. You pick up one mound, dip the rice part into a saucer of soya sauce, turn it over to keep it from dripping, and then place the whole thing on your tongue. Each piece of *sushi* is designed as a single mouthful, but anybody who wants to prolong the delight by nibbling is forgiven—though the rice ball will crumble in his fingers before he finishes.

One portion of *sushi* at a bar consists always of two of these bite-sized balls. Nothing that is sliced must ever be served singly or in threes, for one slice is *hito kire*, which can mean "kill", and three slices, *mi kire*, can mean "kill myself". Since the portions are so small you can sample the entire menu at one sitting, or you can eat as much as you like of your favourite dish. A serving of each variety is priced according to the value of the fish, and you pay only for what you eat. Prawns are usually the most expensive; the cheapest, by volume, is *makizushi* (*page 100*), in which a long sliver of tunny fish, or sometimes cucumber, at the end of a *sushi* meal, is wrapped in rice with an outer sheet of *nori*; this roll is then sliced crosswise, and six or eight squat cylinders are placed before you.

Sushi cuisine has a colourful vocabulary of its own, and the customer who uses the special words for ordering them instead of the standard Japanese vocabulary often gets special treatment as a true *sushi* gourmet. Surprisingly, many Japanese do not know that at a *sushi* restaurant *wasabi* is called *namida*, or tears, because it is hot enough to make you cry, or that octopus is *geso*—meaning "legs", of course. *Sushi* chefs refer to their egg item as *gyoku*, or jewel, to tea as *agari*, meaning "up", for obscure reasons, and to cucumber as *kappa*, the name of a cucumber-fancying river goblin.

Of course, you don't have to go to a *sushi* restaurant to eat *sushi*. The *sushi* shops, as well as the noodle and *domburi* restaurants, do a thriving delivery business. The *sushi* is beautifully arranged in opulent round lacquer boxes, which some aesthetes say enhance the taste, and carried by bicycle and motor cycle to inns, offices and private houses. Moreover the lunch box *bento* that are sold in infinite local and regional variations at railway stations, and at theatres and other places of entertainment contain many *sushi* ingredients although they are not, strictly speaking, *sushi*. Like everything else prepared by the skilled and conscientious restaurant chefs of Japan, they are distinguished by their fine materials, their skilful presentation and by a broad and varied spectrum of flavours.

In Japan, where eating out is a national pastime, people are also fond of ordering prepared dishes to be delivered. Local restaurants do a thriving business delivering food to offices, factories and homes, often by bicycle. In the picture above, a noodle shop delivery boy dexterously balances lacquered boxes and fragile pottery bowls that contain three different kinds of noodles and dipping sauces.

165

A Short but Happy Life

The beer-swilling steer above is enjoying the last months of a pampered existence on a luxurious ranch. Born of prize-winning parents, he was moved as a calf to another farm where the climate, water and grazing offer the best conditions for raising cattle. There he spent his days growing into a perfect three-year-old steer, receiving the sort of loving care which is usually lavished only on thoroughbred horses. He was curried daily and given a hand massage with *shochu* (Japanese gin) to knead his accumulating fat gently through his muscles and so impart the "marbled" look of fine meat. His diet included rice, rice bran and beans. The beer was added shortly before his third birthday, after he reached his last abode, a ranch operated by the Wadakin beef restaurant of Matsuzaka for final fattening into perfect beef. His life is typical of those creatures destined to end up as *shimofuri* (fallen frost) beef, considered by connoisseurs to be the best in the world. This is a remarkable achievement, for the Japanese have developed their unique methods of raising beef cattle only within the past century, after the ancient Buddhist injunction against the eating of meat began to fall into disuse.

Much of the beef raised in the manner described on the left is used in the making of *sukiyaki*. This dish usually serves as the foreigner's introduction to *nabe*, or "one pot" cooking done at the table. To make beef *sukiyaki* (*page 134*) the host first cooks the slices of beef, adding soya sauce as flavouring, then rakes them to one side of the pan. The other ingredients are added and cooked briefly. *Sukiyaki* requires (*opposite, on the right of the beef, from the bottom to the top*): sugar, eggs, soya sauce, soup. On the plate: green onions, bean curd, carrots, onions and mushrooms. Also on the table are a bowl of rice and chopsticks.

Yakimono: GRILLED FOODS

Mushimono: STEAMED FOODS

The recipes in the "yakimono" category are literally "grilled things". The grilling techniques are all familiar and simple, and the cooking times are short. The variations that occur among recipes are mainly in seasonings and combinations of ingredients. Most of the following recipes are suitable for outdoor cooking—over a charcoal fire or on the widely popular hibachi.

Horakuyaki

STEAM-GRILLED PRAWNS WITH CHICKEN, GINKGO NUTS AND MUSHROOMS

This method of grilling—on a bed of coarse salt—is in fact more like steaming or even baking than grilling as foreigners know it, and it gives a delicate flavour to the food.

Although Japanese "horoku" are difficult to find in the United Kingdom, an excellent substitute would be 12- to 14-inch unglazed earthenware casseroles equipped with tightly fitting lids. (See also page 207).

PREPARE IN ADVANCE: 1. Shell the prawns, but leave the last segment of shell and tail attached.

De-vein the prawns with a small, sharp knife by making a shallow incision down their backs and removing the black or white intestinal veins with the point of the knife. Set the prawns aside.

2. Wipe the mushrooms with a damp cloth and cut a small cross on the top of each.

3. Thread ginkgo nuts on each of 4 small (4- to 6-inch) bamboo skewers, and similarly thread 2 or 3 pieces of boned chicken on each of 4 other skewers. Set them aside.

4. Preheat the oven to Mark 6: 400°F. Make a deep cross on the curved top of each chestnut using a sharp, heavy knife. Put the chestnuts on a baking sheet or in a shallow roasting tin and bake in the centre of the hot oven for 10 minutes. Peel off their shells as soon as possible and set the chestnuts aside.

TO COOK: Pour a ½-inch layer of coarse salt into a 12- to 14-inch wide *horoku* or unglazed earthenware casserole. Sprinkle a few drops of water over the salt and place the casserole over a moderate heat for about 5 to 10 minutes, until the salt is heated through.

Now spread a thin layer of the pine needles on the salt and arrange the prawns, mushrooms, skewered chicken and nuts, and chestnuts on top. Scatter about 4 to 6 pine needles over the food, cover the casserole tightly, sealing the edges, if necessary, with a strip of aluminium foil, and steam undisturbed over a moderately high heat for 12 to 13 minutes.

TO SERVE: Remove the pine needles and serve the food directly from the *horoku* or casserole, accompanied by small individual dishes of *chirizu* dipping sauce. *Horakuyaki* will serve four as part of a Japanese meal (*page 198*) or as a first course.

To serve 4

4 medium-sized raw prawns (16 to 20 per lb.)
4 medium-sized white mushrooms
12 canned *ginnan* (ginkgo nuts), drained
1 whole chicken breast, boned (*see pages 176-177*) and cut into 1-inch cubes
8 chestnuts
½ to 1 lb. coarse salt
2 or 3 sprigs fresh pine needles (about 3 tablespoons)

DIPPING SAUCE
¼ pint *chirizu* (*page 94*)

Chestnuts and pine needles add a hint of autumn to an aromatic *horakuyaki*, in which mushrooms, ginkgo nuts, chicken and prawns are steam-grilled on a bed of coarse salt. The cooking utensil is a Japanese *horoku*, an unglazed earthenware casserole.

Miso Zuke 味噌漬

GRILLED MACKEREL IN MISO MARINADE

PREPARE IN ADVANCE: Place the *shiro miso* in a small bowl and stir in the sugar and *mirin* using a wooden spoon. Arrange the fish pieces side by side in a baking dish just large enough to hold them in one layer and spread the marinade evenly over them with a rubber spatula. Cover with a sheet of plastic and refrigerate for 2 days.

TO COOK AND SERVE: Preheat the grill or light a hibachi or charcoal grill. Gently remove the marinade from the fish with a rubber spatula and kitchen paper and discard it. Place the fish about 4 inches from the heat and grill for about 7 to 8 minutes, flesh side towards the heat, until the fish is a light golden brown. Turn the fish carefully with a fish slice or cooking chopsticks and grill for another minute. Serve at once on individual plates, accompanied by the pickled ginger sprouts.

This dish will serve four as part of a Japanese meal (*page 198*) or as a first course or luncheon dish.

To serve 4

1 lb. fillet of mackerel or horse mackerel with skin left on, cut into 2- to 3-inch pieces

MARINADE
⅜ pint *shiro miso* (white soya-bean paste)
2½ oz. sugar
2½ tablespoons *mirin* (cooking *sake*), or substitute 1½ tablespoons pale dry sherry

GARNISH
Hajikami (bottled pickled ginger sprouts)

169

To serve 6 to 8

A 2- to 2½-lb. red snapper,
  cleaned but with fins, head and
  tail left on
Salt
MSG
2½ teaspoons *mirin* (sweet *sake*), or
  substitute 1½ teaspoons pale dry
  sherry

GOMAYAKI (sesame-seed grilled
  fish)
4 teaspoons white sesame seeds
Vegetable oil
1 egg white, lightly beaten

UNIYAKI (fish with sea-urchin
  glaze)
2½ teaspoons bottled *uni* (prepared
  sea urchin)
¾ teaspoon egg yolk
¾ teaspoon *sake* (rice wine)
MSG

Takara Bune   宝舟
TREASURE-SHIP FISH

"Takara bune" means treasure ship, and that is what it is—the steamed shell of a whole fish, shaped like a boat and filled with colourful fish titbits. The recipe in its entirety is suitable for a buffet or formal dinner, but the three different grilled fish can be served as first courses or hors d'œuvre without the treasure ship itself.

TO MAKE THE TREASURE SHIP: Follow the pictures and step-by-step instructions below and opposite.

Preheat the oven to Mark 5: 350°F. Sprinkle both sides of the fish lightly with salt and MSG. Encrust the fins and tail of the fish heavily with salt, pressing it on with your fingers. Using the ends of the skewers as handles, set the fish lengthways across the top of a large roasting tin at least 6 inches deep. Make sure that the tail curls downwards, and place an empty coffee or fruit-juice can against it to prevent it from curling upwards while it steams.

Pour enough boiling water into the tin to come ¼ inch up the sides, and drape two or three damp pieces of kitchen paper over the fish. Place the tin on the floor of the oven and steam for about 45 minutes, until the flesh is firm to the touch. Sprinkle the paper from time to time with hot water to keep it moist.

Remove the fish from the oven and raise the heat to Mark 7: 475°F. Peel off the paper gently, moistening it lightly with cold water if it sticks. Invert

To prepare a "treasure ship" fish, insert the tip of a knife at the back of the head (*above, left*) and cut down to, but not through, the centre bones. Cut along the side to the tail, then across the top (*above, centre*) and down the other side. Remove the fillet (*above, right*), turn the fish over, and repeat on the other side. Wash the fish, pat it dry, and set aside the fillets. Insert 2 long metal skewers along either side of the fish: first down through the neck, then up and down through the centre of the body, finally up at the base of the tail. With strong string, tie a firm knot around the tail and then loop the ends around the head. Bring the ends of the string back towards the tail, catching the fins to spread them, and tie another knot to secure the fish "boat".

the fish on a large ovenproof serving dish—so that the tail curls upwards and the fish forms a basket. Brush the head, tail and skin with *mirin* and return the fish to the oven for about 5 minutes, until it is lightly glazed. Then cool the fish to room temperature. Do not remove the skewers and string.

TO MAKE GOMAYAKI: Preheat the grill to its highest point. Heat a heavy, medium-sized frying pan over a high heat until a drop of water flicked across its surface evaporates instantly. Add the sesame seeds and cook for about 3 to 4 minutes, until they are lightly and evenly toasted. Then chop them finely with a sharp, heavy knife. Spread them out evenly on a sheet of greaseproof paper.

Cut one of the snapper fillets into 1-inch pieces, place them skin side down in a lightly oiled baking dish and grill 3 inches from the heat for 2 to 3 minutes. Turn the pieces over and grill 2 minutes. Remove from the heat, dip the flesh side of the fish into the lightly beaten egg white, then into the chopped sesame seeds. Return to the baking dish and grill for about 1 to 2 minutes longer, until the seeds are a golden brown. Set aside.

TO MAKE UNIYAKI: Put the *uni* with the egg yolk and *sake* into a small mixing bowl. Sprinkle lightly with MSG.

Cut the second snapper fillet into 1-inch pieces and place them skin side down in a lightly oiled baking dish. Grill 3 inches from the heat for 2 to 3 minutes. Turn the fish over with chopsticks and grill another 2 minutes.

A treasure-ship fish, bearing *goma, uni* and *kimeyaki*—pieces of grilled fish (*above and following page*)—nestles on top of a branch of pine.

Brush the flesh side of the fish with the *uni* glaze and grill 1 minute, flesh side up. Brush again with the glaze, grill 1 minute, brush once more with the glaze and grill another minute. Remove and set aside.

TO MAKE KIMEYAKI: Sprinkle the prawns with salt and insert 2 skewers (4 to 6 inches long), about 1 inch apart, crosswise through the middle of each prawn. Grill for about 2 to 3 minutes on each side, until the prawns turn pink. Then brush the curved top of the prawns with egg yolk and grill another 2 minutes. Brush again with egg yolk; grill 2 minutes; brush once more with egg yolk and grill for a final 2 minutes. By this time the top of the prawns should have a rich golden glaze. Remove from the oven, remove the skewers, and set the prawns aside.

TO SERVE: Carefully slide the skewers out of the fish basket and cut away the strings. Fill the hollowed-out centre of the fish with a neatly cut paper doily, rice paper, or a bunch of parsley. Arrange the chunks of grilled fish decoratively in the basket, and serve hot or at room temperature.

KIMEYAKI (fish with egg-yolk glaze)
6 medium-sized raw prawns, shelled and de-veined but with tails left on (*see page 168*)
Salt
1 egg yolk

Yuan Zuke 柚庵漬
GRILLED MACKEREL IN SOYA AND RICE-WINE MARINADE

PREPARE IN ADVANCE: 1. For the marinade, put the *sake* and soya sauce into a medium-sized saucepan and bring to the boil over a moderate heat. Stir in the sugar and *dashi*, return to the boil, then cool to room temperature.

2. Add half the lemon slices and the fish to the marinade and turn them about to moisten them well. Marinate for 2 to 3 hours at room temperature, or in the refrigerator for 5 to 8 hours.

TO COOK: Preheat the grill or light a hibachi or charcoal grill. Remove the fish and lemon slices from the marinade. Discard the lemon and strain the marinade through a sieve into a small saucepan. Grill the fish flesh side first for about 6 to 8 minutes, until golden brown. Carefully turn the fish over with chopsticks, brush with the marinade, and grill for about 2 minutes, until the skin is a deep golden brown.

Meanwhile bring the marinade to simmering point on top of the stove.

TO SERVE: Divide the fish among 4 small serving dishes and moisten each with a teaspoon of the hot marinade. Garnish with fresh lemon slices.

Serve hot, as part of a Japanese meal (*page 198*) or as a first course.

To serve 4

1 lemon, sliced thinly
1 lb. mackerel fillet with skin left on, cut into 2- to 3-inch pieces

MARINADE
4 tablespoons *sake* (rice wine)
4 tablespoons Japanese soya sauce
¾ oz. sugar
¼ pint *niban dashi* (*page 54*)

Dengaku Tofu 田樂豆腐
GRILLED SOYA-BEAN CURD WITH MISO DRESSING

The appearance of skewered "tofu" decorated with white and/or green "miso" is a little like an iced lolly. There, of course, the resemblance ends, although "dengaku tofu" is eaten as a sweet course by the Japanese. The green-coloured "miso" is made, in Japan, with ground "sansho" leaves, which are not available here. Spinach makes an admirable substitute, with packaged "sansho" powder added for flavour.

PREPARE IN ADVANCE: 1. Preheat the grill to its highest point. Place the pieces of *tofu* side by side in a flameproof baking dish just large enough to hold them in one tightly packed layer. Add enough cold water to come half-way up the sides of the *tofu*, then slide the dish under the grill, as close to the heat as possible. Sear the *tofu* for a few seconds, then turn the pieces with a palette knife and sear the other side. The *tofu* will be speckled but

To serve 4

2 cakes fresh *tofu* (soya-bean curd), cut into 8 pieces each ¾ inch wide by 3 inches long
4 oz. fresh spinach leaves, stripped from their stems
4 oz. (6 tablespoons) *shiro miso* (white soya-bean paste)
Kona sansho (Japanese pepper)

Skewered *tofu*, spread with plain and spinach-flavoured soya-bean paste and speckled by grilling, are served as a sweet course.

not evenly browned. Remove the pan from the grill and set it aside.

Bring ¾ pint of water to the boil in a medium-sized saucepan. Add the spinach leaves and boil uncovered for about 2 minutes. Then drain in a sieve and run cold water over the spinach to cool it quickly and set its colour. Squeeze the spinach firmly to remove all its moisture and chop it finely.

Pound or mash the spinach to a paste in a *suribachi* (serrated mixing bowl) or with a pestle and mortar. Then rub it through a fine sieve into a mixing bowl with the back of a wooden spoon.

3. Stir half of the *shiro miso* and a few sprinklings of *kona sansho* into the spinach, continuing to stir until the *miso* paste has turned a delicate green.

4. Place the rest of the *shiro miso* in a small bowl and mix until smooth.

TO COOK AND SERVE: Bring the pan of seared *tofu* (with the water still in the pan) almost to the boil over a moderate heat. Remove from the heat and spoon the green *miso* dressing into a piping bag equipped with a ribbon pipe $\frac{1}{16}$ inch in diameter. Squeeze the *miso* along the top of 4 pieces of *tofu*, covering the top of each piece. (If you do not have a piping bag, spread a thin film of *miso* on each piece of *tofu* with a round-bladed knife, and run the prongs of a fork down the *miso* to create serrated lines.) Cover the remaining *tofu* with the plain *miso*.

Insert two 4- to 6-inch bamboo skewers or small lobster forks half-way through the length of each piece of *tofu*. Return the *tofu* to the water in the baking dish and sear under the grill for a few seconds. Serve at room temperature as the sweet course in a Japanese meal (*page 198*).

173

Two dishes ideal for a summer barbecue: thinly sliced beef *teriyaki* (*above*) and skewered chicken and spring onions.

Gyuniku Teriyaki　牛肉てり燒

GRILLED SLICED BEEF WITH SWEET SOYA-SEASONED GLAZE

Beef "teriyaki", like most of the "yaki" recipes, can be cooked not only under the grill of your own cooker but also on a hibachi or charcoal grill. The sauce may be made in large quantities, covered, refrigerated and kept for as long as a month.

PREPARE IN ADVANCE: 1. To make the sauce, warm the *mirin* or sherry in a medium-sized enamelled or stainless-steel saucepan over a moderate heat. Ignite the *mirin* with a match off the heat, and shake the pan backwards and forwards until the flame dies out. Then stir in the soya sauce and chicken stock, and bring to the boil. Pour the sauce into a bowl and cool to room temperature.

2. To make the glaze, mix 3 tablespoons of the *teriyaki* sauce and 2½ teaspoons of sugar in an enamelled or stainless-steel saucepan. Bring almost to the boil over a moderate heat, then reduce the heat to low. Stir the blended cornflour and water into the sauce. Cook until it thickens to a clear syrupy glaze, stirring constantly. Pour into a dish and set aside.

TO COOK: Preheat the grill to its highest point, or light a hibachi or charcoal grill. Dip the beef, one slice at a time, into the *teriyaki* sauce. Grill 2 inches from the heat for about 1 minute on each side, until lightly browned. For well done meat grill an additional minute.

TO SERVE: Slice the meat into 1-inch-wide strips and place them on individual serving plates. Spoon a little of the glaze over each serving, and garnish each plate with a dab of the mustard and a sprig of parsley. If you prefer, mix the mustard into the glaze before pouring it over the meat.

This will serve 6 as part of a Japanese meal (*page 198*) or 4 as a main course.

NOTE: Any left-over *teriyaki* sauce may be stored in tightly closed jars and refrigerated. Before using, bring to the boil and skim off any scum.

To serve 6

1½ lb. lean boneless beef, preferably fillet or rump, cut in 12 slices ¼ inch thick

TERIYAKI SAUCE

⅜ pint *mirin* (sweet *sake*), or substitute ⅜ pint less 5 teaspoons pale dry sherry

⅜ pint Japanese soya sauce

⅜ pint chicken stock

TERIYAKI GLAZE

3 tablespoons *teriyaki* sauce

2½ teaspoons castor sugar

1½ teaspoons cornflour mixed with 2½ teaspoons cold water

GARNISH

1 tablespoon powdered mustard, mixed with just enough hot water to make a thick paste and set aside to rest for 15 minutes

12 sprigs fresh parsley

Yakitori　燒鷄

GRILLED CHICKEN, SPRING ONIONS AND CHICKEN LIVERS

PREPARE IN ADVANCE: 1. Put the *sake*, soya sauce, sugar and sliced ginger into a mixing bowl and add the chicken livers. Turn them about in the marinade to moisten them well, and marinate at room temperature for at least 6 hours, or overnight in the refrigerator. Then remove the livers from the marinade and cut each one in half. Reserve the marinade.

2. String 4 halved chicken livers on each of 4 small skewers. Alternate 4 chunks of chicken with 3 strips of spring onion on 8 additional skewers.

TO COOK: Preheat the grill, or light a hibachi or charcoal grill. Grill the skewered livers about 3 inches from the heat for about 4 minutes. Then dip them in the *teriyaki* sauce and grill for 4 to 5 minutes on the other side. Set the livers aside on a plate.

Quickly dip the chicken and spring onion skewers into the *teriyaki* sauce and grill on one side for 2 or 3 minutes. Dip again into the sauce, grill for 2 minutes, dip once more, and grill on the other side for an additional 2 minutes. The entire grilling should take 6 to 7 minutes in all.

TO SERVE: Place 1 skewer of chicken livers and 2 skewers of chicken and spring onions on each serving plate. Sprinkle with a little *kona sansho*, and moisten each skewer with a teaspoon or so of the marinade.

To serve 4

2½ tablespoons *sake* (rice wine)

2½ teaspoons Japanese soya sauce

1½ teaspoons sugar

A 1-inch piece scraped fresh ginger root, cut into paper-thin slices

8 chicken livers, trimmed of all fat

2 whole chicken breasts or 4 legs, boned (*see pages 176-177*) and cut into 1-inch pieces

8 spring onions, including 3 inches of the green stalks, cut into 1- to 1½-inch-long pieces

⅝ pint *teriyaki* sauce (*above*)

Kona sansho (Japanese pepper)

175

Tori Teriyaki

鶏てり焼

GRILLED CHICKEN WITH SWEET SOYA-SEASONED GLAZE

To serve 6

6 whole chicken breasts or 12
    chicken legs
1¼ pints *teriyaki* sauce (*page 175*)
3 tablespoons *teriyaki* glaze (*page 175*)
1 tablespoon powdered mustard,
    mixed with just enough hot water
    to make a thick paste, and set
    aside to rest for 15 minutes
12 sprigs fresh parsley

PREPARE IN ADVANCE: Bone the chicken breasts in the following way: Hold the breast skin side down and bend it back until the spoon-shaped keel bone pops up. Pull it out and cut the breast apart with a heavy, sharp knife. One at a time, lay each breast, bone side up, on a chopping board, with the tapered end towards you. Slip the point of a sharp boning knife under the base of the slender single small rib bone attached to the rib cage. Press the flat of the knife up against the bone and cut the flesh away, freeing the bone. Hold the bone in one hand and pull it gently up towards you, meanwhile scraping away the flesh adhering to the adjacent ribs. Continue the scraping and cutting movement until the entire rib cage and adjacent small bones have been detached from the flesh. Pat the boned breast back into shape and repeat the entire process with the other breast. Leave the skin intact on both breasts.

To bone a chicken leg, start at the drumstick end and, using the bone as a guide, cut the meat away from the bone in large pieces. Trim the meat of all cartilage and gristle, but leave the skin intact.

TO COOK: Preheat the grill (or light a hibachi or charcoal grill). Dip the chicken breasts into the *teriyaki* sauce, coating them well, and grill skin side up 3 inches from the heat for about 2 to 3 minutes, until golden brown. Dip the breasts into the sauce again and grill on the other side for 2 to 3 minutes. Dip a third time into the sauce and grill—skin side up—another 3 to 4 minutes. The finished chicken should be a rich golden brown.

TO SERVE: Cut the chicken into 2- to 2½-inch pieces and arrange on individual serving plates. Pour the *teriyaki* glaze evenly over each portion and garnish the sides of the plates with a dab of mustard and a sprig of parsley.

Atsuyaki Tamago

厚燒玉子

BAKED FISH OMELETTE

To serve 8 to 10

2 oz. plaice, flounder or Torbay
    sole
9 eggs
1 oz. sugar
½ teaspoon salt
½ teaspoon MSG
Vegetable oil

PREPARE IN ADVANCE: Put the fish through the finest blade of a meat grinder or purée it in an electric blender. Scrape into a large mixing bowl and beat in the eggs 1 at a time using a whisk or a rotary egg beater. Then beat in the sugar, salt and MSG.

TO COOK: Preheat the oven to Mark 2: 300°F. Lightly oil the bottom and sides of a 2-inch-deep flameproof baking dish or a medium-sized frying pan with a pastry brush or kitchen paper. Heat the pan over a moderate heat until a drop of water flicked across its surface instantly evaporates. Pour in the egg and fish mixture and cook for about 3 minutes, until the bottom is lightly set. Then place the pan in the centre of the oven. Bake for 10 minutes, then turn the heat down to Mark ¼: 200°F. and bake for about 1 hour, until a toothpick inserted into the centre comes out dry and clean.

TO SERVE: Run a sharp knife around the sides of the omelette and place a flat serving dish upside down over the pan. Grasping pan and plate firmly together, quickly turn them over. Rap the plate on a table and the omelette should slide out easily.

Trim the ends of the omelette with a sharp knife and slice the omelette into 1-inch-wide strips. Cut the strips crosswise into ½-inch-wide pieces and serve at room temperature.

Shioyaki 鹽燒
SALT-GRILLED FISH WITH DIPPING SAUCE

"Shioyaki" is perhaps the simplest of Japanese recipes. Salting the fish before grilling causes the fat under the skin to break down, thus adding moisture to the flesh. Fish cooked in this fashion has such an intense natural flavour that many Japanese prefer to serve it without a dipping sauce.

PREPARE IN ADVANCE: 1. To prepare the small whole fish, dip the tail and fins into salt, then wrap them in small pieces of aluminium foil to prevent them from burning. Salt the exposed surface of the fish lightly and let them rest at room temperature for about 30 minutes.

Although the fish may be grilled as they are at once, you may skewer them in the Japanese manner. One at a time, insert the tip of a long skewer completely through the side of each fish at the point where the head meets the body, then force the skewer back through the centre of the body, and out through the base of the tail. The skewered fish will appear to be swimming after grilling.

2. To prepare fish fillets, simply salt them lightly on both sides and let them rest at room temperature for 2 hours.

3. To make the dipping sauce for the whole fish, put the *dashi*, vinegar, a pinch of salt, a sprinkling of MSG and the chopped parsley into a small bowl and mix thoroughly.

4. To prepare the garnish for the fish fillets, mix the grated *daikon*, parsley and soya sauce together in a small bowl.

TO COOK: Preheat the grill, hibachi or charcoal grill. Oil the grill lightly and cook the trout for 5 minutes on each side, turning them carefully with the aid of the skewers. The fish fillets should be grilled with the flesh side exposed to the heat for about 5 to 6 minutes, until a golden brown.

Remove the skewers from the trout and serve the whole fish accompanied by individual dishes of dipping sauce, or the fish fillets accompanied by their garnish.

To serve 4

4 fresh trout, 6 to 8 oz. each, cleaned and scaled but with head and tail left on, or 1 lb. fish fillets of any type with skin left on
Salt
Vegetable oil

DIPPING SAUCE FOR TROUT
2½ tablespoons *ichiban dashi* or *niban dashi* (*page 54*)
1 tablespoon rice vinegar, or substitute 1 tablespoon mild white vinegar
A pinch of salt
MSG
½ teaspoon finely chopped parsley

GARNISH FOR FISH FILLETS
1 oz. finely grated *daikon* (Japanese white radish), or substitute 1 oz. grated icicle radish or white turnip
⅛ teaspoon finely chopped fresh parsley
½ teaspoon Japanese soya sauce

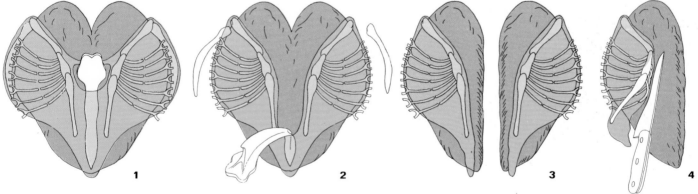

1   **2**   **3**   **4**

TO BONE A CHICKEN BREAST

Hold the breast skin side down and bend it back in half until it is flat (*1*) and the spoon-shaped keel bone in the centre pops up. Pull it out (*2*) and cut the breast apart (*3*). Slip the point of a sharp knife under the base of the slender rib bone (*4*) attached to the rib cage. Press the flat of the knife up against the bone and cut and gently pull the bone up towards you, meanwhile scraping away the flesh adhering to the adjacent ribs. Continue these scraping and cutting movements until the entire rib cage and adjacent bones have been detached from the flesh.

1   Pour a thin layer of egg into an oiled pan, top three-quarters of it with *nori* and cook until lightly set.

2   Using a pair of chopsticks, gently roll the layer of egg over into thirds, enclosing the *nori*.

To serve 1

Vegetable oil

3 eggs, well beaten (about ¼ pint)
    4 tablespoons *niban dashi* or *ichiban dashi* (*page 54*)

⅛ teaspoon salt

MSG

½ teaspoon *usukuchi shoyu* (light soya sauce), or substitute ¼ teaspoon Japanese soya sauce

GARNISH

1 tablespoon finely grated *daikon* (Japanese white radish), or substitute 1 tablespoon grated icicle radish or white turnip

¼ teaspoon Japanese soya sauce

MSG

A sprig of parsley

ISOBE TAMAGO YAKI

1 to 2 sheets *nori* (dried laver)

Tamago Dashimaki   玉子だし巻
FLAKY ROLLED OMELETTE

PREPARE IN ADVANCE: 1. Put the 3 well-beaten eggs with 4 tablespoons of *niban dashi*, ⅛ teaspoon of salt, a few sprinklings of MSG and ½ teaspoon of *usukuchi shoyu* into a mixing bowl.

2. Prepare the garnish in advance by mixing the 1 tablespoon of finely grated *daikon* with the ¼ teaspoon of soya sauce and a sprinkling of MSG. Shape the *daikon* into a ball with your fingers and set aside.

TO COOK: Lightly grease the bottom and sides of a rectangular Japanese *tamago* pan or a large, heavy frying pan, preferably with a non-stick surface, with a pastry brush dipped in oil. Heat the pan over a moderately high heat until a drop of water flicked across its surface evaporates instantly.

Pour in just enough of the egg mixture to coat the bottom of the pan lightly. Tip the pan backwards and forwards over the heat for about 10 seconds, until the eggs begin to set. Then, holding the pan about 2 inches above the heat, roll the omelette over into thirds or quarters, about 2 inches at a time, using chopsticks or a palette knife. Slide the completed omelette to the far end of the pan and lightly oil the pan again. Pour in a little more of the egg mixture, letting some of it run under the first completed egg roll. In another 8 or 10 seconds, you will be able to roll again, this time starting with the first egg roll. Roll it towards you, over the new layer of egg, and roll again, enclosing the new egg as you proceed. Repeat with the rest of the eggs, oiling the pan lightly after each roll is completed and enclosing the whole roll in each new layer.

Transfer the completed rolled omelette to a serving plate with a palette knife and cut it in half crosswise, or in thirds, if it was made in a frying pan. Garnish the omelette with a sprig of fresh parsley and a small ball of the soya-flavoured *daikon*.

TO MAKE ISOBE TAMAGO YAKI, a variation of *tamago dashimaki*: Pass one side of a sheet of *nori* over a flame to intensify its colour and flavour. Cut the *nori* into thirds. Proceed with the omelette as above, but just before rolling up each layer, cover the layer first with a strip of *nori* and then roll them up together. The cut finished omelette will have bands of the greenish-black *nori* between the egg layers.

Serve *tamago dashimaki* for breakfast or with soup as the main course of a light lunch or supper.

178

3 Slide the rolled omelette to the near side of the pan and, with kitchen paper or a pastry brush, lightly re-oil the pan.

4 Slide omelette back to far side, pour in more egg, and lift the first omelette to let the new layer of egg run under it.

5 Top again with *nori* and, starting with the first omelette, roll in thirds. Repeat with remaining egg and nori.

The light, fluffy omelette, halved to reveal its many layers of *nori* and egg, is garnished with grated white radish and served for breakfast or lunch.

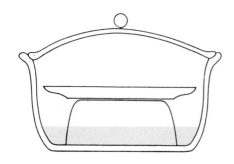

"Mushimono" are steamed foods. They range from such simple combinations as chicken and prawns steamed in egg custard (Recipe Booklet) to the elaborately constructed treasure-ship pumpkin described below.

Oriental steamers can be found in some of the shops listed on page 207, but if you do not have one, a substitute is easily improvised. Pour enough water into a large, heavy pan to come 1½ inches up the sides. Put a heatproof bowl upside down inside and put a plateful of the food to be steamed on top. Bring the water to the boil, cover the pan tightly, and steam the food for the time specified in the recipe.

To serve 8 to 10

1 pumpkin (about 6 lb.)

1 teaspoon *ajishio* (equal parts salt and MSG)

4 medium-sized *shiitake* (dried Japanese mushrooms)

2½ oz. sugar

2½ teaspoons Japanese soya sauce

¾ pint *niban dashi* (*page 54*)

3 tablespoons *sake* (rice wine)

¾ teaspoon *usukuchi shoya*, or substitute ½ teaspoon Japanese soya sauce

18 small prawns in their shells (26 to 30 to a lb.)

Salt

16 to 20 mange-tout, or substitute 16 to 20 French beans

2½ teaspoons *mirin* (sweet *sake*), or substitute 1½ teaspoons pale dry sherry

30 canned *ginnan* (ginkgo nuts)

Takara Mushi   宝蒸

TREASURE-SHIP PUMPKIN WITH PRAWNS, MUSHROOMS, VEGETABLES

PREPARE AHEAD: 1. Scrub the pumpkin vigorously under cold running water with a stiff brush. Cut off the top of the pumpkin with a large, sharp knife to make a lid, leaving the stalk intact as a handle. Remove the lid and scrape the seeds and stringy fibres from the lid and pumpkin shell with a large metal spoon. Scoop out small balls of pumpkin meat, with a melon-ball cutter or small spoon, but leave a ¾- to 1-inch-thick wall of the flesh intact in the shell. Set the pumpkin balls aside.

Sprinkle the flesh side of the lid and the inside walls of the pumpkin evenly with *ajishio*.

To give the pumpkin a preliminary steaming place it and its lid in a colander with small supports, and set the colander in a deep pan large enough to enclose it completely. Pour enough water into the pan to come within 1½ inches of the bottom of the colander, and bring the water to the boil over a high heat. Then cover the pan tightly, and steam the pumpkin for 10 minutes. Remove the colander and pumpkin from the pan and set them aside.

2. Place the *shiitake* in a small saucepan and soak in ⅜ pint of cold water for about 1 hour. Bring to the boil, then simmer uncovered for 15 minutes. Cool to room temperature, strain the liquid into a bowl and set it aside. Remove and discard the hard stalks; cut the mushrooms into 16 or 20 half-inch pieces.

Put 6 tablespoons of the mushroom liquid with ½ oz. of sugar and 2½ teaspoons of soya sauce into a saucepan. Bring to the boil over a high heat, add the mushrooms and, stirring frequently, cook briskly, uncovered, for about 10 to 20 minutes, until all of the liquid has evaporated. Set aside.

3. Put ⅜ pint of the *niban dashi*, 1 oz. of the sugar, ½ teaspoon salt and the pumpkin balls into a medium-sized saucepan. Bring to the boil, stir in 2½ teaspoons of *sake* and sprinkle lightly with MSG. Boil uncovered for 5 minutes, then remove the pumpkin balls with a perforated spoon.

Reduce the liquid in the pan by boiling it over a high heat until it becomes a thick syrup. Watch for any sign of burning and regulate the heat accordingly. Then stir in ¾ teaspoon of *usukuchi shoyu*, remove from the heat, and stir in the pumpkin balls.

4. Bring ¾ pint of salted water to the boil in a medium-sized saucepan, drop in the prawns and boil for 3 to 4 minutes. Drain in a colander and run cold water over the prawns to stop them from cooking. Peel the prawns and make a shallow incision along their backs with a small, sharp knife. Remove the intestinal vein with the tip of the knife. Cut the prawns in half crosswise.

A colourful treasure-ship pumpkin, hollowed out and filled with delicately flavoured prawns, pumpkin balls, mushrooms, mange-tout and ginkgo nuts, is often the highlight of a Japanese banquet. It would be just as dramatic at a Western buffet.

Put 6 tablespoons *niban dashi*, 5 teaspoons *sake*, 1 oz. sugar and $\frac{1}{2}$ teaspoon salt into a medium-sized saucepan and sprinkle lightly with MSG. Bring to the boil and reduce to about half the volume. Remove from the heat. Add the prawns, stir to moisten them thoroughly and set the pan aside.

5. Bring $\frac{3}{8}$ pint of salted water to the boil in a small saucepan. Drop in the mange-tout (or French beans), return to the boil, then drain in a sieve. Run cold water over the peas (or beans) to cool them quickly and set their colour.

Mix 6 tablespoons *niban dashi*, $2\frac{1}{2}$ teaspoons *sake*, $\frac{1}{8}$ teaspoon salt and a sprinkling of MSG in the saucepan and bring to the boil. Drop in the flavoured mange-tout (or beans), return to the boil, then remove from the heat. Cool by putting the pan in a large bowl of cold water.

6. Put $2\frac{1}{2}$ teaspoons of *mirin*, $\frac{1}{8}$ teaspoon of salt, a sprinkling of MSG and the ginkgo nuts into the small pan. Cook over a high heat for 1 to 2 minutes, shaking the pan almost constantly until all the liquid evaporates. Remove from the heat.

TO ASSEMBLE AND STEAM: Cut a thin slice from the base of the pumpkin with a large knife, to prevent it from rocking. Place the mushrooms, pumpkin balls, prawns, mange-tout and ginkgo nuts in the pumpkin, cover with the pumpkin lid, and carefully transfer it to the colander. Return the colander to its pan, add enough water to come within $1\frac{1}{2}$ inches of the bottom of the colander, and bring the water to the boil. Cover the pan tightly and steam 5 minutes, then serve at once.

181

VIII

Magnificent Meals in Elegant Settings

This elegant seven-course meal, served at the celebrated Doi Inn in Kyoto, shows the beauty of the dishes in Japanese cuisine. For example, a low wooden box on a black lacquer tray holds prawn *tempura* (*centre*). Next to it, a red tray holds a small metal-lined hibachi, with two kinds of trout grilling on it.

I remember with pleasure an afternoon in early autumn some years ago when I had lunch at the famous Kitcho restaurant in Kyoto. The lovely garden outside our private dining room and the gently rolling, wooded hills in the distance combined to form a breath-takingly beautiful picture. Noticing my preoccupation with the view, my Japanese host leaned over and asked, "What in particular in that scene attracts your attention?" I nodded towards the hills where the leaves on a few maple trees on the highest ground were beginning to change colour. "I'm fascinated", I said, "with the contrast those small patches of yellow and red provide to all the soft green in the foreground."

My host smiled approvingly, like an art teacher who has received a perceptive answer from a student. "Now", he said, "look at the plate in front of you." I glanced down and was astonished to see an asymmetrically shaped, pearl-grey dish decorated with skilfully painted maple leaves ranging in colour from lush green to pale yellow and then to vivid red.

"This could hardly be a coincidence", I said.

My host shook his head. "Someone once described an artist as a man with an infinite capacity for detail", he said. "I think you will find that the description also fits the owners of the best restaurants in Japan."

I agree whole-heartedly with this observation. In no other nation in the world do the great restaurants make a comparable effort to provide the patron with a rewarding aesthetic experience as well as an excellent meal. The dish that duplicated the autumn scene was an instance of this concern; and matching sets of china, like those prized and used throughout the year in the West, strike the Japanese as the height of monotony. "It is as though you had a wardrobe filled with clothes, all of them of the same material, cut and shade", a Japanese friend once said to me. "Can you imagine yourself wearing the same colour and texture all the year round, and having exactly the same style of dress for a walk in the country and a dinner dance?"

To provide the proper setting for the variety of foods served—in a good establishment ten courses are usually served, but there can be as many as 18 —the best Japanese restaurants have dishes that span the colour spectrum, vary enormously in shape and size, and range in materials from coarse pottery to stoneware to fragile porcelain, basketry, bamboo and lacquered wood.

All these dishes are carefully packed away in boxes after each use, labelled to indicate the season and food for which their contents are appropriate. To equip a restaurant with such tableware obviously requires a substantial investment. In fact, the dishes are sometimes worth more than the combined value of the building and the land on which it stands. "All of us haunt antique shops in search of replacements for the dishes that are inevitably broken and can't be replaced because the artist is dead", one Japanese restaurateur said. "This, of course, is in addition to the commissioning of new work by the finest living artists."

The meticulous choice of tableware is only one of the subtle ways in which an outstanding Japanese restaurant seeks to make dining a pleasant experience for the eye and spirit as well as for the palate. Time favours the very best Japanese restaurants in the achievement of their goals. You simply do not make a spur-of-the-moment decision to have lunch or dinner at such a place; usually a reservation must be made several days in advance. Even then a stranger would probably not have his reservation accepted—though, of course, the refusal will be phrased so politely that the snub will not be immediately apparent. In effect, the first-class restaurants are operated much like private clubs and are supported by a devoted and regular clientele. The club-like atmosphere is heightened by the absence of a bill at the end of the meal; monthly accounts are sent to the customer. A newcomer seeking admission to these temples of eating must be vouched for by a client of long standing whose manners are known to be beyond reproach. But whether the party is to be made up of habitués, novices or a mixture of the two, the restaurant insists on having ample time to create a proper setting and atmosphere and to prepare the many dishes that are to be served; the menu will either be agreed upon in advance or, more often, left to the discretion of the manager. A dinner at an excellent restaurant, like the Hannya-en in Tokyo, will prove that the time required to enjoy the meal has been well spent.

Although the Hannya-en is only a 10- or 15-minute taxi ride from the city's business district, the quiet, dimly lit street in which its classic, 19th-century building stands seems wholly divorced from the frantic hubbub of central Tokyo. When guests enter the Hannya-en, they are greeted at the gate by several of the serving girls, all dressed in handsome kimonos of colours suited to the season. The patrons remove their shoes inside the door, are given felt slippers to wear, and then are led through a series of corridors to their private dining room. This, incidentally, is one of the principal ways in which the great Japanese restaurants differ from their western counterparts; each group of guests have their own room, even if there are only two in the party.

Once in the dining room, the eye is struck by a lovely garden, so skilfully landscaped that it seems like a happy accident of nature. All the rooms at the Hannya-en look out on this garden with its ancient pine trees, beautiful shrubs and flowers, winding streams and great, fantastically shaped rocks. But the garden has been so designed that each room enjoys an unobstructed and seemingly private view of a particular area. If the weather is chill, the view is seen through floor-to-ceiling glass doors, but if the temperature is mild, the doors will be open and the guest is free to wander outside before the meal is served. At night, when the garden is softly lit by the traditional Japanese stone lanterns, it takes on an oddly dream-like quality, like a stage setting for an ancient oriental legend.

The room itself is simply but richly furnished. A low lacquered table about 18 inches high is in the centre. This is flanked by floor-level cushioned chairs, each with its own armrest to lean against. Inset in one wall is a *tokonoma*, the ever-present alcove in which is hung an elegant picture scroll, and beneath it, a delicately executed flower arrangement that complements the painting. The entire setting creates a mood of timeless tranquillity.

Once the guests are seated, serving girls enter with baskets of *oshibori*—steaming face towels, frequently scented with cologne. After everyone wipes his hands and face, the towels are returned to the basket and removed by the girls. When they return, each bears a tray holding small dishes for soya sauce, chopsticks and a small earthenware bar on which to rest the chopsticks between courses. There is a rare kind of grace in the way in which one of these well-trained girls serves the guests. Supporting a lacquered tray with the palms of her hands, she advances to within three feet of the table, kneels and places the tray gently with both hands on the mat-covered floor, lets her hands rest momentarily on her knees, and bows to the guests. Somehow the effect is one of unbroken movement. Incidentally, the girls will be with the guests through most of the meal, leaving only to return dishes to the kitchen after a course is finished and then to bring in the next course. If encouraged by the customers, they will join in the conversation and, since the party probably will be comprised exclusively of men, even flirt a little. Except for a few fortunate western women who, under suitable auspices, have had the pleasure of dining in this grand style, the patronage of the great, expensive restaurants in Japan is as exclusively male as that of the clubs of St. James's.

To see what is included in a fairly typical dinner at the Hannya-en, I would like you to join me as I recall the delights of a meal I had there with some Japanese friends. The first course was *sakizuke*, appetizers consisting of cashew nuts, an arrow-root cracker, a dried fish called *kisu*, fried sea tangle and crunchy ginkgo nuts carved in the form of a hexahedron. An hors d'œuvre followed. Each guest was served a hard-boiled quail egg rolled in bacon, a chicken ball, a cod-roe canapé, a raw oyster and salmon eggs nesting in a piece of melon carved into the shape of a ship.

Then in a black and gold lacquer bowl came a clear soup with a slice of carrot, cut in the shape of a maple leaf. A spectacularly served *sashimi*,

Continued on page 193

185

The working day at the
Kitcho ("Good Omen")
restaurant in Kyoto begins
(*above*) with a top-level
conference about menus.
Gathered round the low
table, the master chef Koji
Yuki, in white, his wife
Junko (*left*) and Sosei
Takahara (*right*), the Kitcho's
tea-ceremony expert, listen
as bespectacled Teiichi Yuki
asks their opinions before
making a decision.

Hospitality as a Fine Art

Patrons of Japan's finest restaurants expect—and receive—much more than the mere
gratification of their appetite. Starting with the selection of raw ingredients, the
proprietors meticulously supervise every detail in order to satisfy all five senses
of the diner and above all to create an atmosphere of tranquillity. Thus the appeal
to the customer's eye extends beyond the room by providing him with a view of a
garden and of part of the natural landscape. In their effort to avoid any jarring
note that might disrupt this peaceful ambiance, the great restaurants train their
staffs in the skills of preparing and serving foods that are both beautiful and good,
over and beyond this the employees are schooled in comporting themselves with
charm and grace. The décor, the table service, the aesthetics of food preparation
and the serving rituals are based largely on the rules laid down in the 16th century
for the tea ceremony. Shown here and on the following pages are a few behind-
the-scenes glimpses of the work that precedes the serving of meals at the Kitcho,
a famous Kyoto restaurant, considered to be one of the best in Japan.

Flower arrangement is a highly regarded art in Japan, and the Kitcho calls upon the services of an expert, Sosei Takahara (*above right*), to decorate the *tokonoma* in one of the dining rooms. Mrs. Takahara, the wife of an Osaka tea-ceremony master, also gives the staff a weekly lesson in tea-ceremony ritual (*right*). As the tea-kettle in front of her steams, she demonstrates the proper handling of the napkin used to wipe the tea utensils, while apprentice chefs in white jackets and kimonoed serving maids look on. The apprentice farthest to the right is the first Japanese woman to be accepted for training as a master chef.

Two serving maids kneel in attendance as visiting American patrons begin the second course of a New Year's luncheon at the Kitcho. Even though they are at the moment intent on their bowls of clear soup, the diners are always aware of the garden outside and of the rustic ceiling inside. The preceding course consisted of sliced abalone, the next one will be *sashimi* and the fourth a dish of assorted foods, each of which has a symbolic connection with the New Year. As arranged on the plate on the left, they are (*counter-clock-wise from the bottom*): egg patties; bean-curd patties; *chisha*, a Japanese vegetable; bamboo shoots; black beans on pine-needle skewers; salmon eggs in kumquat shells; boiled prawns; and raw fish wrapped in seaweed.

The chef-patron Koji Yuki (*opposite*) drops in to wish his guests a prosperous year to come. The festive baskets on the table contain various titbits from the New Year's dish on the left.

188

190

A diner at the Doi, a
fashionable Kyoto inn,
takes his eyes from the
entertainment long enough
to refill his *sake* cup, a
gesture that ordinarily
would be performed by one
of the dancing geisha. The
two girls who strike the
stylized traditional poses are
maiko, or apprentice geisha,
who dance to the music
provided by the samisen
player in the corner. At the
Doi, well-known for its food
and comfortable lodgings,
geisha entertainment is not
a regular feature. But like
all good restaurants and inns,
the Doi will bring in the girls
at the request of patrons.
When they have finished
dancing, the geisha return
to converse, play table
games, pour drinks and light
cigarettes for the guests.

191

This geisha displays the proper blend of docility and reserve as she presents a light to a diner in a Tokyo restaurant.

succulent slices of raw fish, was next. In the setting of a miniature seashore —small potatoes entirely covered with seaweed serving as black rocks, polished white rice grains suggesting sand and pebbles adding an authentic touch—the chef had placed slices of raw tunny fish, sea bream, young yellowtail and shell-fish. The fifth course, served in a shallow red lacquer bowl with a cover, was *tempura* that included prawns, eel, *kisu* (an Asiatic fish), asparagus and ginkgo nuts.

A beef dish with noodles, onions, grilled bean curd, Chinese cabbage, bamboo shoots and an egg served with a Japanese green pepper was the next offering brought in by the serving girls. Then came a lighter dish—a delicious salad of crab meat and fresh vegetables. *Chawan mushi*, a hot egg custard made of eggs, chicken, lily bulbs, boiled fish paste, ginkgo nuts and trefoil greens, followed the salad. The ninth course was fruit: melon, a peeled and sliced orange, and flawless, superbly succulent strawberries.

The tenth and last course consisted of two kinds of tea, a powdered, opaque variety that is served with a bean cake with a chestnut centre, and a clear tea. Although such a meal seems gargantuan in the retelling, it doesn't require a ploughboy's appetite. The portions are small and the food is eaten at a leisurely pace. My own experience is that I usually feel pleasantly satisfied but not over-fed after such a banquet. The price of a dinner like this at Hannya-en or any of the other leading restaurants was about £19 a head, not including drinks.

Sake, the rice wine, which is generally served warm, is more or less the national drink, and a fine dinner is incomplete without repeated rounds of this beverage. Since it has an alcoholic content of about 15 per cent, making it slightly stronger than European table wines, the atmosphere around the table can become extremely jovial by the time the last morsel of food has been eaten—especially since the diners often alternate tall glasses of the excellent Japanese beer with the tiny cups of *sake*.

The visitor who wishes to sample Japanese cuisine at its highest level can do so in the course of a dinner at one of the great restaurants and then return to his Western-style hotel to sleep and—perchance—to dream of exquisite dishes in endless profusion. But if he wishes to have a truly Japanese experience, I heartily recommend a stay at one of the superb Japanese inns whose reputation for an all enveloping hospitality equals the excellence of its table. There are only a limited number of hostelries that can meet both of these requirements: the Doi in Kyoto, one of this select group, was where an American couple I know recently spent a few days.

"When my wife and I arrived at the Doi", the husband told me, "we were met at the door by Kakuko Yamada, one of the inn's five serving maids. Following instructions, we removed our shoes and replaced them with slippers set out on the floor. This pleasant custom, we learned, serves the hygienic purpose of leaving all street-soiled footwear outside, and also protects the delicate *tatami* matting inside the inn from damage caused by sharp-edged heels. Then Kakuko led us into a kind of drawing room and served us clear tea. After we had drunk this ceremonial refreshment, which is a traditional indication of the visitor's intention to stay, she led us to our second floor room whose large windows offered a fine view of the Doi's serenely classical inner garden on one side, and the briskly modern Kyoto skyline on the other. Like all traditional Japanese rooms, this one served both as a living room and as a bedroom. Its furnishings were sparse—a lacquered table about two feet high in the centre of the room, four cushioned chairs without legs, and a *tokonoma*, with its elegant yet simple adornments. At night, as we discovered later, Kakuko would push the table and low chairs to one side and in their place set up beds.

"Kakuko then made us sit at the table and served us with a powdered green tea. As we drank it, she kneeled next to the table, a Japanese-English dictionary by her side, and asked us about our travels, our family and other matters. Soon, of course, we were asking her questions about herself. She was never intrusive, merely friendly and eager for us to enjoy ourselves. At about five in the afternoon Kakuko announced it was time for our baths."

The first stop in a Japanese bathroom is the dressing room, decorated with a Japanese print and a flower arrangement, and furnished with brushes, combs and cosmetics. Sliding doors open on to the bath itself, a steamy room of about seven by twelve feet built entirely of carefully joined cypress planks. This aromatic wood adds its fragrance to the vapours rising from the hot water and gives the room a wondrous aroma of the forest. The sunken tub is about seven feet long, four feet wide and four feet deep—ample for two. But before getting in, the bather observes a very sensible Japanese custom: he washes himself with soap and hot water and then rinses himself until no soap suds remain to defile the clean water of the bath.

To western skins, the temperature of the water seems better suited for boiling lobsters than for bathing. Surprisingly, the body does make an adjustment after a few moments. At one end of the pool there is a small bench raised a few inches from the bottom. Seated on this slat, with only his neck and head above the surface of the water, the bather soaks luxuriously, feeling the tensions of the day melting away in the heat of the water. When he emerges, he gets into the Japanese clothes provided by the inn.

When my friends arrived in their room, Kakuko again made them sit at the table and took their orders for drinks. This was the only ordering done; the meal had been arranged beforehand. In a few moments she was back with glasses, bottles and an ice bucket. The bar and kitchen were on the first floor, which meant that she made about a dozen trips on the stairs just to serve that one meal. Yet despite all the climbing and kneeling, she continued to look as fresh as she had when she first appeared.

The dinner began with boiled prawn on a slice of lemon, accompanied by a cube of *daikon* that had been hollowed out and filled with bean paste. Raw sea bream and crisp celery followed, served in exquisite blue-and-white Ming bowls. A clear fish soup with half a mushroom and strips of bright-green spinach stems floating on the surface was the next dish offered by Kakuko. After another trip to the kitchen, she returned with mushrooms covered with egg and a small button-like morsel of fish paste. A delicious *tempura* was next. Now Kakuko brought in two charcoal braziers on which she grilled sliced mushrooms and fish coated with the white of an egg. Also served with this course were pieces of roast quail. Next, Kakuko brought on a pungent soya-bean soup called *akadashi*. Pickled vegetables—aubergine, cucumber and radish leaf—served with fluffy white rice were next. Then came fresh fruit and, finally, tea.

"It was a magnificent dinner", the husband said later, "but the atmosphere contributed enormously to our enjoyment of it. The lights in the garden projecting shadows of maple leaves on the window, the simple elegance of the room, the graceful service, the moments of absolute silence when even the distant voices faded away—together they induced the great sense of intimacy which is an essential part of a fine meal in Japan."

The artistic serving of excellently prepared food in a gracious atmosphere is, as we have seen, a serious art in Japan's outstanding restaurants. Like all great art, the finished product rarely betrays the effort that went into its making. We can get some idea of the care required to produce the best Japanese food by following the manager of one of these establishments as he selects the raw materials for his chef's masterpieces.

Shortly after 5 a.m. on most days, Koji Yuki, master of the Kitcho in Kyoto—there are also Kitcho restaurants in Tokyo and Osaka—is in his estate car rolling down the Kyoto-Osaka motorway *en route* for the market. Koji has two major reasons for making these trips: to confer with his father-in-law, Teiichi Yuki, who owns and retains overall supervision of the Kitcho restaurants, and to get fish for the Kyoto branch. All the fish for the three branches come from the small fishing village of Akashi, some 30 miles down the coast from Osaka. By 4 a.m., the previous day's catch is delivered to Kitcho's headquarters in Osaka; the fish destined for Tokyo has already gone off by air by the time Yuki has reached Osaka to pick up the portion ear-marked for him. Although Japan teems with excellent fish markets, the Kitcho restaurants cling to this expensive system to be certain that they are serving the best and the freshest fish available.

The same care is shown in the buying of vegetables. For instance, on many mornings Yuki loads his car with locally produced vegetables before leaving for Osaka. "Some of the vegetables are better in Kyoto than anywhere else", he explains, "particularly bamboo shoots and mushrooms." But no matter where the best vegetables are grown, the owners of Japan's best restaurants, or their representatives, will be there as buyers.

Fruit is especially cultivated and packed for these restaurants. As growing peaches, grapes and pears ripen, they are tied in little paper bags to protect their skins from birds and bees. When the fruit is picked, each piece or bunch is cradled in white cotton-wool and carefully placed in small wooden boxes only one layer deep to avoid bruises or gashes during shipment.

The master chefs who perpetuate their restaurants' fame usually serve a ten-year apprenticeship before they are accorded this honoured title. Serving maids, too, must serve an apprenticeship, although the period is much shorter than for chefs. Anyone who has ever observed the ballerina-like movements of these girls knows that the training is effective.

All the chefs, serving maids and apprentices at Kitcho's in Kyoto live in quarters provided by the management, and when the work is finished at night, they gather with Koji and his wife, Junko, to watch television. Every staff member takes an interest in all aspects of Kitcho's operation, from the menus to the flower arrangements. This clannishness is a hang-over from the long Japanese feudal tradition, but the Kitcho is not entirely bound by the past. One of the apprentice chefs is a girl in her twenties, the first of her sex to wield a knife in any of the Kitcho kitchens.

195

Kitcho's staff does not include geisha but, like most of the great restaurants in Japan, Kitcho is happy to bring in geisha at the request of a patron. The geisha acts as both entertainer and companion. She may dance, sing, play musical instruments, recite poetry or draw pictures for the guests, talk with them or listen sympathetically to their troubles, light their cigarettes, pour their drinks and, if invited, drink with them. But casual amorous advances are against the rules.

Although the average age of the geisha is about 27, neither youth nor beauty is necessary for the profession. One popular geisha is in her eighties. "Sometimes our clients ask for her specifically", I was told by a Tokyo restaurant owner. "She treats them like sons, and if they want to reminisce about the good old days, she can tell them about the romantic scandals involving the political figures of the pre-war period."

At one time, girls were apprenticed to the profession when they were six; now the law requires that they attend secondary school, so that the average starting age is 16. The apprentice, called a *maiko*, is supposed to be a virgin, and she wears a kimono with an extra fold over each shoulder to denote her maidenhood. As a fully-fledged geisha, she will probably acquire a rich patron who will take over responsibility for her debts to the *okiya*, the training school for geisha, and help to pay for her expensive wardrobe.

The training period usually lasts for several years and emphasizes the development of poise, charm and wit. During this time, the apprentice also studies flower arrangement and the tea ceremony, learns to perform the classical geisha dances and becomes proficient in playing various instruments. She must also master the elegant and circuitous vocabulary used in *karyukai*, "the world of flowers and willows", of which she will be a part. When customers relax with a geisha in the evening, they enjoy the brilliant word play implicit in the poetic, evocative Japanese language. In the otherworldly atmosphere of a great restaurant or geisha house, *shoyu*, for instance, is far too blunt a word for soya sauce. One should ask for *murasaki*, "the purple". Even salt has a lyrical name: *nami no hana*, which means "crest of the wave".

After completing her training, much of the geisha's work will be done in geisha houses. Since his firm will pay all his expenses, the businessman has no objection to the geisha's fee of about £1. 7s. 6d. per hour—the current rate in most big cities. She receives the entire amount; the house makes its money on the sale of food and drinks. But though geisha houses serve food, most of them bring it in from near-by restaurants where standards are usually not as high as those of the really good restaurants.

The ideal arrangement, therefore, is to have dinner at an outstanding restaurant like the Kitcho and enjoy the company of geisha there. I must quickly acknowledge that if you are a Western woman a good deal of what you will learn about geisha parties must be learnt from Japanese and Western men friends. While women have indeed attended such affairs, it is quite evident that their presence has an inhibiting effect on the festivities.

Geisha parties will often start at a geisha house where the men may stay for a short time and have a few drinks and some light-hearted conversation with the girls before they go on to a restaurant or a night-club. But if the party begins at a great restaurant, it will probably end there.

196

Once in the private room which has been reserved by the host, the guests relax with *sake* and beer, take off their jackets and loosen their ties; some of them may shed all their Western clothing and get into a comfortable kimono. The geisha, resplendent in their gorgeous finery—a single kimono can cost as much as £5,000—welcome the guests with smiles and bows and small talk.

Now the wonderful Kitcho food is brought in, course after exquisite course, and the party grows noisier as the *sake* cups are refilled with graceful gestures by geisha whose trained eyes immediately spot any empty cups. Faces grow flushed, and jokes, puns, snatches of poetry are flung to and fro across the long low table. By this time the geisha, too, glow as the warm *sake* they have been offered makes itself felt. The jokes become more elliptically suggestive. The food disappears and more is brought in. When the Western guest protests that he can no longer keep up with his Japanese friends and their nearly continuous cries of "kampai!"—bottoms up—his half-serious complaint produces boisterous laughter and a challenge by one of the geisha to try his hand at a game. A tiny *sake* cup is placed before him and the girl fills it half-way to the brim. Tilting a *sake* flask, the Westerner adds a little wine to the cup. Then the geisha does the same. After a few turns, the cup is full, then brimming, and then the convex surface of the wine trembles slightly as, drop by drop, the players strive to avoid adding the fatal dash that will make the bulging cup overflow. For the loser will have to drink a tall cup of *sake* with everyone at the table, guests and geisha alike. With a roar of delight the company watches the geisha's last move create a small cascade on the table. She bows to the foreign guest, compliments him on his steady hand, and with wonderful aplomb exchanges drinks with each member of the happy group.

As the meal reaches its end, an older woman comes in carrying a samisen, a lute-like instrument, bows and seats herself at one side of the room. The other geisha have gathered at the end of the room and stand in picture-book postures. The music begins and the girls dance, a highly formal set of graceful movements recapitulating a thousand years of tradition. When the dance is over, the guests applaud vigorously, and the geisha perform another stylized dance. Again they acknowledge the compliments, and after one more dance they return to the table and rejoin the guests.

More toasts are proposed, and other games are played. Some of them are ingenious puzzles like the one in which match-sticks are rearranged into prescribed patterns by adding or moving a limited number of sticks. Others involve great delicacy of touch in manipulating carefully erected but teetering structures made of cigarettes without destroying the entire creation. Always there is good-humoured laughter when one of the players loses, and loud praise when he wins. Finally it is time to go. The men get back into their dark suits, and the American or European visitor is astounded by the swift transformation of his recently dishevelled dinner companions into sedate Japanese businessmen, clothed in the respectability demanded by the world outside. Thinking about the party back in the quiet of his hotel room, he realizes that he has once again been made aware of the Japanese gift for living—their talent for harmonizing everything that contributed to each aspect of the atmosphere of the occasion.

How to Use Japanese Recipes

One day a famous Kyoto chef visited a Zen monk.

"Tell me in a few words", the monk said, "the reasoning behind your cuisine."

"To reflect nature precisely."

The monk was silent. "Is it only nature you reflect", he corrected gently, "or is it your awareness of nature? When you slice a radish, shouldn't you be aware of where it grew, of the rain that fell on it, of the farmer whose toil produced it?"

This tale—true, not apocryphal—sums up the reason why Japanese cuisine is so satisfying on so many levels. As you begin to introduce Japanese dishes into your menus, you will find yourself shopping with an increasing awareness of the foods that nature provides to celebrate the seasons of the year; even in this age when most foods are available either frozen or canned all the year round you can find ways to bring the seasons to your table. Handling your ingredients in the kitchen, you will be more conscious of their shape, texture and colour, since the Japanese believe—and who would contradict them?—that food should look as good as it tastes. The Japanese cuisine is a challenge to all the senses.

It is, however, far from an overwhelming challenge. Anyone starting on Japanese cuisine for the first time will find that there is a wonderful clarity to almost every dish. Though some ingredients may seem unfamiliar, they are obtainable from oriental food stores (*page 207*), and all except a few fresh vegetables can be stored almost indefinitely. If an ingredient proves to be totally unavailable in your area, you can often use a substitute. Even if the recipe calls for an item as commonly used as spinach, you can substitute watercress, for example, and a new taste will have been added by your own ingenuity.

For obvious reasons, most foreigners would not even want to try to reproduce the atmosphere of a Japanese room, with its *tatami* mats, sliding wood panels, and scroll hanging in the *tokonoma*. But there is no reason why you should not try, if you wish, to serve your foods on different plates, bowls and saucers. Even small, decorative ashtrays can be used to serve dipping sauces or garnishes. As the photographs in this book show, the Japanese aim at a direct yet delicate balance of colour and form.

Basic Rules of Meal Planning

The Japanese do not divide their meals as we do into one main course preceded by soup and accompanied by a salad and vegetables. The order of the Japanese formal meal often puts soup near the end, and usually includes both fish and meat, or several kinds of fish and a number of vegetables treated in different ways. In this sense, the Japanese meal is like that of the Chinese, which it consciously imitated many centuries ago.

We are likely to think of such menus as "a large number of small dishes". So at first it may be wise to plan your Japanese meal much as you would a European one, by selecting a main dish and building up around it. Most of the lunches and dinners listed on this page have, in fact, been planned around one main course. While it will be understandably tempting to decide on one of the more familiar *teriyaki*, *tempura* or *sukiyaki* dishes for the

main course, you should not overlook the less familiar *nabemono* (one-pot) dishes, which are delicious and relatively simple to make.

A word here about salads and sweet dishes. The Japanese do not eat salads in our sense of raw salad greens tossed with a dressing. The *aemono* and *sunomono* dishes (*Recipe Index*) are roughly the equivalent of salad, and several of them appear in these sample menus. They may be served as you would serve a salad, or they could serve as a vegetable course or even as a first course.

There is no sweet-dish section in this book, since the Japanese normally end their meals with fresh fruit. A sliced orange or pineapple, mandarin oranges or strawberries will make a fitting close to any of the menus presented on this page.

Experimenting with Japanese Food

Since an all-Japanese meal requires a careful balance of foods, it might be a good idea to use the recipes in this book—at least to start with—to supplement a European meal. There are many Japanese soups, salads and main dishes that can be used instead of one of the courses of a European meal. In this way, you can perfect your Japanese cooking techniques one at a time.

One great advantage to experimenting with Japanese recipes is that so many of the dishes may be served at room temperature; consequently they may be prepared at leisure, long before serving.

A cautionary note: The number of guests that a dish will serve depends on whether it is part of a Western or a Japanese menu. Western-style portions generally tend to be larger, and the Japanese dishes may serve fewer people than the number indicated in the recipe.

Planning an All-Japanese Menu

Don't be afraid of trying meals of several courses. It's not really that much harder to prepare half a dozen small courses than it is to make three large ones—if you plan your cooking in advance. The trick is not to be caught at the last minute with too many unfamiliar operations under way at once. This is true in all cooking, but it is particularly so in Japanese cuisine. A dish like *tempura* will demand all your attention while you're frying the prawns and vegetables. The heat must be adjusted so that the temperature of the oil doesn't drop; the oil must be kept clean; the frying time must be quite precise. Consequently, if *tempura* is to be the main course, it might be preceded and followed by dishes that can be made hours in advance —leaving you free for a virtuoso performance as a *tempura* cook.

The various courses in a Japanese dinner are usually brought to the table at the start of the meal. If you wish to eat as the Japanese do, you can give each of your guests an individual tray containing the various courses and accompany the meal with warm *sake*, which has about the same alcoholic content as most European table wines. If you are preparing a more elaborate dinner with five or seven courses, you'll probably find it easier to serve two courses at a time. If the course is a big one, like *zensai*, Japanese hors d'œuvre, it might be more convenient to serve it by itself.

Sample Japanese Menus

Spring luncheon:

Kinome-ae: bamboo shoots with green soya dressing

Mazezushi or *fukusazushi*: vinegared rice mixed with vegetables and seafood

Aka misoshiru: red *miso*-flavoured soup

Autumn luncheon:

Shira-ae: *tofu* and sesame-seed dressing with French beans

Shioyaki: salt-grilled fish with dipping sauce

Satsuma jiru: *miso*-flavoured stew

Gohan: steamed rice

Winter luncheon:

Suzuko mizore-ae: red caviar with "sleet" dressing

Tori gohan: chicken and rice with mushrooms

Chawan mushi: chicken and prawns in egg custard

Summer luncheon:

Kani kyuri ikomi: cucumber stuffed with crab meat and pickled ginger

Sashimi: sliced raw fish

Hiyashi somen: cold summer noodles

Spring dinner:

Nuta-ae: seafood and spring onions in *miso* dressing

Hamaguri ushiojitate: clear clam soup with mushrooms

Sashimi: sliced raw fish

Kamo yoshino-ni and *fuki no nitsuke*: duck and coltsfoot simmered in *sake*-seasoned sauce

Tori teriyaki: grilled chicken with a sweet soya-seasoned glaze

Gohan: steamed rice

Summer dinner:

Domyoji age: deep-fried prawns coated with rice

Kamo sukamushi: *sake*-steamed duck

Kimin: *sake*-seasoned prawns with egg-yolk glaze

Nigiri zushi: vinegared rice and fish "sandwich"

Autumn dinner:

Igaguri: thorny prawn balls filled with sweet chestnuts

Sumashi wan: clear soup with *tofu* and prawns

Tatsuta age: sliced beef with red pepper and radish garnish

Yuan zuke: grilled fish in soya and *sake* marinade

Umani: chicken and vegetables simmered in seasoned broth

Gohan: steamed rice

Buffet:

Yakitori: grilled chicken, spring onions and chicken livers

Nanban zuke: fried fish in vinegared sauce

Domyoji age: deep-fried prawns coated with rice

Zensai: assorted hors d'œuvre

Oden: winter casserole with fish cake, *tofu* and vegetables

Makizushi: vinegared rice and vegetables rolled in seaweed

Takara mushi: treasure-ship pumpkin, filled with prawns, mushrooms and ginkgo nuts

A Guide to Ingredients in Japanese Cooking

Most of the basic ingredients in Japanese recipes can be found at any food store. Exceptions, described below, can be bought through one of the shops listed on page 207, or try any shop that stocks oriental provisions in your neighbourhood. Except for a few foods, such as daikon *and* tofu, *Japanese ingredients can be stored at room temperature, many for as long as a year. If an ingredient is not available and a substitute is not named, the best course is to omit it from the recipe.*

AJI-NO-MOTO: Japanese trade name for MSG (monosodium glutamate), a flavour-enhancing agent used in very small quantities. MSG is available as Aji-no-moto or Asahi-Aji in oriental shops, or sold elsewhere as Ac'cent, Stress, or MSG.

AONORIKO: Powdered green laver, a member of the seaweed family. Used as a seasoning agent. Available in bottles in Japanese food shops.

AZUKI: Red beans, usually cooked in rice or made into a sweet dish. Available in Japanese shops.

BENI SHOGA: Red pickled ginger root, available bottled in Japanese food shops. Used slivered or sliced as flavouring agent or garnish. Once opened, will keep refrigerated for several weeks if bottles are reclosed.

DAIKON: Japanese white radish, available fresh in Japanese food shops, in sizes ranging from sections of 6 inches to several feet. It may be refrigerated for up to two weeks. A substitute is icicle radish, which most closely approximates the taste and texture, or white turnip.

DASHI NO MOTO: Instant *dashi*, available in packets in Japanese food shops. *Dashi* is a basic soup and cooking stock and is made from powdered *katsuobushi* and *kombu*. Only cold water and MSG need to be added.

FU: Light cake made of wheat gluten, available in packets in different sizes, shapes and colours. Used principally as a soup garnish.

GINNAN: Ginkgo nuts, available canned in oriental food shops and delicatessen shops. The opened ginkgo nuts may be refrigerated, tightly closed, for weeks.

GOBO: Burdock, a long, slender root popular as a vegetable in Japan. Available fresh in Japanese shops, *gobo* may be kept for two weeks in the refrigerator.

GOMA: Sesame seeds, both black and white, available in boxes. A popular spice in Japanese cooking, sesame seeds are generally warmed in a pan to release their aroma and flavour, and are often ground. Italian sesame seeds are a good substitute.

GOMA-ABURA: Sesame-seed oil, available canned or bottled in oriental shops. Middle Eastern sesame-seed oil, which may be more easily available, has a different taste and weight but may be used if diluted with lighter vegetable oils.

HAKUSAI: A Chinese cabbage that has 12- to 16-inch-long smooth white stalks and large green leaves. Sold fresh by the bunch or by weight in oriental shops. Will keep for one week refrigerated in a plastic bag. Substitute celery cabbage or white cabbage.

HARUSAME: Bean-gelatine noodles; literally, "spring rain". This vermicelli, also called bean-thread or transparent noodles, is available in oriental shops. Usually softened in water before using.

HICHIMI TOGARASHI: Seven-pepper spice, available in small bottles. Powdered blend of hot mustard seed, sesame seed, pepper leaf, poppy seed, rape seed, hemp seed and dried tangerine peel.

HIYAMUGI: Thin noodles, usually eaten cold. Available in bags or boxes at Japanese food shops. Substitute Italian vermicelli.

JUNSAI: Wild delicacy sold in glass bottles in Japanese food shops. Translated as "water shield", *junsai* has a slippery coating and is used as a vegetable garnish in soups.

KANPYO: Dried gourd shavings, available in packets in Japanese food shops. Usually softened before being used as a garnish.

KATSUOBUSHI: Dried bonito. Pre-flaked *katsuobushi* is available in bags or boxes in Japanese food shops primarily for use in *dashi*—the basic soup stock. Keeps indefinitely, even after opening.

KOMBU: Dried kelp, a species of seaweed. Comes in hard black sheets, which are usually cut into pieces, washed, and used in stock. Keeps indefinitely.

KONA SANSHO: Ground pepper from *sansho* (prickly ash) leaf.

Substitute ground black pepper.

KONNYAKU: A hard, translucent loaf made from the starch of tubers of the devil's tongue plant. Available canned in Japanese food shops. Once opened, may be refrigerated for weeks.

MATSUTAKE: Large Japanese mushrooms, available canned.

MIKAN: Mandarin oranges, canned in syrup. Widely available. Served as a sweet dish.

MIRIN: Sweet *sake* (rice wine), used only for cooking. Available on special order from Mikadoya. A good substitute is pale dry sherry, used in lesser amounts than the *mirin* called for in recipes.

MISO: Soya-bean paste, made from the fermentation of cooked soya beans, wheat or rice, and salt. The basic types are *aka miso* (a reddish colour) and *shiro miso* (white). Used as a flavouring in soups and as the base for a dressing for vegetables. Available in containers in Japanese food shops. Will keep, even opened, for as long as a year at room temperature.

MSG: *See* Aji-no-moto.

NAMEKO: Tiny wild mushrooms with a slippery wet coating, available in cans in Japanese food shops.

NORI: Dried laver, a species of seaweed. Available in thin greenish-black sheets resembling carbon paper. When warmed, becomes crisper and more purplish in colour. Used as garnish or to roll around rice or fish. Sold in packets in Japanese food shops. Will keep for up to six months once opened.

RENKON: Lotus root, sold fresh in sections about 2 to 3 inches in diameter and 4 to 6 inches long, and canned in various sizes. Store in the refrigerator.

SAKE: Although called rice wine, *sake* is more closely related to beer. When used as a beverage, it is usually heated gently in the bottle before serving. It is also an important seasoning ingredient in cooking. Available at Mikadoya and Cydilda.

SHIITAKE: Japanese mushrooms, available dried in bags or packets in oriental food stores. Can be stored indefinitely in their packets. They are usually reconstituted by soaking in water for at least 30 minutes before using.

SHIRATAKI: Literally, "white

waterfall". Shredded form of *konnyaku*, long vermicelli-like threads available canned or in small cartons in Japanese food shops.

SHOGA: Gnarled, brown fresh ginger root, about 4 inches long, available fresh in oriental speciality shops. Will keep for a few weeks wrapped in kitchen paper in the refrigerator.

SHOYU: Japanese soya sauce, a pungent brown liquid made of fermented soya beans, barley, yeast and salt. Japanese soya sauce is more delicate and less salty than the Chinese brands.

SOBA: Thin buckwheat-flour noodles, available packaged in Japanese food shops.

SOMEN: Fine white wheat-flour noodles, usually eaten cold. Available in Japanese food shops. A substitute is very thin spaghetti.

SU: Rice vinegar, available bottled or canned, in various sizes, at oriental food stores. A good substitute is cider vinegar, but a mild white vinegar will suffice.

TAKENOKO: Young bamboo shoots, available whole in cans in oriental food stores. Chinese sliced bamboo shoots are more widely available.

TOFU: Custard-like cake of soya-bean curd, about 3 inches square. Sold fresh in Japanese food shops. Will keep for two to three days if refrigerated and kept in fresh cold water, changed every day. *Tofu* is also available canned and in instant powdered form.

UDON: Thick wheat-flour noodles, available in Japanese food shops. A good substitute is medium-thick spaghetti ($\frac{1}{16}$ inch diameter).

UMEBOSHI: Small pickled plums, available bottled and vacuum packed in Japanese food shops.

UNI: Prepared sea urchin, available bottled in some Japanese food shops.

WAKAME: Long, curled, dried strands of seaweed. Available packaged in oriental food stores. Reconstitute by soaking in water, then strip the leaves from the tough centre vein and use as a garnish.

WASABI: Green horse-radish, available canned in powdered form. No substitute.

ZUKEMONO: Pickled, vegetables, in bottles and vacuum packs in Japanese food shops.

199

Recipe Index: English An R preceding a page reference refers to the Recipe Booklet.

Stocks and Soups
Basic soup stock . . . . .54; R 2
Clear clam soup with mushrooms .58; R11
Clear soup with rolled egg, vegetables and fish . . . . .60; R 6
Clear soup with sea bass . . . . .58; R 9
Clear soup with sea bream . . . . .61; R 8
Clear soup with soya-bean paste 59; R12
Clear soup with *tofu* and prawns . . . . .55; R 4
Clear soup with winter melon and prawns . . . . .58; R 5
Cooking stock for vegetables . . . . .54; R 3
Miso soup garnishes 59; R12
Miso-flavoured pork and vegetable stew 61; R10

Picnic Food and Hors d'Oeuvre
Chestnuts cooked in green tea .70; R16
Cooked kelp R21
Miso-marinated asparagus 70; R22
Prawn *sushi* with egg yolk 69; R18
Prawns wrapped in seaweed R17
Red-bean cake R24
Sake-seasoned clams 73; R15
Sake-steamed duck 68; R14
Steak and spring-onion rolls 73; R22
Steamed fish loaf 68; R20
Sweet-cooked abalone 73; R16
Sweet-cooked clams 73; R15
Sweet-cooked snails R17
Taro potatoes rolled in crumbled seaweed R21
Thorny prawn balls filled with sweet chestnuts 70; R19
Turnips in vinegar dressing R23

Mixed Foods and Vinegared Salads
Aubergine with mustard and *miso* dressing R25
Bamboo shoots with green soya dressing 67; R32
Chicken and parsley with horse-radish sauce R30
Crab meat in vinegared dressing 62; R36
Cucumber stuffed with crab meat and pickled ginger 66; R34
Daikon and carrot in vinegar dressing 64; R35
Mackerel in vinegar dressing 65; R36
Red caviar with "sleet" dressing .64; R28
Rice-vinegar and soya dipping sauce 64; R29
Seafood and spring onions in *miso* dressing R30
Seaweed-flavoured fish with lemon sauce R37
Slippery mushrooms with "sleet" dressing 65; R29
Soya and sesame-seed dressing with French beans 62; R27
Spinach with toasted sesame seeds R33
Tofu and sesame-seed dressing with vegetables 63; R26
White *miso* dressing 67; R31

Sliced Raw Fish
Delicate soya-based dipping sauce for *sashimi* 94; R41
Sashimi wrapped in laver 94; R40
Sliced raw fish 90; R38
Spicy dipping sauce for *sashimi* 94; R40
White-radish and red-pepper garnish 94; R41

Vinegared Rice Dishes
Rice in vinegar dressing 95; R42
Vinegared rice and fish balls 95; R48
Vinegared rice and fish "sandwiches" 101; R44
Vinegared rice and vegetables rolled in seaweed 100; R43
Vinegared rice mixed with vegetables and seafood 96; R46

Rice
Chicken and rice with mushrooms 125; R52
Chicken omelette on rice 124; R50
Dipping sauce for *domburi* 125; R50
Mixed rice and vegetables 126; R51
Red-cooked festival rice 126; R53

Steamed rice 124; R49

Noodles
Buckwheat noodles with laver 131; R57
Cold noodles with prawns and mushrooms 128; R58
Cold summer noodles R59
Dipping sauce for noodles 128; R58
Fox noodles 127; R56
Hot noodles and broth R55
Hot noodles and chicken in broth 130; R54

Fried Foods
Deep-fried prawns and vegetables in batter 103; R60
Deep-fried prawns coated with rice 105; R64
Deep-fried prawns in noodles R65
Deep-fried *tofu* in soya sauce 105; R68
Fried aubergine with *miso* dressing R67
Fried fish in vinegared sauce R66
Lemon and salt dip 104; R61
Mirin and soya dipping sauce for *tempura* and noodles 104; R62
Mixed deep-fried pancakes 104; R63
Sliced beef with red-pepper and radish garnish R68

Foods Cooked in Seasoned Liquid
Chicken and vegetables simmered in seasoned broth 123; R74
Chicken simmered with white-radish threads R73
Coltsfoot in *sake*-flavoured sauce R73
Duck simmered in *sake*-seasoned sauce R72
Fresh sardines cooked in *sake*-flavoured sauce 122; R70
Sake-seasoned broad beans R75
Sake-flavoured prawns with egg-yolk glaze 122; R71
Salted mackerel in *miso* sauce .R72
Sweet chestnuts 123; R75
Winter casserole with fish cake, *tofu* and vegetables R76

One-Pot Cookery
Beef and vegetables cooked in broth with dipping sauce 135; R80
Beef and vegetables simmered in soya sauce and *sake* 134; R77
Bubbling *tofu* 132; R83
Chicken and vegetables cooked in broth with *pon-su* dipping sauce . .134; R78
Pan-grilled duck and vegetables with dipping sauce R84
Seafood and vegetables in broth 132; R82
Temple of Jade *nabe* R81

Grilled Foods
Baked fish omelette 176; R95
Fish with egg-yolk glaze: *See* Treasure-ship fish
Fish with sea-urchin glaze: *See* Treasure-ship fish
Flaky rolled omelette 178; R94
Grilled chicken, spring onions and chicken livers 175; R89
Grilled chicken with sweet soya-seasoned glaze 176; R88
Grilled fish fillets in rice-wine sauce R93
Grilled mackerel in *miso* marinade 169; R91
Grilled mackerel in soya and rice-wine marinade 172; R90
Grilled sliced beef with sweet soya-seasoned glaze 175; R87
Grilled soya-bean curd with *miso* dressing 172; R98
Salt-grilled fish with dipping sauce 177; R85
Sesame-seed grilled fish: *See* Treasure-ship fish
Steam-grilled prawns with chicken, ginkgo-nuts and mushrooms . .168; R92
Treasure-ship fish 170; R96

Steamed Foods
Chicken and prawns in egg custard R101
Sake-steamed fish with *tofu* and spinach R102
Seasoned egg custard R103
Steamed chicken, mushroom and ginkgo nut parcels R102
Steamed prawns, mushrooms, chicken and ginkgo nuts R104
Treasure-ship pumpkin with prawns,
    mushrooms and vegetables 180; R99

Recipe Index: Japanese

Dashi and Owanrui (Stocks and Soups)

Botan wan ....58; R 9
Hamaguri ushiojitate 58; R11
Ichiban dashi ....54; R 2
Misoshiru 59; R12
Misoshiru no-mi 59; R12
Niban dashi ....54; R 3
Satsuma jiru 61; R10
Sumashi wan ....55; R 4
Togan-to ebi ....58; R 5
Umewan ....60; R 6
Ushio jiru ....61; R 8

Bento and Zensai (Picnic Food and Hors d'Oeuvre)

Achara zuke R23
Awabi sakani 73; R16
Ebi isobe yaki R17
Ebi kimizushi 69; R18
Gyuniku negimaki 73; R22
Hamaguri sakani 73; R15
Hamaguri shigure-ni 73; R15
Igaguri 70; R19
Kamaboko 68; R20
Kamo sakamushi 68; R14
Karashi zuke 70; R22
Koimo nori-ae R21
Mizuyokan R24
Shibu kawa-ni 70; R16
Shiro bai R17
Tenjo kombu R21

Aemono and Sunomono
(Mixed Foods and Vinegared Salads)

Goma joyu-ae 62; R27
Horenso hitashi R33
Kani kyuri ikomi 66; R34
Kani sunomono 62; R36
Kinome-ae 67; R32
Kobujime R37
Namasu 64; R35
Nameko mizore-ae 65; R29
Nasu karashi sumiso-ae R25
Neri shiro miso 67; R31
Nuta-ae R30
Sambai-zu 64; R29
Shime saba 65; R36
Shira-ae 63; R26
Suzuko mizore-ae 64; R28
Toriwasa R30

Sashimi (Sliced Raw Fish)

Chirizu 94; R40
Isobe zukuri 94; R40
Sashimi 90; R38
Some oroshi 94; R41
Tosa joyu 94; R41

Sushi (Vinegared Rice Dishes)

Fukusa zushi: See Mazezushi
Makizushi 100; R43
Mazezushi 96; R46
Nigiri zushi 101; R44
Sushi 95; R42
Temarizushi 95; R48

Gohan (Rice)

Domburi ni shiru 125; R50
Gohan 124; R49
Maze gohan 126; R51
Oyako domburi 124; R50

Sekihan 126; R53
Tori gohan 125; R52

Menrui (Noodles)

Hiyamugi 128; R58
Hiyashi somen R59
Kitsune udon 127; R56
Menrui no dashi 128; R58
Su udon R55
Tori nanban 130; R54
Zarusoba 131; R57

Agemono (Fried Foods)

Agedashi 105; R68
Ajishio 104; R61
Dengaku nasu R67
Domyoji age 105; R64
Ebi kobore matsuba age R65
Kaki age 104; R63
Nanban zuke R66
Soba tsuyu 104; R62
Tatsuta age R68
Tempura 103; R60
Ten tsuyu: See Soba tsuyu

Nimono (Foods Cooked in Seasoned Liquid)

Fuki no nitsuke R73
Kamo yoshino-ni R72
Kimini 122; R71
Kiriboshi daikon R73
Kuri fukume-ni 123; R75
Miso-ni R72
Nitsuke 122; R70
Oden R76
Otafukumame shoga-ni R75
Umani 123; R74

Nabemono (One-Pot Cookery)

Hakusai nabe R81
Okaribayaki R84
Shabu shabu 135; R80
Sukiyaki 134; R77
Tori mizutaki 134; R78
Yosenabe 132; R82
Yudofu 132; R83

Yakimono (Grilled Foods)

Atsuyaki tamago 176; R95
Dengaku tofu 172; R98
Goma yaki: See Takara bune
Gyuniku teriyaki 175; R87
Horakuyaki 168; R92
Kimeyaki: See Takara bune
Kinome yaki R93
Miso zuke 169; R91
Shioyaki 177; R85
Takara bune 170; R96
Tamago dashimaki 178; R94
Tori teriyaki 176; R88
Uniyaki: See Takara bune
Yakitori 175; R89
Yuan zuke 172; R90

Mushimono (Steamed Foods)

Chawan mushi R101
Kabura mushi R104
Sakamushi R102
Takara mushi ....180; R 99
Tamago dofu R103
Tori mushiyaki R102

General Index
Numerals in italics indicate a photograph or drawing of the subject mentioned.

Abalone, *35, 79,* 80, *188;* diving for, 77; sliced and cooked in *sake* and soya sauce, *72*

Aemono (mixed foods in dressing), 48, 62, 108, 116

Agemono (frying), 48-49, *102*-103

Agriculture, 10, *12-13, 14-15,* 29, *30-31,* 39

Aji-no-moto (MSG), *45,* 48, 110, 199

Akadashi (red soya-bean-paste soup with radish and spring-onion garnish), *35, 56*

Aka miso (red soya-bean paste), *45*

Akashi, 195

Algae. *See* Seaweed

Ama (diving girl), 77

Antarctic, 76

Aomori, *map* 11

Aonoriko (powdered green seaweed), 43, *45,* 199

Asia, 12, 16

Asparagus: garnish for raw fluke, *148;* marinated in *miso, 72*

Atlantic Ocean, 76, 80; Gulf Stream, 75

Aubergines, 110, *111,* 115, 163

Awabi. See Abalone

Ayu (freshwater fish), 28-29, 32, 76, 140, 147; fishing for with trained cormorants, 29, *81,* salt-grilling, 29

Azuki (red beans), 43, *44,* 120, 199

Bamboo: leaves, *34;* stalks, 19, 128, *129;* teaspoon, *141-143;* whisk, *141-143*

Bamboo shoots, 27, *35,* 43, *44,* 106, 107, 147, *148, 188;* cutting techniques for, 52, *53*

Bancha (tea), 28

Bando, Mitsugoro, *112*

Banquet, 181; wedding, *118-119*

Barley tea, 32

Barracuda, 38

Bass, 90, *91, 92,* 99; how to slice, *93,* in clear soup with wild vegetables and lime, 110, *111*

Batayaki (food grilled in butter), 161

Bean, 166; black, 43, *44,* 188; green powder, 27; lima, *148; mame,* 121; paste, 27; red, 43, *44,* 120

Beef, 22, 38, 46, 76, 108, *157, 159, 166,* 193; beer-fed cattle, *166;* Kobe, 161; Matsuzaka, 161;

rolled beef with spring onions, *72; teriyaki, 174. See also* Beef; Liver; Pork; *Shabu shabu; Sukiyaki*

Beer, 162, 193, 197; fed to cattle, *166*

Bento (lunch or picnic box), *24, 25, 40,* 41, 68, 109, 165

Bering Sea, 76

Blow-fish. *See* Globe-fish

Boiling, 43; in seasoned liquid, 46-47, 122

Bonito, 32, 76, *79,* 80; dried, *45,* 87, 110, 152. *See also Katsuobushi*

Botan wan (clear soup with sea bass, wild vegetables and lime), 110, *111*

Brazier, *141-143*

Breakfast, 109, 179; soup, 41, *56-57,* 109, 110, 138

British Isles, 16

Broth, 46, 116, *159;* beef, 116; chicken, 43, 116; kelp, 147

Buckwheat noodles, 38, *130*

Buddhism, 16, 17, 22, 86, 120, 162, 166; Zen, 137, 146

Buffet, 181, 198

Burdock root, *35,* 42, 43, *44. See also* Gobo

Cabbage, 49, 82, 162; Chinese, 38, *149*

Cake: in cherry leaves, 27; Children's Day, 120; Girls' Day, 120; funeral, 121; nightingale, 26-27; rice cakes, 27, 36, 38, 121

Carp, 82, 161; symbolism of, 86, 121

Carrots, *40,* 41, 50, *51, 57, 133,* 163, 166, *167;* cutting techniques for, *52*

Cattle, *166*

Caviar, red, *40, 41, 99, 130*

Chakin (linen tea cloth), *141-143*

Chameshi ("tea rice") restaurants, 162

Chasen (bamboo whisk), *141-143*

Chasenmura, 143

Chashaku (bamboo teaspoon), *141-143*

Chawan (tea bowl), *141-144*

Chawan mushi (food steamed in egg custard), 47-48

Chazuke (rice soaked in tea), 110; restaurants, 162

Chefs: apprenticeship, 195. *See also* names of chefs

Cherry: leaves, 27; trees, 8, *9,* 27, *114*

Chestnuts, *24, 25,* 36, 121, 140, *169;* in deep-fried prawn balls, *40, 71*

Chicken, 22, *34,* 38, 43, 47, 109, 112, 140, *169, 174,* grilled with chicken liver and spring onions, 161; broth, 43; grilled, *158;* grilled with spring onions, *174;* how to bone a chicken breast, *177;* scrambled with *tofu* and peas, *160,* 161

Children's Day festival, *34,* 86, 120

China, 10; early influence on Japan, 16-17, 19; origin of tea ceremony, 137

Chirashi (loose rice covered with fish), 154, *155*

Chopsticks, *33, 34, 35, 40, 66, 85,* 109, *111, 112, 113, 114,* 116, 129, *130, 131, 148-149, 150, 154, 156, 159, 160,* 163, 166, *167, 169, 187,* for cooking, 50, 71, *105,* 132, *178-179;* how to use, 47

Chrysanthemums, 29, *30-31,* 121

Clams, *24, 25,* 76, 77, *79;* soup, *57,* 118

Cod, 76

Coffee shops, 27

Cooking clubs, 188

Cooking methods, 10, 23, 41, 43; boiling, 43, 46-47, 122; food cooked at dining table, 46, 132, 166, *167;* frying, 43, 48-49, *102, 103, 105;* grilling, 29, 43, *158-159,* 161, 168, *173;* ingredients kept separate, 10; "interrupted cooking", 47; simmering, 41, 46; steaming, 43, 47-48, 115, *125, 169,* 180. *See also Aemono; Agemono; Mushimono; Nabemono; Nimono; Shioyaki; Sukiyaki; Umani*

Cooking schools, 108

Cooking utensils, *50, 51;* automatic electric rice cooker, *125;* brazier, *141-143;* chopsticks, *50, 66, 105,* 132, *178-179;* for tea ceremony, *141-144, 145-146, 147, 148-149, 187;* hibachi, 37, 132, *182, 183; horoku,* 48, 169; improvised steamer, *180; kushi,* 161; *nabe,* 108, 132; *suribachi, 50, 63; teppan,* 157

Cormorant fishing. *See Ayu*

Cottage cheese, 110

Cotton-seed oil, 49

Crabs, 76, 80, 82, 86, 110, 147; cucumber stuffed with, *66, 111;* restaurants, 161

Cucumber, *34, 35,* 48, 49, *98,* 110, *111,* 115, 165; cutting techniques, 52, *53;* in *sushi,* 154, *155*

Cutting techniques: chicken breast, *177;* display, *40, 41;* raw fish, *92-93,* vegetables, *52-53*

Cuttle-fish, 80

Daidai. *See* Orange

Daikon, 199. *See also* Radish

Dashi (soup stock), 32, 35, 38, 47, 48, 76, 87, 89, 109, 112, 116, 152, 162, 198

Dinner, 56, 110, *111,* 112-113, 115, 116, 185 193

Dipping sauces, 47, 110, 128, *129,* 132; for noodles, 36, 165; *pon-su,* 46, 82, 90, *91,* 152; *sambaizu,* 65; *sashimi, 91;* for *shabu shabu, 159;* for steak, 46; for *tempura,* 49; *yuzu* juice, soya sauce and *sake,* 116

Dishes: seasonal table service, 26; tea ceremony, *141-144, 145-146, 147, 148-149,* 198

Dobin mushi (steamed chicken, fish, *matsutake* and ginkgo nuts), 36

Doi Inn, Kyoto: baths, 194; description, 183, *193-195;* food, 194; geisha party, *190-191;* meal at, *182*

Domburi (bowl), 112, 162

Domyoji age (deep-fried prawns encrusted with dried rice and served with green pepper, aubergine and lemon), 110, *111*

Drinks, 32, 193. *See also* Beer; Gin; *Mirin; Sake;* Whisky; Tea

Duck, *24, 25, 34, 114, 115,* 161; and chrysanthemum leaves, 110, *111;* grilled duck liver, *158;* with noodles, spring onions, caviar and radish, *130*

Eating habits, 16, 19, 165; aesthetic influence, 26, 33, 110, *111,* 120, 138; food in season, 26-32, *33-35,* 109; restaurant entertaining, 107, 152; Western influence, 22

Edo, grilled, 32

Eels, *35,* 76, 87, 140; grilled, 29; eel day, 29, 32; medicinal properties, 29; restaurants, 32, 163

Eggs, 35, 49, 56, 81, 110, 112, 115, *159*, 166, *167*; cold noodles topped with prawn, mushroom and egg, *129*; custard in soup, 26; fried in sesame oil, 43, 46; patties, *188*; quail, *24, 25*; prawns stuffed with egg yolk, *148*; egg custard, 47-48. *See also* Omelette

Emperor of Japan, 16; birth of grandson, 120

Empress of Japan, 16

Europe, 16, 19

F erns, *35*, 147, *149*

Festivals: chestnut, 36; Children's Day, 34, 86, 120; fish, 10; Girls' Day, or Doll Festival, 120; harvest, 16; mushroom gathering, 36; New Year, 121, 147, *188-189*; Tsukimi, 35

Fish, 8, *9*, 16, 19, *24, 25*, 28, 38, 49, 75, 79, 80-83, *84-85*, 86-88, 110, 115, *150*, 151, 163, *188*, 195; auction, *78*, 79, 80; boning and slicing knives, *50*; cooking methods, 43; dried, 87, 88; flavour, 75; festival, 10; how to fillet, *93*; market, 76, *78*, 79, 80-81; paste, 87, 121, 147, *148*; preparation of "treasure ship" fish, *170-171*; raw, 26, *92-93*, 154, *155*; vinegared rice and fish "sandwich", *99, 101*; salad, 48; sausage, 87; uses for, 87; variety and abundance, 75-76. *See also* Abalone; *Ayu*; Barracuda; Bass; Bonito; Cod; Cuttle-fish; Flounder; Fluke; Globe-fish; Halibut; Herring; Mackerel; Salmon; Sardines; *Sashimi*; Sausage; Sea bream; Sea urchin; Shad; Snapper; Snipe; *Sushi*; Trout; Tunny fish; Whale; Whitebait; Whitefish; Yellowtail

Fishing, 75; for abalone, 77; for *ayu* with cormorants, 29, *81*; industry, 76-77, 80, 87

Flounder, 82

Flour, 49

Fluke: fried and seasoned with vinegar sauce, *72*; salted raw, *148*

Fowl, 42. *See also* Chicken; Duck; Quail

France, 10, 23

Fruit, 10, 19, 36, 193; grown for restaurants, 195; in season, 26; introduced from West, 36. *See also* Cherries; *Fuki*; Kumquats; Lemons; Limes; Melon; Oranges; Persimmons; Plums; Strawberries; Tangerines

Fu (wheat-gluten croûtons), 41, 43, *45*, 199

Fugu. See Globe-fish

Fuji, Mount, 19, *map* 11

Fuki (vegetable), *148*

Fukiyose (nuts, prawns, mushroom and vegetables), 36

Fukugen restaurant, Tokyo, *85*

Fukuoka, *map* 11

Fukusa (silk napkin), *141-143*; *bassami* (silk bag), *141*

Fukusa zushi (rice, seafood and vegetables wrapped in an omelette), *97*

Furikake (bottled sauce for rice), 110

Furo (brazier), *141-143*

Futaoki (rest for tea-kettle lid or dipper), *141-143*

G arnish, seaweed, 89; white radish and red pepper, 90

Geisha, 108, *192*; party, 196-197; training and duties, *190-191*, 195-196. *See also* Maiko

Germany, 23

Gifu, *map* 11, 28, 29, 81

Gin, 166

Ginger, 32, *34*, 43, *45*, 46, 161, 163, 164; grated, 65; red pickled, *66*, *97*, 110

Ginkgo nut, 36-37, *40*, 41, 43, *44*, 156, *169, 181*

Ginnan (ginkgo nuts), 43, *44*, 199

Ginsen restaurant, Tokyo, *157*

Ginza, 80, 162

Girls' Day cake, 120

Giseidofu (uncooked *tofu* topped by strips of deep-fried *tofu*), *160*, 161

Globe-fish, 25, 38, 76, *84-85*, 86, 87, 152; expense, 83; poisonous qualities, 83, 85

Gobo (burdock root), 42, 43, *44*, 199; cutting technique, *52, 53*

Gohan (rice), 37

Goma (black and white sesame seeds), 43-44, *170-171*, 199; *-abura* (sesame oil), 43, *44*, 199

Gourd, *100*; dried, 42

Grater, *50*

Grilling, 43, 168; salt-grilling, 29, 43, *169. See also* Hibachi

Ground-nut oil, 49

Guji. See Sea bream

H akusai (Chinese cabbage), 38, 199

Halibut, 76

Hamaguri (clam soup), 118; *ushiojitate* with mushroom and lime garnish, *57*

Hangetsu (half-moon box), *114*, 115

Hannya-en restaurant, Tokyo: description, 184-185; typical dinner, 185, 193

Harusame (transparent noodles), 43, *45*, 199

Heian shrine, Kyoto, *114*, 115

Herbs, 19

Herring roe, 121

Hibachi, 37, 132, *182*, 183

Hichimi togarashi (seven-pepper spice), 43, *45*, 199

Hijiki (seaweed), 89

Hiroshima, *map* 11, 80; Bay, 19

Hishaku (water dipper), *141-143*

Hiyamugi (thin noodles served cold), 43, *45*; topped with prawn, mushroom and egg, *128, 129*

Hiyayako dofu (uncooked *tofu* with spicy soya sauce), *160*, 161

Hokkaido, 10, *map* 11, 80

Holland: early traders, 19

Honshu, 10, *map* 11, 38, 87

Horakuyaki (food steamed on salt), 48, *169*

Horenso. See Spinach

Horoku (unglazed pottery bowl), 48, *169*

Hors d'œuvre, *34, 66, 72*, 185. *See also* Bento; *Zensa*

Horse-radish, 81; green, 42, 82, 109

I ce-cream, 22, 32

Igaguri, 40, 41, *71*

Inari, the rice god, 13, 37

Indian Ocean, 76, 80

Inland Sea, 10, *map* 11, 29, 75, 80, 151

Inn. *See* Doi

Innoshima Islands, 29, *30-31*

Iodine, 89

Iridofu (*tofu* scrambled with chicken and peas), *160*, 161

Ishiyaki (grilled food) 161

Isogen restaurant, Tokyo, 154-*155*

Italy, 23

J apan, 10, *map* 11; Chinese influence, 16-17, 19; dairy products, 10; description, 10, 12-13, 75; expense-account spending, 153; fishing industry, 10, 76-77, 79, 80; food, 8, 10, 16, 19, 22, 23; history, 12-19; philosophy of harmony with nature, 13, 33, 86, 138; symbolism and superstition, 86, 116, 120-121; visual appeal of food, 8, 10, 12, 110, *111. See also* Eating habits

Japan Current, 75

Japan Sea, 27

Jesuits, 19

Jimmu, first emperor of Japan, 13

Junidanya restaurant, Tokyo, *159*

Junsai (slippery vegetables), 43, *44*, 199; in soup with sea bass, 110, *111*

K abayaki (grilled eel), 29, 32

Kaiseki ryori. See Tea ceremony

Kaki. See Persimmon

Kamaboko (fish paste), 87, 121

Kamameshi (pot rice), 162

Kamasu (barracuda), 38

Kani kyuri ikomi (cucumber rounds with crab meat, watercress and red pickled ginger), 110, *111*

Kanname Sai. See Festivals

Kanpyo, 199. *See also* Gourd

Kansai, 36

Karashi (mustard), *45*

Karibayaki (grilled food), 161

Katsuobushi (dried bonito), 32, *45*, 76, 87, 89, 110, 112, 116, 152, 162, 199

Kawamasu. See Trout

Kawataro restaurant, Kyushu, *150*, 151

Kazunoko. See Herring roe

Kelp (*kombu*), 25, *45*, 74, 75, 87-89, 116, 121; broth, 147; symbolism, 120, 121

Kensui (bowl for waste water), *141*

Kimeyaki, 40, 41, *170, 171*

Kimini (prawns boiled in *dashi*, *sake*, sugar and salt), 47

Kitcho restaurant, Kyoto: description of, 183; geisha party, 196-197; marketing for, 195;

staff, *186-187*, 195-196
Koban (box), *114*, 115
Kobe, *map* 11
Kobukusa (silk napkin), *141*, *144*
Kocha. See Tea
Kombu, 45, 199. *See also* Kelp
Kome (Japanese rice), 43, *44*,
Kona sansho (Japanese pepper), 43, *45*, 199
Konnyaku (vegetable), *35*, 43, *44*
Korea, 12
Koya, Mount, 147
Koyadofu (dried *tofu* boiled in soya-sauce soup with mushrooms), *160*, 161
Kumquats, salmon eggs in, *188*
Kuromame (black beans), 43, *44*
Kusamochi (green cake for Girls' Day), 120
Kushi (bamboo skewer), 161
Kushizashi (brochette-grilled food), 113
Kyogashi. See Sweets
Kyoto, 8, *map* 11, 13, 19, 28, 36, 120, 139, 143, 152; Doi Inn, *182*, *183*, *190-191*, 193-195; Heian shrine, *114*, 115; Kitcho restaurant, 183, *186-189*, 195-196
Kyushu, 10, *map* 11, 87

Laver, 26, 88, 108, 109. *See also Nori*
Lemons, 110, *111*, 161; juice and soya sauce, 46
Limes, 26, *40*, 41, *57*; in clear soup with sea bass and wild vegetables, 110, *111*; juice and soya sauce, 46
Liver: chicken, 161; duck, 161
Lobster, *79*, 82, 112, *113*, 121, *133*, 150, 151; symbolism of, 120
Lotus root, 43, *44*, 163; cutting technique for, 52, *53*; leaf, 121
Lunch, 56, 109, 110, 179; New Year, *188-189*

Maguro (tunny fish), 82
Maiko (apprentice geisha), *190-191*, 196
Mackerel, 38, *65*, 80
Makizushi (vinegared rice wrapped in seaweed), *98*, *99*, *100*, 109, 154, *155*, 165
Mame beans, 121
Mandarin orange. *See* Tangerine
Mange-tout, *181*

Marinade, 41, 42; for *teriyaki*, 43
Marriage ceremony, *117-119*
Marrow pickles, 147, *149*
Matsunoh shrine, Kyoto, *18*, 19
Matsutake, 199. *See also* Mushroom
Matsutake Meshi (rice with mushroom), 36
Matsuyama, *map* 11
Matsuzaka, 166
Meat, 42, 110. *See also* Beef, Pork, Liver
Medicinal uses for food, 36, 38; eels, 29, 32; globe-fish, 83, 86
Mediterranean Sea, 76
Melon, 115
Mikan, 199. *See also* Tangerine
Mirin (rice wine), 42, 43, *44*, 121, 152, 162, 199; and soya-sauce marinade, 43
Miso (fermented soya-bean paste), 41, *45*, 48, 138, 146, 147, 199; -marinated asparagus, *72*
Misoshiru (soya-bean paste soup), 41, *56-57*, 109, 110, 138
Mizusashi (cold-water jar), *141-143*
Mizutaki (simmered chicken), 38, 108, 116
Mochi. See Rice cake
Mochi-tsuki (rice-pounding ceremony), 121
Molluscs, 79
Monosodium glutamate, *45*, 48, 110. *See also* Aji-no-moto
Morimoto, Toshio, *4*, 50, *51*
MSG. *See* Monosodium glutamate
Mugicha (roasted barley-grain tea), 32
Mushi (steamed food), 47-48
Mushimono (steamed food), 115, 180
Mushiyaki (steaming without water), 48
Mushrooms, *34*, *35*, 43, *44-45*, 128, *129*, 161, 163, 166, *167*, *169*, *181*; *matsutake*, 32-33, 36, 43, *44*, 140, 199; *nameko*, 43, *44*, 199; *shiitake*, 32, *37*, 42, 43, *45*, 199
Mustard, *35*, *45*, 115

Nabe (pot or saucepan), 108, 132, 166, *167*
Nabemono (food cooked at table), 46, 116, 132, *133*, *159*, 166, *167*
Nagara river, *81*
Nagasaki, *map* 11
Nagoya, 10, *map* 11, 28
Namashoyu dofu (*tofu* boiled in soya

sauce flavoured with lemon and ginger), *160*, 161
Namasu (salad), *65*
Nameko. See Mushrooms
Nara, 10, *map* 11
Nara zuke (melons pickled in *sake* lees), 115
Natsume (tea caddy), *141-143*
Natto (fermented soya bean), 115
New York City, 145
Nigiri zushi (vinegared rice and fish "sandwich"), *99*, *101*
Nihon-cha. See Tea
Niiname Sai. See Festivals
Nikko, 117, 161
Nimono (boiling in seasoned liquid), 46-47, 110, *111*, 122
Noodles, 43, *44-45*, 71, *133*; buckwheat, 32, 38, *130*; cold, with prawn, mushroom and egg, 128, *129*; duck, spring onions, caviar and radish, *130*; restaurants, *154*; shops, 25, 165. *See also Harusame; Hiyamugi; Somen; Udon*
Nori (dried laver), 32, *34*, *45*, 88, 89, *97*, *98*, *99*, *100*, 109, 110, 112, *131*, 152, 162, 165, 199; gathering, *88*; omelette, *178-179*
Nuts, 36. *See also* Chestnuts; Ginkgo nuts

Obi (sash), 26
Octopus, *35*, 76, 77
Odori (live prawns), 82-83
Oil: for *tempura*, 49, 103; sesame, 43, *44*. *See also* Olive oil; Cotton-seed oil; Ground-nut oil; Sesame-seed oil
Okama (tea-kettle), *141-143*
Okinawa, 76
Okiya (geisha training school), 196
Okonomiyaki (do-it-yourself grilling), 161
Olive oil, 49
Omelette, 46, 110; as wrapping, *97*, 165; to roll, *178-179*; rectangular pan, 50, *178-179*
Onigiri (rice in seaweed), 89
Onions, 166, *167*
Oranges, 121
Osaka, 10, *map* 11, 36, 186, 195; food in, 162
Oshibori (damp towel), 110, *111*, 164, 185

Otomo restaurant, Tokyo, *157*
Oyako domburi (chicken and egg over rice), 112
Oysters, 76, 80; baby, 77; boat, 19, *20*

Pacific Ocean, 10, *map* 11, 76, 80
Parsley, 128
Peas, with chicken and *tofu*, *160*, 161
Pepper, 43, *45*; red, 45, *84*, 90, 140
Pepper leaf (*sansho*), *45*, *57*, 147, *148*, 157
Persimmon, 28, 36
Philippines, 19
Pickles, 43, *44*, 112, 115; squash, 147, *149*, 198
Pine needles, *169*
Plum: cucumber stuffed with plum paste and raw prawns, *34*; red pickled, 109
Pon-su (soya sauce and citrus juice), 46, 82, 90, 152; with spring onion and radish garnish, 83, *91*
Pork, 22, 112; cutlet, 162
Portugal: early traders, 19
Poultry. *See* Chicken; Fowl
Prawns, 22, *34*, *35*, *57*, 76, *79*, 81, *99*, 128, *129*, *133*, *154*, 162, *169*, *181*, *188*; deep-fried and encrusted with dried rice, 110, *111*; deep-fried shrimp balls, *24*, *25*, 71; dried, *88*; eating alive, 82-83; to prevent curling, *69*; stuffed with egg yolk, 147, *148*; wrapped in seaweed, *72*. *See also Tempura*
Pumpkin, *181*

Quail, 161; eggs, *24*, 25

Radish, 26, *130*; cutting techniques for, *52*; in dipping sauce, 83; Japanese (*daikon*), *35*, 42, 43, *45*, 46, 48, 49, 50, *51*, *52*, *56*, 82, 90, 108, 109, 115, 147, *179*, 199; yellow, *98*
Renkon (lotus root), 43, *44*, 199
Restaurants, 12, 22, 23, 25, 26, 27, 29, 36, 38, 42, 46, 76, 80, 81, 83, 88, 107-108, 109, 110, 112, *150*, *153*, 186, *192*; *chameshi*, 162; *chazuke*, 162; cleanliness, 164; eel, 32, 163; entertaining at, 152; expense-account clientele, 153; *fugu*, 25, 83, *85*, 86; rice, 162; *sashimi*, *157*; speciality, *154-*

160, 161; steak houses, *157*,161-162; *sushi*, 81, *155*, 164-165; *tempura*, *156*, 163; *tofu*, *160*, 161; *yakitori*, *158*, 161. *See also* names of restaurants

Restaurants: Fukugen, Tokyo, *85*; Ginsen, Tokyo, *157*; Hannya-en, Tokyo, 184-185, 193; Isogen, Tokyo, 154-*155*; Junidanya, Tokyo,*159*; Kawataro,Fukuoka, Kyushu, *150*, 151; Kitcho, Kyoto, 183, *186-189*, 195-197; Otomo, Tokyo, *157*; Sasagayuki, Tokyo, *160*, 161; Ten-ichi, Tokyo, *156*, 163; Tori-gin, Tokyo, 162; Torishige, Tokyo, *158*; Wadakin, Matsuzaka, 166, *167*; Yabuizu, Tokyo, *154*

Religious ceremonies, 86-87

Rice, 8, *9*, 10, 19, 26, *34*, 35, 37-38, 43, *44*, 81, 87, *97*, *101*, 109, 110, *111*, 112, *114*, 115, 140, 147, *148-149*, 154, *155*, 162, 165, 166, *167*; electric rice cooker, *125*; bran, 166; cakes, 26, 27, 109,121; dried,110; fields, *14-15*; historic importance, 13, 37, 42; red, 120. *See also Sake*; *Sushi*

Rikyu, Sen, 137, 146

S*ake* (rice wine), 13, 25, 26, *34*, *35*, 36, 38, 42, 43, *44*, 46, 47, 83, 86, 115, 116, 128, *129*, 146, 162, *190-191*, 193, 197, 199; at wedding ceremony, *118-119*; blessing, *18*, 19; food wagon, *159*; game, 197; shops, 87. *See also Mirin*

Sakizuke. See Hors d'œuvre

Salad, 48; crab meat and vegetables, 193; mixed, 48

Salmon, *34*, 82; eggs in kumquat shells, 188

Salt, 42, 110; for steaming, 48, *169*

Sambai-zu (dipping sauce), *65*

Samisen (musical instrument), *190*, 191, 197

Samma (mackerel), 38

Sampei jiru (salmon soup with vegetables), 38

Samurai, 17, 19, *34*

Sano, Masaki, *112*

Sansankudo (wedding ritual), *118*

Sansho (pepper) leaf, *45*, *57*, *148*

Sapporo, 10, *map* 11

Sardines, 76, 80, 161

Sasagayuki restaurant, Tokyo *160*, 161

Sashimi (slices of raw fish), 26, 27, 43, *65*, 80-83, 86, 90, *91*, 108, 112, 138, 146, 152; restaurant, *157*, 161, 185, 188; knife and scabbard, *50*; popularity, 81; preparation, 81-82, *92-93*

Sauces, 38, 86, *112*; for rice, 110; for salad, 48; *tare*, 29, 113. *See also* Soya sauce; Dipping sauces

Sausage: fish, 87

Sayori (snipefish), 112

Sea bream, *34*, 35, *57*, 76, *79*, 80, 82, 110, 120, 147, *149*, *150*, 151; symbolic importance of, 86, 121

Seafood, 42, 56, *57*, 81, *97*, *102*, *105*, *150*, 151, 156, 164; variety and abundance, 75-76. *See also* Fish; Octopus; Shell-fish; Seaweed; Squid

Sea of Japan, *map* 11

Seasonal themes, 10, 26, 33-35; autumn, *35*, *40*, 41; spring, 10, *24*, 25, *34*, *120*, 147, *148-149*; summer, *34*; winter, 35

Seasonings, 42, 47. *See also* Aji-no-moto; Monosodium glutamate; Pepper; Salt

Sea-urchins, *34*, 43, *45*, 76, 80, 115

Seaweed, 8, *9*, *34*, 76, 81, 88-89, *188*; for *sushi*, 89, *98-99*, *100*, 154, *155*; garnish, 89; medicinal value, 89; powdered, 43, *45*; with prawns, *72*. *See also Hijiki*; Kelp; Laver; *Nori*; *Wakame*

Sekihan (red rice): symbolism, 120, 121

Sendai, *map* 11

Sensu (fan), *141*

Sesame: oil, 42, 43, *44*, 49; seeds, 38, 48, *63*, 110, *159*

Shabu shabu (simmered beef), 38, 108, 116, *159*

Shad, 82

Shell-fish, 8, 75-76, 77, 82, 115, *150*, 151, 163; salad, 48. *See also* Clams; Crab; Lobster; Molluscs; Oysters; Prawns; Scallops; Snails

Shiitake, *45*, 199. *See also* Mushrooms

Shikiita (protective tile),

141-143

Shikoku, 10, *map* 11

Shimofuri (beef), 166, *167*

Shimonoseki, 87

Shincha (tea leaves), 27

Shinmai (rice), 37

Shinto: gods, 38, 121; prayer, 16, 76; priests, *18*, 19; religion, 13, 19; shrines, *18*, 19, *117-118*; wedding, *117-119*

Shioyaki (salt grilling), 29, 41, 43

Shirataki (vegetable), 42, 43, *44*

Shiro dashi (white soya-bean flavoured soup with gourd and hot mustard), *56*

Shiro miso (white soya-bean paste), *45*, 199

Shisha (vegetable), *188*

Shiso (beefsteak plant), 147, 162

Shiumani (vegetables with chicken), 47

Shizuoka, 27, 38

Shochu (Japanese gin), 166

Shoga (ginger root), 43, *45*

Shoyu, *44*, 199. *See also* Soya sauce

Shrines: Matsunoh, Kyoto, *18*, 19; Toshogu, Nikko, 117-118

Siberia, 12

Skimmer, *50*

Snails, *72*

Snipe-fish, 112

Soba (buckwheat noodles), 38, 147, 199

Sodare (bamboo mat), *50*, *100*

Somen (wheat noodles), 43, *45*, 199

Some oroshi (white radish and red pepper), 90, *91*

Soup, 75, 115, *130*, *154*, 166; burned rice, 147, *149*; clam, *57*, 118; clear, 56-*57*, 110, *111*, 147, 185, 188; egg, 26; flavoured with soya-bean paste, 41, *56-57*, 109, 110, 138, 147, *148*; salmon, 38. *See also* Broth; *Dashi*; *Miso shiru*

Soya bean: curd, 32, *34*, *35*, 41, *45*, 108, *159*,*160*, 161, 166, *167*, 188; fermented soya-bean paste, 41, 109, 115, 147, *173*, green, *34*; importance of, 16; red paste, 35, *45*; white paste, 45. *See also Miso*; *Tofu*; Soya sauce

Soya sauce, 26, 32, *35*, 36, 41, *45*, 48, 90, *91*, 116, *160*, 161, 166, *167*, 196; with fish, 81, 82; ingredients, 42; and *mirin*, 43, 46, 162; multiple uses, 42. *See*

also Pon-su

Spain, 19

Sparrow, 161

Spice, 43, *45*

Spinach, 87; *horenso*, 140; salad, 48

Spring onions, 32, *56*, 109, 113, 116, *130*, *133*, 163, *174*; grilled with chicken and chicken livers, 161; in dipping sauce, 83; with rolled beef, *72*

Squash pickles, 147, *149*

Squid, 76, *79*, 80, 82, *92*, *99*, 163; "fire fly", 27; to cut, *92*; and pickled cod roe, *72*

Steaming: 47-48, *180*; over *sake*, 47; steam- or salt-grilling, 29, 43, *169*

Stock, 46; fish, 116. *See also Dashi*

Strawberries, 25-26, 32, 38, *39*

Su (rice vinegar), 43, *44*, 199

Sugar, 46, 166, *167*

Suimono (clear soup), 110; wedding, 121

Sukiyaki (simmered beef), 22, 26, 27, 36, 38, 41, 108, 116, 152, 161, 166, *167*; origin, 46

Sumo (wrestlers), 22

Sunomono (vinegared salad), 48, 108, 115

Suribachi (serrated bowl), *50*, *63*

Sushi (vinegared rice), 8, *9*, 26, 77, 80, 81, 89, *98-99*, *100*, 108, 110, 115, 163; popularity of, 81; restaurants, 81, 154, *155*, 164-165; vocabulary, 165

Suzuko mizore-ae (red caviar and radish), *130*

Sweets, *34*, 120

T*ableware*, 183-184

Tai. See Sea bream

Takahara, Sosei, *186*, *187*

Takano tjume (red peppers), 43, *45*

Takenoko (bamboo shoot), 43, *44*

Takuan (pickled radish over rice), 115

Tamago dashimaki (rolled omelette with grated *daikon*), 46, 110, *179*

Tamago dofu (egg custard in soup), 26

Tangerines, 10, 38

Tare (sweet soya sauce), 29, 113

Taro, 110, *111*, 140

Tatami (straw matting), *148-149*, 152, 193

Tea, 17, 27-28, 38, 110, *111*, 112, 162, 164, 193; black, 27; green, 27, 32, *144*; harvest, *12-13*; plantations, *12-13*, 27; preparation of, 27-28, *141-144*. *See also Bancha*; *Shincha*; Tea ceremony

Tea ceremony, 17, *136*, 137-147; aesthetics, 136, 138-139, 141, 145-146, 147; food, 26, 143, 145-147, *148-149*; leaf for, 27; masters, 137-138, 141, 142, 143, 145, 146, 147; menus, 145, 146, 147, 186; origin, 137; preparation, *141-144*; rules, 138, 144, 147; schools and lessons, *139*, 145, *187*; utensils and dishes, *141-144*, 145-146, 147, *148-149*, *187*

Temarizushi, *40*, 41

Temples: Sojiji, near Tokyo, 86-87. *See also* Shinto

Tempura, 19, 38, 43, 115, 116, 152, 162, 163, 193; dips, 49; ingredients, 49, *102*; oil, 49, 102; origin, 19, 22; preparation, 48-49, *102*, *105*, 163; restaurants, *156*, 163; prawn, *182*, 183

Ten-ichi restaurant, Tokyo, *156*, 163

Teppanyaki (grilled meat and chicken), *157*, 161, 162

Teriyaki ("shining grill"), 43, 152, 161, *174*

Tofu (soya-bean curd), 32, 36, 41, 42, *45*, 48, 87, 108, 109, 110, 116, *133*, 147, *148*, 152, *160*, 161, *173*, 199; powdered, 42; restaurant, *160*, 161; slicing knife, 50; uses, 42, 161; with dried bonito, spring onions,

ginger and soya sauce, *32*

Togarashi, 199. *See also* Pepper

Tokonoma (alcove), 10, 26, 86, 108, 152, 185, *187*, 193

Tokyo, 10, *map* 11, 22, 27, 32, 77, 86, 107, 110, 115, 162; Bay, 87; fish market, 76, 79, 80-81; Imperial Hotel, 138; Shinjuku district, 83; restaurants, *155-160*, 161, 162, 163, 184-185, *192*, 193

Tonkatsu (pork cutlet), 162

Tori-gin restaurant, Tokyo, 162

Torishige restaurant, Tokyo, *158*

Toro (belly of tunny fish), 152

Toshogu shrine, Nikko, 117

Toyama, *map* 11; Bay, 27

Trout, 28, 183; grilled rock trout, *35*; river, *34*; salt-grilled 27. *See also Ayu*

Tsuji, Kaichi, 12, 33

Tsukemono (pickles), 43, 44, 115, 152, 162, 198-199

Tsukiji Central Market, Tokyo, 76, *78*, 79, 80-81

Tsukimi Festival, 35

Tsukudani (fish and kelp), 87, 89

Tsunokakushi (headdress), *117*

Tunny fish, 76, 81, 82, *92*, *99*, 154, *155*, 165; buying, *78*, 79, 80; how to slice, *93*; red, 82, 90, *91*, *98*; vinegared rice and tunny "sandwich", *101*

Turnips, 71; cutting technique for, 52, *53*

Turtle, 161

Udon (wheat noodle), 38, 43, *45*

Uguisu mochi (nightingale cake), 26-27

Ujidawara district, 13

Ukai (cormorant fishing). *See Ayu*

Ukemochi-no-kami (food goddess), 13

Umani (boiling method), 47

Umeboshi (pickled red plum), 43, *44*, 109

Uni (sea-urchin), 43, *45*, 170

United States: influence on Japanese food, 22, 23

Urasenke (tea-ceremony school), 145

Vegetables, 29, *30-31*, 42, 47, 48, 57, 71, 75, 81, 89, 109, 110, 116, *156*, *157*, 159, 163, 195; canned, 43, *44*; cutting knife, *50*, *51*; cutting techniques for, *52-53*; pickled, 110, *111*; slippery, 43, *44*; soaked, 115; steamed, 47; wild, 110, *111*. *See also* Asparagus; Aubergines; Bamboo shoots; Beans; Burdock; Cabbage; Carrots; Cucumber; Mangetout; Ginger; Gourd; Lotus root; Marrow; Mushrooms; Onions; Peas; Potatoes; Pumpkin; Radish; Rice; *Shirataki*; *Shisha*; *Shiso*; Soya bean; Spinach; Spring onions; Taro; Turnips; Watercress

Vinegar, 72; rice, 8, 42, 43, *44*; salad dressing, 48

Vitamins: A, 29; C, 89

Wadakin restaurant, Matsuzaka, 166, *167*

Wakame (seaweed), *45*, 89, 109, 110, 199

Warabi (fern), 147, *149*

Wasabi (green horse-radish), 42, 82, 90, *91*, 108, 115, 152, 165, 199

Wasabi zuke (vegetables pickled in green horse-radish and mustard), 115

Watanabe family, *114*, 115

Watercress, *98*, *100*, 110, *111*; cucumber stuffed with crab meat, watercress and ginger, *66*

Whale, 76, 79; restaurants, 161

Wheat, 29, *30-31*, 42

Whitebait, *79*

Whitefish, 76

Wine, 42. *See also Sake*; *Mirin*

Wright, Frank Lloyd, 138

Yabuizu restaurant, Tokyo, *154*

Yakitori (food grilled on skewers over charcoal), *158-159*, 161, *175*

Yamada, Kakuko, 193-194

Yellowtail, 82

Yokohama, 10, *map* 11

Yosenabe (fish, vegetables, *tofu* and *dashi*), 116, *133*

Yudofu (simmered soya-bean curd), 116

Yuki, Koji, *186*, 188, *189*, 195; Junko, *186*; Teiichi, 195

Yuto (burned rice soup), *149*

Yuzu (citrus fruit) 26, 109, 116

Zarusoba (buckwheat noodles), 32, *129*

Zen. *See* Buddhism

Zensai (hors d'œuvre), 68, *72*, 198

Zuiki. *See* Taro

Where to Find Japanese Foods

One or another of the shops listed here will be able to provide many of the foods called for in the recipes and described on page 199. Importers and retailers of specifically Japanese foods include Mikadoya, with shops at 250 Upper Richmond Road, Putney, London S.W.15, and 529a Finchley Road, London N.W.3, and Cydilda & Co., whose shop at 61 Wimbledon High Street, Wimbledon Common, London S.W.19, is called the Nippon (Japan) Food Centre.

Cydilda will fill mail orders, something Mikadoya is not yet set up to do, but both of these importers will be happy to reply to inquiries. Imported *sukiyaki* sets can be ordered from Mr. Butterfield, The Anglers Hotel, Runnymede, Surrey.

Japanese restaurant cooks in London bring much of their equipment with them from Japan, and so far Japanese kitchen utensils are not imported in any significant quantity. But you can try the Chinese provision stores listed here for utensils that approximate to those used in Japanese cooking, and you will also find that these shops stock many of the ingredients you will need. The list is reprinted from *The Cooking of China*, a previous Foods of the World title.

Cheong-Leen Supermarket,
4/10 Tower House,
Tower Street,
London, W.C.2

Loong Fung Chinese Provisions,
37/38 Gerrard Street,
London, W.1

Oriental Stores,
5 Macclesfield Street,
London, W.1

Chinese Emporium,
22 Rupert Street,
London, W.1

Bombay Emporium,
70 Grafton Way,
London, W.1

Hong Kong Emporium,
53 Rupert Street,
London, W.1

Far East Food Centre,
34 Greek Street,
London, W.1

Chung Nam Provisions,
88 Jamaica Row,
Birmingham, 5

Wing Lee Company,
14 Nelson Street,
Liverpool, 1

Benny and Company,
7 Great George Street,
Liverpool, 1

Quong Tai Young and Co. Limited,
24/26 Nelson Street,
Liverpool, 1

Chung Wah Trading Company,
8/8a Grenville Street,
Liverpool, 1

Wei Shang Tong,
34 Nelson Street,
Liverpool, 1

Shing Cheong Oriental Food Co.,
116 North Street,
Leeds, 2

Li-Kar Yuen Stores,
3 Hoxton Street,
Bradford, 8

Shai Hing Emporium,
26 Russell Street,
Middlesbrough,
Yorkshire

Picture Credits and Acknowledgements

The sources for the illustrations in this book are shown below. Credits for the pictures from left to right are separated by commas, from top to bottom by dashes.

All photographs by Eliot Elisofon except: 4—Horace Bristol, Monica Suder—Charles Phillips, Monica Suder. 11 —Map by Kiyoshi Kanai. 14, 15—Brian Brake from Rapho Guillumette. 28—T. Tanuma. 30, 31—Orion Press from Free Lance Photographers Guild. 39—T. Tanuma. 46, 47 —Drawings by Albert Sherman. 51, 52, 53—Richard Jeffery. 63, 66, 69, 71—Clayton Price. 81—S K Slide Company Ltd. 84, 85—T. Tanuma. 92, 93—Clayton Price, drawings by Matt Greene. 97, 100, 101, 105—Clayton Price. 117, 118, 119 —Ernest Heiniger from Rapho Guillumette. 125 —Anthony Donna. 139—John Launois from Black Star. 153—Norman Wightman courtesy Japan National Tourist Organization. 154, 158—T. Tanuma. 159—*top*, Jerry Cooke. 160—T. Tanuma. 170—Clayton Price. 177 —Drawings by Matt Greene. 178, 179—*top*, Clayton Price. 180—Drawing by Elise Hilpert.

For their help in the production of this book the editors wish to thank the following: *in Japan*, Takiko Kato, Ernest Satow, Mrs. Sochitsu Sen, Mr. and Mrs. Akira Watanabe, and the Ajinomoto Company, Inc.; *in New York City*, The Japan Society, Inc.; Hisashi Yamada, Director of the Tea Ceremony Society of Urasenke, Inc.; Genichiro Inokuma; Sondra Meadow; Mary Evans for her assistance on the tea ceremony chapter; Teiji Tamaru; Maureen Herbert, Japan Airlines; Takatoshi Terahira, Japan Food Corporation; H. Hamano, Japan National Tourist Organization; Japan Trade Center; Ellen Sakata and Myyo Enoki, Japanese Foodland; Tatsuro Miyoshi, Miya Company, Inc.; Irwin Vladimir, Van Brunt & Company.

Sources consulted in the production of this book include: *They Came to Japan*, edited by Michael Cooper; *Typical Japanese Cooking*, by Tomi Egami; *Things Japanese*, by Mock Joya; *The Book of Tea*, by Okakura kakuzo; *Japan Past and Present*, by Edwin O. Reischauer; *Japan, a Short Cultural History*, by George B. Sansom; *Japanese Inn*, by Oliver Statler; *The Romance of Tea*, by William H. Ukers; *We Japanese*, published by Fujiya Hotel, Ltd.

✠

Typesetting by C. E. Dawkins (Typesetters) Ltd., London, S.E.1
Smeets Lithographers, Weert
Bound by Proost en Brandt N.V., Amsterdam
Printed in Holland